Introduction to the Social Services

Introduction to the Social Services

Fifth Edition

W. E. Baugh

MACMILLAN
EDUCATION

First edition 1973
Second edition 1975
Reprinted 1976
Third edition 1977
Reprinted (with revisions) 1979
Fourth edition 1983
Reprinted 1985 (twice)
Fifth edition 1987

Published by
MACMILLAN EDUCATION LTD
Houndmills, Basingstoke, Hampshire RG21 2XS
and London
Companies and representatives
throughout the world

Printed in Hong Kong

British Library Cataloguing in Publication Data
Baugh, W.E.
Introduction to the social services.—5th ed.
1. Public welfare—Great Britain   2. Social
service—Great Britain
I. Title
361'.941   HV245
ISBN 0–333–44820–0 (hardcover)
ISBN 0–333–44821–9 (paperback)

To Joyce, Vivien and Richard

Contents

Preface to the Fifth Edition   xiii
Abbreviations   xv

1 The Social Services   1

Definition   1
The Main Social Services   1
Administration   3
The Aim of the Book   3

2 The Historical Background   5

Summary   9

3 The Origins of Social Security   12

The Poor Law   12
The Changed Attitude to Poverty   13
The Rise of Social Services Outside the Poor Law   15
Developments in Social Security in the Interwar Years   19
Developments in Social Security since 1939   21
Summary   25

4 Social Security Today   29

National Insurance   29
Supplementary Benefit   32
Child Benefit   35
Family Income Supplement   35
Miscellaneous Allowances   36
Housing Benefit   37
Social Security Advisory Committee (SSAC)   38
Redundancy Payments   38
Summary   39

**5 Problems of Social Security (Including the
  Government's Reform Proposals)**   **41**

  Who are the Poor?   41
  Policies to Reduce Poverty   43
  Means-testing   52
  The Poverty Trap   54
  Government Proposals for the Replacement
    of Supplementary Benefit   55
  Summary   58

6 Health   **64**

  Development of the Health Services   64
  The Basic Principles of the National Health Service   70
  Summary   71

7 The National Health Service Today   **73**

  The Personal Practitioner Services   74
  The Hospitals and Community Health   76
  Community Health Services   79
  Local Authority Social Services Department
    Services (linked with Health)   82
  Summary   84

8 Current Problems in the Health Service   **86**

  Reorganisation of the National Health Service   86
  Finance   89
  Allocation of Resources   93
  The Family Doctor   95
  Primary Health Care Services   97
  Complaints   98
  Summary   100

9 Welfare   **105**

  The Elderly   105
  Mothers and Young Children   109
  Schoolchildren   112
  Handicapped Children   114

Maladjusted Children   115
Children in Need of Care and Protection   115
Physically Handicapped People   122
Mentally Disordered People   124
Community Care   128
Summary   131

10 Education   **135**

History   135
Summary   143

11 The Organisation of Education Today   **146**

Education provided by Local Authorities   146
Private Education   147
Handicapped Children   149
Finance of Education   149
Administration   150
Summary   152

**12 Developments in Education since 1945 and
Current Problems**   **154**

Higher Education   154
Secondary Education   160
Primary Education   167
Independent Schools since 1945   167
Education for Leisure   168
Value for Money?   169
Equality of Opportunity   169
Summary   173

13 Youth Service   **176**

Definition   176
History   176
Administration Today   177
Some of the Problems of the Youth Service   178
Summary   181

14 Employment Services **184**

Employment Offices 184
Vocational Training 185
Industrial Training Boards 186
Services for Disabled People 186
The Unemployed 188
Ethnic Minorities 190
Women 190
Health and Safety at Work 191
Employment Protection 192
Careers Service 192
Some Problems 193
Summary 197

15 Housing **200**

History 200
Housing Policy since 1945 201
The Administration of Housing 204
Substandard Housing 205
Summary 206

16 Planning **211**

History 211
Planning Administration 212
New Towns 213
Urban Renewal 214
The Countryside 217
Regional Planning 219
Problems Today 219
Summary 221

17 Probation and After-Care Service **225**

History 225
Administration 229
Problems Today 229
Summary 231

18 The Future of the Social Services **235**

Appendices

1 *Some of the main social security weekly benefit rates*   243

2 *Expenditure on social security benefits for Great Britain, 1985–6 and estimated number of recipients, 1979–80 and 1985–6*   245

3 *Cost of the health and personal social services for Great Britain 1985–6*   246

4 *Manpower in the National Health Service in the United Kingdom in 1979 and 1983*   247

5 *Education: numbers of students in 1984 in the United Kingdom*   248

6 *Pupils in secondary education in 1984 in England, Wales, Scotland and Northern Ireland*   249

7 *Students in further education in 1983–4 in the United Kingdom taking courses up to 'A' level and intermediate professional level*   250

8 *Public expenditure on education for the United Kingdom 1983–4*   251

9 *Stock of dwellings by tenure in the United Kingdom 1951, 1961, 1971, 1981, 1984*   252

10 *Persons supervised by the probation service: by type of supervision in England and Wales 1971, 1981, 1984*   253

Index   254

Preface to the Fifth Edition

This edition, like previous editions, gives a brief historical survey of each of the social services, their current operation and some of the problems affecting them and their users. It covers some further developments within the social services since the last edition arising from the commitment of the Thatcher government to a monetarist economic policy. Some of the more important of these developments are the proposed reform of the social security system should the Government win the next election; the new management structure in the National Health Service and the privatisation of some of its domestic services; the growing centralisation of the education system and planning system; the continuing proliferation of schemes to help the unemployed. Another development of a general nature which has unfolded over the years is the application of the Government's viewpoint, in line with its economic philosophy, that for each of the social services the private sector has a role to play of benefit to that service; that the private and public sectors are not rivals but complement one another. The degree of controversy this viewpoint engenders depends on the service.

As in the Fourth Edition, I have given some assignments to encourage students to find things out for themselves although I appreciate teachers have their own ideas on what assignments to give.

I thank all the public servants who answered my queries but emphasise again that mistakes and wrong judgements are my own.

December 1986   W. E. B.

Acknowledgement

The author and publishers are grateful to the Controller of Her Majesty's Stationery Office for permission to quote statistics from the 1986 edition of *Social Trends*.

xiii

Abbreviations

ACAS   Advisory, Conciliation and Arbitration Service
AHA   Area Health Authority
CBI   Confederation of British Industry
CEDP   Committee for the Employment of Disabled People
CHC   Community Health Council
Cmnd   Command (Paper)
CNAA Council for National Academic Awards
COI   Central Office of Information
CPAG   Child Poverty Action Group
CTC   City Technical College
DES   Department of Education and Science
DHA   District Health Authority
DHSS   Department of Health and Social Security
DMA   Diploma in Municipal Administration
DMT   District Management Team
DRO   Disablement Resettlement Officer
FE   Further Education
FIS   Family Income Supplement
FPC   Family Practitioner Committee
GNP   Gross National Product
GP   General Practitioner (Medical)
MSC   Manpower Services Commission
NAB   National Advisory Body for Public Sector Higher
          Education
NCVQ National Council for Vocational Qualifications
NHS   National Health Service
RAWP Resource Allocation Working Party
RHA   Regional Health Authority
SEC   Secondary Examinations Council
SRN   State Registered Nurse
SSAC   Social Security Advisory Committee

SSP	Statutory Sick Pay
TOPS	Training Opportunities Scheme
TUC	Trades Union Congress
TVEI	Technical and Vocational Education Initiative
UBO	Unemployment Benefit Office
UGC	University Grants Committee
YOP	Youth Opportunity Programme

1 The Social Services

Definition

It is difficult to give a definition of a social service to which one can refer for precise guidance on whether a service is, or is not, a social service. But a social service can be defined as a service provided by the community to help those in need – need not necessarily being need of money. A state with many statutory social services can be called a *welfare state*. (For other definitions of a welfare state see William A. Robson (1976) *Welfare State and Welfare Society: Illusion and Reality*, and also Norman Furniss and Timothy Tilton (1979) *The Case for the Welfare State*, ch. 1.)[1]

The Main Social Services

1. *National Insurance*, which is compulsory and which provides partial cover against interruption of earnings during a person's lifetime.
2. *Supplementary Benefit*, which is a payment made to a person not in full-time work whose income is below what is considered necessary for the person's requirements. The actual payment is the difference between the person's income and his or her requirements.
3. *Child Benefit*, which is a cash payment to families with one or more children.
4. *Family Income Supplement*, which is a cash payment made to poor families where the wage-earner is working and there is at least one dependent child.

[1] Fuller references to works cited in this book can be found in a reading section at the end of chapters.

5. *Redundancy payments*, which are cash payments given to workers as compensation for being made redundant.
6. The *National Health Service*, which provides a virtually free health service for everyone. It has three branches:
   (a) Family (personal) practitioner services (doctors, dentists, pharmacists, opticians)
   (b) Hospital services
   (c) Community health services.
7. *Local welfare services*, now better known as *personal social services*, run by local authorities and voluntary organisations.
8. *Children's services*, which include services for children in need of care and protection and the education of disabled children.
9. The *education service* provided by the state (although there is a fairly large private sector as well).
10. *Youth service*, which covers all kinds of youth work run by voluntary organisations and local authorities.
11. *Employment services*, which include not simply help in getting a job but training for a job and special services for the disabled and the young and special schemes for the unemployed.
12. *Housing*, which is included as a social service because an adequate home is considered a basic human need.
13. *Planning*, which is concerned with making our environment as pleasant as possible bearing in mind all the human needs which have to be satisfied.
14. The *Probation and after-care service*, which, among other things, is concerned with looking after an offender who is put on probation instead of being sentenced, and the after-care of prisoners released from prison.

Under the 1986 Social Security Act, effective from April 1988, providing the Government wins the next General Election, there will be changes to services 1, 2 and 4 above. Within the National Insurance system there would be modifications to the State Earnings-related Pension Scheme (SERPS) and widows' benefits. Supplementary benefit would be replaced by a system known as Income Support to include a discretionary Social Fund to meet special requirements, replacing the statutory single payments now paid under the supplementary benefit scheme, although certain changes to the system of single payments became operative from August 1986. Family Income Supplement (FIS) would be replaced by Family Credit. These proposed changes are discussed in Chapter 4.

Administration

The main social services are provided by the state working through central government departments, local authorities and *ad hoc* boards, but important social services are also provided by voluntary organisations. All were pioneered in the first place by voluntary effort.

The Aim of the Book

The aim is to give the basic facts about the above social services – how they operate, how they developed and some of the current problems in relation to each of them.

Assignments

1. List the statutory social services in your area and, against each one, the administrative body responsible for it and the address of its main local office.
2. List as many as possible of the voluntary organisations in your area. Which, in your opinion, are providing a social service? Give their official titles and the services they provide. (The names of many voluntary bodies can be obtained from your local library.) Find out from the Chief Executive's department of your local authority which of the voluntary bodies receive financial help from the local authority.
3. What would you say are the main criteria for deciding whether a service is or is not a social service?

Reading

Jonathan Bradshaw, 'The Concept of Social Need', *New Society* (30 March 1972).

D. V. Donnison and Valerie Chapman, *Social Policy and Administration* (Allen & Unwin, 1965) ch. 2.
Norman Furniss and Timothy Tilton, *The Case for the Welfare State* (Indiana University Press, 1979) ch. 1.
Julian le Grand and Ray Robinson (eds), *Privatisation and the Welfare State* (Allen & Unwin, 1984) ch. 2 by Alan Walker
David C. Marsh, *The Future of the Welfare State* (Penguin, 1964) ch. 1.
William A. Robson, *Welfare State and Welfare Society: Illusion and Reality* (Allen & Unwin, 1976).

2 The Historical Background

Over the past 200 years Britain has developed from a comparatively poor country into a comparatively rich country. This has been due to the introduction of power-driven machinery to make goods previously made by hand, to better farming methods and to a greatly improved system of transport, all of which have led to a much greater output of food and goods at lower costs. Britain was the first country in the world to pioneer the new industrial techniques, and she became the richest country in the world and remained so until the end of the nineteenth century. But after 1870 her relative position in the world began to decline and has been declining ever since. At the beginning of the twentieth century the USA and Germany were beginning to overtake her in *per capita* income and, since 1945, she has slipped even further down the league-table of wealth. This is not to say that since 1870 Britain has been getting poorer. On the contrary, Britain is richer than she has ever been. It simply means that other countries have been getting richer at a faster rate (see Aldcroft, 1978, ch. 5).

The new machinery came first to the textile industry in the late eighteenth century and, to begin with, was powered by water, but, later, steam power was used. Coal was needed to make the steam power and so industry moved to the areas of the coalfields, leading to a drift of population to the north. In the twentieth century there has been, and still is, a drift of population to the south due to the fact that the development of electricity as a source of power has made possible the location of new and expanding industries in the south, while the older, basic industries around the coalfields in the north – textiles, heavy engineering, shipbuilding, iron and steel, coal – have contracted.

Parallel with the developments of the new industrial and farming techniques there was a rapid rise in population. For England and Wales the population figures (to the nearest million) are as follows: 1801 – 9 million; 1851 – 18 million; 1911 – 36 million; 1961 – 46 million; 1981 – 49 million. This rapid growth of population (it quadrupled in just over 100 years) led to the rapid growth of towns and gave rise to problems of public health (now called environmental health), especially in the industrial areas where, as well as the natural population growth, there was an influx of people from the countryside seeking work.

The new industrial system was initially resented by most working people. Previously goods were made in people's homes or in small workshops attached to the home, and this domestic system of industry was usually combined with a little farming. Although the home worker normally worked for a middleman who provided materials and sometimes tools, and although working hours were long and piecework paid poorly, at least there was a feeling of being one's own boss. But the new power-driven machinery was too big to be used in the home and had to be housed in buildings called mills or factories. In the factory, even though more money could be earned, workers had to work hard in humid conditions under strict discipline. They lost their sense of independence. To mitigate some of the worst evils of the factory system, especially child labour, Factory Acts were passed in spite of much opposition from most of the factory owners. But they did not become of general application or reasonably effective until the latter half of the nineteenth century. Those people who carried on with domestic industry had to accept less and less for what they produced because they had to compete with the machine-made product, which was cheaper. Is it any wonder that many workers hated the new textile machinery and some of them (e.g. the Luddites) went round in gangs smashing it up?

On the land the new farming methods led to a speeding up of enclosures because it was only by having all the land in one compact holding that farmers could please themselves how they farmed and introduce new farming methods. Under the open-field strip system, farming was done communally and an individual farmer could only bring in a new farming technique if all the other farmers agreed. In the main, enclosures were forced through against the wishes of the majority of working people. They were resented because much of the common land was enclosed and the people of the village could no longer use it, and those people who lived on it had to seek shelter elsewhere. Many small farmers could not afford the cost of enclosure – the fencing, the ditching, the legal fees – and sold up and became farm labourers or sought work in the towns. On the other hand, enclosures eventually made possible a much greater output of food, of great importance in view of the rapidly rising population.

Thus the industrial and agricultural changes upset a way of life that had been settled for centuries. Changes brought insecurity; insecurity made people think afresh about their lives and their position in society. As a result, many people became sympathetic to the ideas of the French Revolution which broke out when these changes were beginning to have some impact on British society. It is from this period that the history of the modern working-class movement begins. The working class campaigned for political rights, but at the same time practised self-help by forming friendly societies, trade unions and, later on, co-operative societies. After 1850 both the trade-union movement and the co-operative movement had become well established, but it was not until 1867 that the first categories of working men received the vote. In 1918 all working men over 21 and all women over 30 received the vote. In 1928 women, like men, received the vote at 21. But it was not until 1948 that we had 'one man, one vote', when the business vote and university vote were abolished.

By 1850 the main economic changes had been completed – railways were established, the new farming methods introduced in the seventeenth and eighteenth centuries and others introduced later were in general use and the mechanisation of the major industries was well under way. People began to get the benefit of these new industrial and farming techniques, and living standards for those in work, between 1850 and 1900, rose fairly rapidly. Apart from the period between 1900 and 1914, when prices rose faster than wages, living standards have been rising ever since, especially since 1945. And even allowing for the rapid increase in inflation since 1970 and a world recession since 1974, the real disposable income of the majority of those in work has continued to rise according to statistics based on the index of retail prices and increases in average earnings. But the recession has meant a slowing down in the production of wealth and a rapid rise in the number of unemployed. The firms that produce and distribute the much greater output of goods have grown greatly in size, many of them operating on an international scale, especially since the railway and the steamship opened up the continents of the world to commerce from around 1870 onwards.

In spite of much greater wealth and higher living standards there is still much poverty in Britain although what is called poverty today is a higher living standard than what was called poverty in the inter-war years. Put another way, the poverty line is higher than it was then.

In accounting for the origin of the welfare state the sociologist emphasises the impact of technological change on the family. Thus before the Industrial Revolution society was less complicated. The family worked together as a unit and a person in need looked to the family for help. But the new industrial society led to a much greater division of labour, the family ceased to be the unit of production and more of its members sought work away from home, many in distant parts. The role of the family as provider and sustainer diminished. The state had to take over part of the sustaining role previously done by the family.

On the other hand, the political scientist, in seeking the origins of the welfare state, emphasises the growing role of the state in the nineteenth century, made necessary, in spite of the prevailing theory of *laissez-faire*, to mitigate the evils created by the new industrial society which the private enterprise system left untouched. Thus from almost the beginning of the nineteenth century Factory Acts had been passed to control working conditions in the factories to be followed later in the century by Acts regulating working conditions in mines. From 1848 the state was very much concerned with public health legislation to combat the insanitary conditions of the rapidly growing towns. A state system of education was introduced in 1870 to give support to the private system of education. By the end of the nineteenth century state interference to help the weaker members of the community (quite apart from the Poor Law, which had been in operation since the sixteenth century) was accepted, and in the first decade of the twentieth century the state ceased to play simply a regulatory role but developed a more positive and constructive role in relation to its citizens. The development of an efficient civil service and local government service after 1870 made this increasing state role workable. From state interference in the nineteenth and early twentieth centuries on behalf of the poorer members of society, there developed in the 1930s, because of the world-wide depression, state interference on behalf of the harassed businessman.

Nowadays the state, in the interests of everyone, not only manages a welfare state but also a comparatively prosperous economy. But the way the welfare state will develop in the future is now more uncertain than at any time since 1945. The main reason for this is that because of a world recession political parties have had to rethink their economic strategies. Hence for the first time since 1945 the broad consensus between the parties on economic stategy based on the economic teachings of the English economist, J. M. Keynes, has collapsed. The Conservative government, elected in 1979, adopted an economic policy that goes back to the pre-Keynesian era. The policy is based on the belief that the main cure for the country's economic ills is a strict control of the money supply. Hence the economic theory on which it is based is called *monetarism*, associated with the American economist, Milton Friedman. In spite of this, at the end of 1985, the annual rate of increase in the money supply was higher than when the Government came to power. Furthermore, contrary to its monetarist aims, the Government has failed to reduce overall public expenditure as a proportion of the Gross Domestic Product. But the Chancellor of the Exchequer in his annual autumn statement on 12 November 1985 claimed that in the three financial years 1986–7 to 1988–9 public expenditure will be 'more or less flat in real terms' and would decline as a proportion of national output (i.e. GDP). Where the Government has broken with Keynesian economics is in its refusal to reflate the economy to reduce unemployment. There has been a modest growth in output since 1981 but this has been obtained without a fiscal stimulus. One aspect of the Government's economic strategy consistent with monetarism has been to reduce State control of the economy by means of denationalisation and privatisation programmes.

Summary

Britain has developed in the last two hundred years from a comparatively poor country to a comparatively rich country due to the introduction of power-driven machinery and better farming methods and a greatly improved system of transport. By 1900 she had become the richest country in the world. In the twentieth century other countries, having adopted many of Britain's industrial methods and having developed their own, have become richer than Britain, though Britain is today richer than she has ever been, supporting a population six times greater than it was 200 years ago and in much greater comfort.

The industrial and agricultural developments created social problems – sanitation problems in the rapidly growing towns, long hours of work and child labour in the factories, embittered relations between employer and worker – leading successive governments in the nineteenth century to pass regulatory legislation to try to mitigate these problems. In the meantime the workers had developed trade unions, co-operative societies and political organisations as a form of self-help.

Positive government assistance to help the weaker members of society, leading to the modern welfare state, began at the beginning of the twentieth century and was a natural development from the regulatory legislation of the nineteenth century. The reduced role of the family as a provider for its members in need, due to its fragmentation by increased division of labour, made this new positive role of government very necessary. Because of high inflation and recession in recent years, combined with low productivity, political parties are rethinking their economic strategies on much more fundamental lines. Hence the progress of the economy and the future of the welfare state are more uncertain than at any time since 1945.

Assignments

1. Briefly trace the development in your local area or geographical region of one of its major industries.
2. What do you understand by the phrase 'Victorian *laissez-faire*'? How do you reconcile it with increasing government intervention in social matters from the 1830s onwards?
   [INTERMEDIATE DMA 1964]

Reading

Derek H. Aldcroft, *The European Economy 1914–1970* (Croom Helm, 1978) ch. 5.
Paul Barker (ed.), *Founders of the Welfare State* (Heinemann, 1984).
Ronald Fletcher, *The Family and Marriage in Britain*, 3rd edn (Penguin, 1973) ch. 2.
C. P. Hill, *British Economic and Social History*, 5th edn (Arnold, 1985).

3 The Origins of Social Security

The Poor Law

In the nineteenth century there were two main sources of help for the poor – the state system of poor relief dating from the sixteenth century, and charity provided by voluntary organisations.

The administration of the state system of poor relief was based on the 1834 Poor Law Amendment Act. The country was divided into Poor Law unions, each administered by locally elected Guardians of the Poor, who worked within a framework of regulations laid down by a central authority. But the central authority often found it difficult to enforce its decisions, due partly to the Victorians' dislike of the growing encroachment of central government into local affairs, an encroachment made necessary by the social problems created by the Industrial Revolution. Until 1847 this central authority comprised three Poor Law Commissioners, and then it was replaced by a Poor Law Board responsible to Parliament. In 1871 the Local Government Act set up a new department of state called the Local Government Board which, among other things, took over the work of the Poor Law Board. In 1919 the newly created Ministry of Health took over the work of the Local Government Board and remained the central authority until the Poor Law was officially abolished in 1948.

The assumption behind the Poor Law Amendment Act was that if you were fit and a pauper then it was your own fault. Hence fit paupers, including a male pauper's wife and children, were to be given relief in the workhouse where conditions were to be 'less eligible' than those of the lowest-paid worker outside. In this way it was thought that poverty among the able-bodied would be abolished because, rather than go into a workhouse, the able-bodied pauper would get a job. Even so, in a few unions material living standards were better than those of some farm workers.

Men, women and children were kept separate, which meant wives were separated from their husbands, and even children (except babies) from their mothers. Sick paupers could obtain relief outside the workhouse and, in fact, out-relief was never completely abolished even for the able-bodied and their dependants, but usually before relief was given in such cases so many hours' labour had to be done – breaking stones, for example. The administration varied in this respect between one union and another. For example, in parts of Lancashire and the West Riding, where workers' opposition to the workhouse was most bitter, out-relief continued to be given in many areas without a commitment to do work in return. This was partly a recognition by the authorities that relief for these industrial workers was a temporary measure to tide them over a period of recession. Some unions continued to give out-relief to the able-bodied because they found it cheaper than keeping paupers in the workhouse. (Derek Fraser, *The Evolution of the British Welfare State* (p. 52), quoting statistics from the annual reports of the Poor Law Commissioners, reveals, rather surprisingly, that between 1840 and 1870 the proportion of paupers receiving indoor relief was never greater than 15½ per cent.)

The 1867 Metropolitan Poor Act and the 1869 Poor Law Amendment Act empowered Boards of Guardians to build separate hospitals for the sick poor. But even as late as 1900, in some workhouses, sane and insane shared the same facilities. However, by 1870, the central authority had approved the boarding out of children should a Poor Law union desire it.

The Changed Attitude to Poverty

In the last quarter of the nineteenth century there was a growing realisation that poverty, even among the able-bodied, was not necessarily the individual's fault.

The heavy unemployment Britain experienced for the first time between 1873 and 1896, when Britain ceased to be the 'workshop of the world', brought home to many people the fact that impersonal economic forces could be the cause of poverty.

Many old people were seen to be poor yet known to have worked hard all their lives. In the 1890s the Poor Law authorities reported that 40 per cent of the working class over 65 were on poor relief.

There was also growing evidence that poverty was on a much wider scale than realised. This was due to a number of causes:

1. Education was made compulsory in 1880, and for the first time all the nation's children were on view to the authorities. Many were seen to be badly clothed and fed.
2. Strikes by unskilled workers in the 1880s gave publicity to to their low wages.
3. Writers like Dickens, Kingsley and Disraeli had hinted at a vast underground sea of poverty, and Henry Mayhew in the 1850s had given detailed descriptions of it. But it was the social investigations of the Reverend Andrew Mearns, Charles Booth and Seebohm Rowntree in the last two decades of the nineteenth century that had the greatest impact and brought home to people the terrible poverty in their midst, especially Mearns's pamphlet *The Bitter Cry of Outcast London*, published in 1883. Booth confirmed Mearns's findings on the extent of poverty in his great work *The Life and Labour of the People of London*, the first volume of which was published in 1889. The main causes of poverty, Booth reported, were unemployment and old age. About a third of the people of London were poor, and of these 28 per cent had not sufficient food and clothing to maintain physical efficiency and the remainder 'live under a struggle to obtain the necessaries of life', but with some of these 'it may be their own fault'. Rowntree made his first survey into poverty in York in 1899, and using a more precise method than Booth of assessing a minimum income needed to keep a person above the poverty line found that 28 per cent of the people were poor due mainly to low wages; 10 per cent of the people had such a low income that it was impossible for them to keep physically fit; and 18 per cent were in secondary poverty in that although in want they could with more 'careful' spending have maintained an income to buy the bare necessities to maintain physical efficiency.
4. The final confirmation of widespread poverty came with the Boer war, which broke out in 1899 – about a quarter of the volunteers had to be rejected because they were medically unfit.

But the changed attitude to poverty was not simply due to an appreciation of its cause and extent but to its injustice, especially in the midst of so much wealth. The point was driven home by middle-class socialists, trade unionists, working-class socialists, radical parsons and certain academic philosophers, and they all looked to the state to do something about it. To the prevailing *laissez-faire* philosophy that any increase in state activity would diminish individual liberty, Oxford philosopher Thomas Hill Green replied that liberty was not simply freedom from restraint but 'doing what one desires' (John Stuart Mill's definition). State activity could actually increase liberty by removing the obstacles to doing what one desires. One of the obstacles was certainly poverty and the state should therefore get rid of it. Green saw the general role of the state as providing an environment within which the individual could make the most of his abilities. Here was the theoretical justification for a welfare state.

The 1867 Reform Act and the 1884 Representation of the People Act, by giving the vote to a large section of the working class, made its coming inevitable.

The Poor Law becomes less harsh

By the end of the nineteenth century old people were receiving help from the Poor Law Guardians in their own homes and those old people still in workhouses were receiving little luxuries like tea and tobacco; more and more pauper children were sent to ordinary boarding schools or boarded out with foster parents; workhouse hospitals began to compare with the voluntary hospitals and working-class people were using them. The 1885 Medical Relief (Disqualification Removal) Act permitted people receiving poor relief for medical reasons to vote, but other paupers remained disenfranchised until the 1918 Representation of the People Act. The 1894 Outdoor Relief (Friendly Societies) Act authorised Poor Law Guardians to ignore sums of up to 5 shillings a week from a friendly society received by an applicant for relief.

The Rise of Social Services Outside the Poor Law

The foundations of the modern welfare state were laid by the Liberal governments of 1905–15. The assumption behind the social services they created was that poverty was not necessarily individuals' fault and that society had an obligation to help them. The Poor Law was an unsuitable means of help because of its deterrent principle, being based on the assumption that poverty among the able-bodied was the individual's fault. Before these governments, attempts had been made to provide public-work schemes for the unemployed, and the 1905 Unemployed Workmen Act (passed by a Conservative government) authorised financial assistance to local distress committees which provided jobs for the workless. But these public-work schemes were not a success.

The Liberal Government's main social services legislation

The 1906 Education (Provision of Meals) Act permitted local authorities to introduce school meals in elementary schools. Although parents were supposed to pay a contribution towards them, meals were not withheld from children whose parents could not afford to pay. This was done outside the Poor Law and was, in fact, the first breach in the Poor Law. In 1914 it was made obligatory for local authorities to provide school meals.

The 1907 Education (Administrative Provisions) Act introduced medical inspection of schoolchildren in elementary schools. Under the Act it was obligatory for local authorities to ensure medical inspection of schoolchildren at least three times during their school career. But it was not until the 1918 Education Act that it was made obligatory for local authorities to provide facilities for treatment. This Act also extended medical inspection to secondary schools. Treatment could be charged for, but payment for treatment was eventually abolished by the 1944 Education Act.

These Education Acts arose from the report of the Inter-Departmental committee on Physical Deterioration. Because of the large number of volunteers for the Boer war who failed the fitness test, this Committee was set up in 1903 to investigate whether the nation was deteriorating physically.

Local authorities received financial help from the Central Government for providing the meals and the medical services for schoolchildren and this dependence of local authorities on Central Government for money to help pay for services they were given to administer continued to grow as the century progressed.

The 1907 Probation of Offenders Act laid the foundations of the Probation and After-Care Service by providing for the creation of probation officers by the courts to look after offenders put on probation instead of being sentenced.

The 1908 Children Act abolished imprisonment for children under 16 and introduced juvenile courts to keep children away from criminals. It also introduced remand homes to prevent children from going to prison while awaiting trial.

The 1908 Old Age Pensions Act gave pensions, paid for out of taxation, to people over 70. There was a means test and the maximum pension per person was 5 shillings (25p) a week.

Since the social investigations in the last century had revealed much poverty among the old, schemes for preventing their 'falling into the clutches of the Poor Law' had been put forward. Because of the need for speed, there was no time to create the administrative machinery for a contributory scheme.

The 1909 Labour Exchanges Act inaugurated a system of labour exchanges, later called employment exchanges, throughout the country to help overcome local unemployment. The first statutory ones were those set up by the London boroughs in 1902. Some voluntary ones were in existence prior to that.

The 1909 Trade Board Act gave the government powers to set up boards to fix minimum wages in 'sweated trades' – mainly tailoring and box-making and later mining.

This Act was part of a developing pattern of legislation to protect the worker which began in the first half of the nineteenth century with the Factory Acts. The 1911 Shop Act continued this protection for shop assistants. It established half-day closing once a week.

The 1911 National Insurance Act, which introduced health insurance and unemployment insurance, was the most important social legislation of the Liberal governments. All workers earning less than £160 a year (and all manual workers whatever their pay) had to be in the health insurance scheme (£160 was chosen because it was the limit for exemption from income tax). It provided:

(a) sickness benefit of 10 shillings (50p) a week (7s 6d (37½p) for women) for 13 weeks and 5 shillings (25p) for the following 13 weeks

(b) disability benefit not covered by any time limit and which began when sickness benefit ended

(c) maternity benefit

(d) the right to treatment in a TB sanatorium

(e) payment of the doctor's fee including the prescription charges.

Health insurance was administered and benefits paid out by insurance companies, friendly societies and trade unions, collectively known as *approved* societies.

Part 2 of the Act gave compulsory unemployment insurance to workers in seven occupations particularly vulnerable to the ups and downs of trade. A minimum of 26 weeks' contributions qualified a person for 15 weeks' unemployment pay within a period of 12 months at 7 shillings (35p) a week. The benefits were paid at labour exchanges.

The cost of the benefits for both parts of the Act were paid for by the contributions from workers, employers and the government. But the benefits were only to supplement private effort. They were not intended to be sufficient to live on.

The purpose of the state insurance scheme was to cover those workers not covered by private insurance.

Lloyd George and Winston Churchill were the ministers chiefly responsible for the Acts (Lloyd George, health insurance; Churchill, unemployment insurance). Both had previously visited Germany and had been much impressed with its state insurance scheme for pensions and health. Britain, however, was the first country to have unemployment insurance.

The Royal Commission on the Poor Law

This Commission was set up in 1905 before the Liberals came to power, but it reported during the Liberals' term of office in 1909. The two main reasons for setting it up were the Poor Law Board's strong objection to relief being given outside the Poor Law and the increasing cost of the Poor Law per head of the population. There was a Majority and a Minority Report. The Majority Report wanted the Poor Law to continue but it was not against the Liberal government's policy of developing other forms of aid outside the Poor Law, but it preferred such aid to be organised mainly by voluntary bodies, with a more humane Poor Law taking care of those that voluntary action could not deal with. The Minority Report wanted the Poor Law abolished and the various categories of need to be dealt with by appropriate specialised public agencies. For example, it was against separate facilities run by the Poor Law for the sick pauper, and wanted all sick people, whether paupers or not, to be helped by the same administrative body. The specialised public agencies would be committees of the local authorities. But the unemployed (i.e. the able-bodied poor) should be dealt with by a department of central government. Both reports recommended that local authorities should take over the administration of the Poor Law, and this was eventually enacted in 1929.

The Relief Regulation Order 1930 officially ended the principle of deterrence, which both reports had opposed, by instructing local authorities to adopt a more constructive approach to the needy.

Developments in Social Security in the Interwar Years

Health Insurance

In 1919 the income maximum for compulsory health insurance (Part 1 of the 1911 Act) was raised to £250. By 1939 it had been raised to £420, which, in effect, meant it covered the vast majority of workers. Inflation was the main reason for the rise in the income limit, but not entirely – the real income limit had been raised to some extent.

In the 1930s there were special arrangements made for the unemployed who could not keep up with their contributions.

The weakness of the health insurance scheme in the interwar years was that workers' dependants were not covered. Thus married women who did not go out to work (and most of them did not in those days) had to pay for their medical treatment. This was not remedied until the creation of the National Health Service after the Second World War.

Unemployment Insurance

The 1920 Unemployment Insurance Act extended unemployment insurance to virtually all workers except certain categories who were considered to be in stable employment, though some of these, like farm workers and domestic servants were included in the 1930s. The 1921 Unemployed Workers' Dependants Act introduced unemployment benefits for dependants. In 1921 the unemployment benefit period was extended from 15 weeks to 47 weeks.

Payments outside the Unemployment Insurance Scheme

In the interwar years unemployment rarely averaged less than 10 per cent of the working population. In 1932, the worst year, it averaged 23 per cent. Many workers continued to be out of work beyond the expiry of the benefit period. Long-term unemployment on such a large scale had not been anticipated when the 1911 Act was drawn up. However, instead of forcing the unemployed worker to seek Poor Relief after the expiry period, extra payments were made, beginning with payments to returning soldiers during the war. The 1927 Unemployment Insurance Act, based on the Report of the Unemployment Insurance Committee (the Blanesburgh Committee), made these payments of unlimited duration and called them *transitional benefit*. The 1931 National Economy Act introduced a household means test for those claiming transitional benefit to be administered by the public assistance committee of the local authorities which had taken over the administration of the Poor Law from the Guardians of the Poor in 1929. A household means test meant that the income of the whole family was taken into consideration and not just the income of the applicant. This means test was one of a number of economy measures introduced because of the financial crisis in 1931. It was abolished in 1941.

The Unemployment Assistance Board

A Royal Commission on Unemployment Insurance (the Gregory Commission) set up at the end of 1930 made its final report in 1932. In order to stop the drain on the insurance fund, it recommended that transitional payments should be financed by the Treasury. The government accepted this recommendation (it had, in any case, been the practice since 1930) but not the recommendation that transitional payments should continue to be administered by local authorities. Instead it gave the administration of transitional benefit under the 1934 Unemployment Act to a specially created Unemployment Assistance Board.

In setting up a special board to administer transitional payments the government was influenced by the fact that certain public assistance committees had been, in its view, over-generous. A national board would make for efficiency and standardised treatment. The fact that the board was not subject to parliamentary questions, in connection with its discretion in applying the standard benefits approved by Parliament, meant that the details of its administration were taken out of the political arena.

Contributory old-age pensions

After the war pensions were raised to take account of inflation. The 1925 Widows, Orphans and Old Age Contributory Pensions Act introduced contributory insurance for old-age pensions, including pensions for widows. Those who paid national health insurance were, in the main, covered. The basic pension was 10 shillings (50p) per week to the insured or his widow at 65, but, on reaching the age of 70, a person receiving a contributory pension transferred to the 1908 non-contributory pension now payable to people reaching 70 without a means test. The Act also gave a pension to the guardian of each motherless orphan child of an insured man until the child reached the age of 14.

The increasing cost of the non-contributory scheme was one reason for going over to a contributory scheme. The increasing cost was mainly due to the increasing proportion of old people in the population. (This proportion will continue to increase up to the late 1980s and is due to a fall in the birth rate from the 1880s onwards plus medical advance.) But many people argued that a contributory scheme was a good thing in itself as pensioners would feel more self-respect in receiving something they had paid for.

A large number of widows had been created by the disasters of the First World War and it was realised that, if over a certain age, it would be difficult for them to find work and hence they were brought into the contributory scheme.

Developments in Social Security since 1939

The creation of the National Assistance Board

Because of the price rise during the Second World War, older people could not live on their pensions alone and, at the beginning of the war, it was supplemented, subject to a means test, by the public assistance committee of the local authorities. The 1940 Pensions Act introduced a nationally financed and administered scheme of supplementary pensions which took them out of the hands of local government and gave them to the Unemployment Assistance Board, now renamed the Assistance Board. This Act also reduced the age a woman could receive a pension under the Contributory Acts from 65 to 60. Local government continued to administer the Poor Law, which still included workhouse relief. The Poor Law was officially abolished in 1948, when the National Assistance Act set up the National Assistance Board with duties which included those of the previous Assistance Board and the Poor Law.

The Beveridge Report

In June 1941 the government appointed a committee under the chairmanship of Sir William Beveridge 'to undertake, with special reference to the interrelation of the schemes, a survey of the existing national schemes of social insurance and allied services, including workmen's compensation and make recommendations'. Beveridge's famous *Report on Social Insurance and Allied Services* (Cmd 6404) was published in November 1942. It was a best-seller!

The Report recommended a unified system of social insurance to replace 'the tangled maze and administration' of the then existing social insurance.

The system should be comprehensive in that all should be insured, including the self-employed.

All should pay the same flat-rate contribution and all should receive the same flat-rate subsistence benefits.

The Report presupposed full employment, a national health service and a system of family allowances if, as it stated, the five 'giants' of 'ignorance, squalor, disease, idleness and want' were to be slain.

The principles underlining the Beveridge Report were:

1. The benefits should be given against contributions, thus supporting the insurance principle and avoiding any humiliation in accepting benefit as one could accept it as of right.
2. The benefits should be enough to live on at subsistence level without any other source of income. Obtaining an income above this level was the individual's responsibility.
3. Everyone should pay the same contributions and receive the same benefits.

4. Those people who had not paid sufficient contributions to qualify for subsistence benefits or who were not covered at all by insurance should have their income supplemented to subsistence level by national assistance.

But it was expected that as the insurance benefits were to be at subsistence level and all workers had to be insured as well as the self-employed, only comparatively few people would have to seek national assistance and their number would diminish. In other words, national assistance was seen as a safety-net only for the minority not covered or not covered adequately by national insurance.

The legislation embodying most of the ideas in the Beveridge Report was passed within three years of the conclusion of the war.

The 1945 Family Allowances Act provided weekly payments for each child beyond the first until such time as the child commenced work.

The 1946 National Insurance Act and the 1946 National Insurance (Industrial Injuries) Act operative from 5 July 1948 provided, on a compulsory basis, insurance against loss of earnings and gave, among other things, unemployment, sickness and disablement benefit and old-age pensions.

The 1946 National Health Service Act introduced a virtually free health service for everyone, operative from July 1948.

The 1948 National Assistance Act abolished the Poor Law, and hence workhouses, and set up a National Assistance Board to provide payments to people over 16 not at school or in work whose income was below the level considered necessary to meet that person's requirements.

At the same time the government had committed itself to a full-employment policy made possible by a revolution in economic theory largely due to the writings of a famous British economist, John Maynard Keynes (1883–1946).

The failure of National Insurance

If one takes the Beveridge principles as the criteria for success, then the national insurance scheme has failed.

The benefits have never been sufficient to live on without any other source of income, and thus a large number of people, dependent solely on insurance payments, have had to seek national assistance (now called supplementary benefit). And because supplementary benefit is means-tested, many people, especially pensioners with memories of the Poor Law and means-tested transitional payments in the 1930s, have refused to claim it. Others have failed to claim because of ignorance. However, it depends what is meant by 'sufficient to live on'. National insurance benefits today are above Beveridge's basic minimum. Hence by his standards they are more than enough to live on without any other source of income. The reason is that general living standards have risen rapidly since 1945 and, over the years, increases in national insurance benefits have meant that, in spite of inflation, benefits are higher in real terms than they were in 1945. But, at the same time, the poverty line, as denoted by the supplementary benefit level, has been raised because of increases in the rate of supplementary benefit, and national insurance benefits have remained below supplementary benefit payments when the housing allowance is taken into consideration. Hence we still say that people living solely on national insurance benefit have not enough to live on (see Carter and Wilson, 1980, p. 26). Even so, it is still correct to speak of the failure of national insurance because, as originally intended by Beveridge, national insurance benefit was supposed to be equal to the basic minimum, whatever that was considered to be, to avoid people having to undergo a means test. In other words, Beveridge envisaged security against want without a means test and a rising poverty level.

The finance of the Insurance Fund was undermined right from the start due to the government agreeing to a full pension to those reaching pensionable age after only ten years' contributions, and to give full pension to existing pensioners. Beveridge intended that only a full subsistence pension should be given to a person who had made the required number of contributions over a period of twenty years. Others should receive a pension appropriate to their contributions and have it made up to subsistence level from national assistance.

And far more people are outside the insurance scheme than Beveridge envisaged. For example, Beveridge never planned for a big rise in one-parent families, nor a return to mass unemployment. Thus payments have had to be made outside the insurance scheme to help certain categories of people with special needs. Finally, the government contribution to the Insurance Fund has not been as generous as Beveridge originally envisaged.

The abandonment of the Beveridge principles

Beveridge's principles of the same contribution from everyone and the same benefit for everyone has been abandoned. There are two main reasons for this:

(1) Living standards have improved considerably since 1945, and for a person to go from the income he has been used to down to a near-subsistence income was considered too big a drop. Hence, as well as the flat-rate scheme, graduated (i.e. earnings-related) schemes have been introduced, whereby those who earn more pay more but receive bigger benefits.

(2) As living standards have risen and continue to rise, the subsistence level of benefit is considered too low, but, in order to increase it, the employee's and employer's shares of the contributions have to be increased. But the poorer employee paid the same flat-rate contribution as the richer employee and hence there was reluctance to increase the flat-rate contribution to provide larger benefits because of the financial burden this placed on poorer people. In other words, the flat-rate contribution had to be set at a level the lower-paid worker could afford and this was not high enough to give the income from contributions to provide adequate benefits. Inflation aggravated the problem. (Those on wages below a certain level pay no contribution.) The earnings-related schemes are a way of providing more income to enable larger benefits to be paid. At the same time, they provide some subsidising of the poorer contributors by the richer contributors.

Summary

The legislation of the Liberal governments on 1905–15 laid the foundations of the welfare state by introducing social services outside the Poor Law to help those in need. It was a response to the growing sympathy for the poor and a desire for greater social justice. It was only a matter of time before national insurance and old-age pensions, introduced to a limited category of people in the original legislation of 1911, were extended to a wider range of people, and this came in the interwar years.

The First World War accelerated the process. Ordinary men and women, having made great sacrifices during the war, were less prepared to accept their old status and relationships. Furthermore,

Lloyd George, the Prime Minister, in an attempt to rekindle flagging national morale, had raised the aspirations of the working class by making promises of a better world after the war with 'homes fit for heroes'. The 1918 Representation of the People Act gave the vote to all men over 21 and women over 30 and thus increased the political power of the working class and ensured that their raised aspirations would at least have to be partially met.

After the short boom period to 1920, fear of revolutionary violence by large sections of the working class was one of the reasons which led the government to introduce transitional payments outside the insurance scheme – an admission that every worker had the right to be protected from poverty caused by unemployment.

Mistaken views on how to deal with economic depression, including the insistence on a balanced budget and need for economy, shared by both Labour and Conservative governments, restricted the development of the social services, and in 1931 crisis year the introduction of household means-tested transitional payments created great bitterness.

In the interwar years the Labour party replaced the Liberal party as the chief opponent of the Conservatives. Although in office for only two short spells, the fact that it was waiting in the wings to take over government perhaps made the Conservative governments more sensitive to the need for social reform.

The Second World War again stimulated interest in social reform, but this time it was not only the war but also the wish not to go back to the bad old days of the 1930s. That was one of the reasons why there was so much interest in the Beveridge Report. Inspired by this, the next major advance was made by the Labour governments from 1945 to 1951. National insurance, to guard against loss of earning power, was made compulsory for everyone, even the self-employed.

At the same time its administration was centralised in a new government department – the Ministry of National Insurance. The system of approved societies was abandoned and the new department supervised the contributions and the benefits. The free medical service provided by the original insurance scheme, which did not, however, cover dependants, was superseded by a comprehensive and virtually free National Health Service. The Poor Law was replaced by a more humane system of national assistance intended as a safety-net for those not adequately covered by national insurance. But as the insurance benefits were insufficient (and still are insufficient) to live on, without any other source of income based on the prevailing poverty line, far more people had to claim assistance than originally intended. In the meantime, just prior to the Labour party coming to power, the coalition government had introduced family allowances.

In recent years graduated insurance has replaced the original flat-rate scheme. Also, since 1975, the main social security benefits have been index-linked to the rate of inflation.

Assignments

1. By making use of the reference books in the library, write short biographical accounts of the following people: Charles Booth, Seebohm Rowntree, William Beveridge.
2. Go to the reference library and ask to see a copy of the Beveridge Report (*Report on Social Insurance and Allied Services*, HMSO, 1942). Read pages 2 to 20 of the Report and answer the following questions:
   (a) What was the third of the three guiding principles of the Report's recommendations?
   (b) What was 'the main feature of the Plan for Social Security' in the Report? What were its six fundamental principles?
   (c) Why did the report stress the insurance principle (i.e. 'benefit in return for contributions rather than free allowances from the State')?
   (d) Why did only the Chairman of the Committee (Beveridge) sign the Report?
   (e) Who was the Minister who set up the Committee?
   (f) Who was the Secretary of the Committee?
   (g) To which Minister was the Report submitted, and the date?
3. Using the cost-of-living index in Whitaker's Almanack, make an estimate of the value of the retirement pension in 1914 at present-day values.
4. What is meant by 'the awakening of the social conscience in later Victorian times'? [INTERMEDIATE DMA, 1959]

28   *Introduction to the Social Services*

Reading

Paul Addison, *The Road to 1945* (Quartet Books, 1977).
Paul Barker (ed.), *Founders of the Welfare State* (Heinemann, 1984).
Corelli Barnett, *The Audit of War – the Illusion and Reality of Britain as a Great Nation* (Macmillan, 1986) chs 1 and 2.
Beveridge Report, *Report on Social Insurance and Allied Services*, Cmd 6404 (HMSO, 1942).
Janet Beveridge, *Beveridge and his Plan* (Hodder & Stoughton, 1954).
Maurice Bruce, *The Coming of the Welfare State* (Batsford, 1971).
Maurice Bruce (ed.), *The Rise of the Welfare State: English Social Policy 1601–1971* (Weidenfeld & Nicolson, 1973).
Charles Carter and Thomas Wilson, *Discussing the Welfare State* (Policy Studies Institute, 1980).
D. V. Donnison and Valerie Chapman, *Social Policy and Administration* (Allen & Unwin, 1965) ch. 2.
Derek Fraser, *Evolution of the Welfare State*, 2nd edn (Macmillan, 1984).
S. Gand and E. O. A. Checkland (eds), *The Poor Law Report of 1843* (Penguin, 1974).
Bentley B. Gilbert, *Evolution of National Insurance in Great Britain* (Michael Joseph, 1966).
Bentley B. Gilbert, *British Social Policy 1914–1939* (Batsford, 1973).
Brian Inglis, *Poverty and the Industrial Revolution* (Hodder & Stoughton, 1971).
Norman Longmate, *The Workhouse* (Temple Smith, 1974).
David C. Marsh (ed.), *An Introduction to the Study of Social Administration* (Routledge & Kegan Paul, 1965) ch. 2 by Joan L. M. Eyden.
T. H. Marshall, *Social Policy*, 5th edn (Hutchinson, 1985).
Robert Pinker, *Social Theory and Social Policy* (Heinemann, 1971).
Robert Roberts, *The Classic Slum*, 3rd impression (Manchester University Press, 1978).
Michael E. Rose, *The Relief of Poverty, 1834–1914*, 2nd edn (Macmillan, 1986).
Pat Thane, *The Foundations of the Welfare State* (Longman, 1982).

4 Social Security Today

Social security is concerned with ensuring, for all citizens above school-leaving age, a basic income when they cannot earn enough money to maintain themselves and their dependants.

The main social security services are:

1. National insurance.
2. Supplementary benefit.
3. Child benefit (formerly family allowance).
4. Family income supplement.
5. Miscellaneous allowances.
6. Redundancy payments.

National Insurance

Like any other form of insurance, people in the national insurance scheme contribute to a fund out of which payments are made to those who suffer loss providing the contribution conditions are satisfied. In the case of national insurance, loss is 'loss of income by interruption of earnings'.

The 'risks' which can cause loss of earnings and which are covered by national insurance are as follows:

(a) sickness during working life, including chronic sickness – long-term sickness benefit is called *invalidity benefit* and is paid after six months of sickness. From 6 April 1986, under the 1985 Social Security Act, the employer pays the first 28 weeks of sickness benefit (called statutory sick pay). After that, if still sick, an employee goes on to invalidity benefit. Those not entitled to statutory sick pay claim the State national insurance sickness benefit. For most people, therefore, national insurance sickness benefit has been privatised.

29

(b)   unemployment
(c)   industrial accidents, including disablement
(d)   old age (a 'desirable risk')
(e)   maternity
(f)   widowhood.

(Maternity benefit is called maternity allowance but there are other maternity benefits outside the national insurance scheme in that they are non-contributory – for example, maternity grant and paid maternity leave. From April 1987, under the 1986 Social Security Act the maternity grant of £25 now paid (1986) to all mothers will be abolished and a new grant of around £75 will be introduced for low income families only (see p. 56). Furthermore, under this Act starting in April 1987, a new statutory maternity pay scheme, administered by employers is to come into operation. It will bring together the separate schemes of maternity allowance run by the DHSS and maternity leave run by the Department of Employment. But those women who do not qualify for statutory maternity pay may still get maternity allowance from the DHSS.

Widowhood in the insurance scheme covers widow's allowance, widow's pension and widowed mother's allowance. The 1986 Social Security Act would in 1988 abolish the widow's allowance which is, at the time of writing, paid to widows for 26 weeks at £54.20 a week and, instead, they would receive a tax-free lump sum of £1,000. Widows with children and any widow over 45 would also get a weekly benefit. At the time of writing a widow age 40 or over with no dependent children or who is 40 or over when widowed mother's allowance ends receives a pension. The 1986 Act would raise the pension age to 45 and the full pension age to 55 – previously 50.)

All workers, even the self-employed, have to be in the national insurance scheme. Before 1961 all categories (i.e. under-18s, employed, self-employed) paid the same flat-rate contribution and all received the same flat-rate benefit. But the National Insurance Act 1959 introduced a pension scheme with earnings-related contributions and benefits which came into operation in April 1961. It did not cover the self-employed and an employee could opt out if he or she was in a sound private scheme. It was discontinued on 5 April 1975 but rights to graduated pension already earned have been preserved. The National Insurance Act 1966 introduced earnings-related contributions and benefits for unemployment, sickness and widowhood. These were compulsory for all (except the self-employed) in the national insurance scheme – no opting out was allowed. These earnings-related schemes were extra to the flat-rate contributions and benefits which still continue to be made. The 1975 Social Security (Pensions) Act introduced a new pension plan operative from April 1978 and made all national insurance contributions, except those of the self-employed, earnings related as from 6 April 1975. In January 1982 the earnings-related supplement for the following short-term benefits – sickness, unemployment and widows' allowance – was abolished. For these, new claimants only receive the flat-rate benefit. But the earnings-related addition has been retained for retirement pensions, widows' pensions and invalidity benefit. Since 1975, the main insurance benefits have been index-linked – pensions to prices or wages, whichever had the biggest percentage increase during the year, and unemployment and sickness benefit to prices. In 1981 the link was made to prices only for pensions so that pensioners' benefits keep pace with inflation but do not increase in real terms. Unemployment benefit and supplementary benefit paid to registered unemployed have been taxable since 5 July 1982. In view of this, these benefits at the uprating in November 1980 were increased by 11½ per cent, i.e. 5 per cent less than the 16½ per cent inflation rate.

National insurance is paid for by:

(a) contributions from employees
(b) contributions from employers as they pay part of the employee's contribution
(c) an Exchequer contribution paid for out of taxation
(d) interest on investments of the Insurance Fund.

Benefits under the national insurance scheme are paid for as of right – there is no means test.

National insurance is administered directly by the Department of Health and Social Security (DHSS) and the minister in charge is the Secretary of State for Social Services. He is aided by junior ministers, one of whom is Minister for Social Security. He is advised by the civil servants in his department and by a Social Security Advisory Committee (SSAC). There is a separate Industrial Injuries Advisory Council which advises the minister on matters relating to industrial injuries. There are also medical appeals tribunals which hear appeals against the decisions of medical boards in relation to assessment of disablement.

If insured persons are dissatisfied with the benefits received or are denied benefit, they can appeal to a local social security tribunal. The tribunals are independent of the government. The procedure is friendly and it costs the claimant nothing. Three people usually sit on the tribunal – the chairman, who normally has legal qualifications, one person from the management side of industry, and one from the trade-union side.

Supplementary Benefit

Supplementary benefit (called supplementary allowance and to those of pensionable age supplementary pension) is a payment made to anyone over 16 who is not at school or in full-time work or on strike (but an amount is paid to strikers' families) whose income is below a certain minimum considered necessary by Parliament for that person's requirements and with capital of not more than £3,000. But this figure will increase to take account of inflation. And 16–19-year-olds in full-time education can get supplementary benefit in exceptional circumstances. The actual benefit is the difference between income and requirements. There are long- and short-term supplementary benefit rates. The short-term rate is less than the long-term rate. This is because it is assumed that a person newly coming on to supplementary benefit will have some resources to fall back on but those on supplementary benefit over a long period will have dissipated those resources and will need extra help. The long-term rate commences after twelve months on the short-term rate except for the unemployed who never receive the long-term rate. In addition, people on supplementary benefit are automatically entitled to free school meals for their children, free milk and vitamins for expectant mothers and children under school age, exemption from charges for prescriptions, dental treatment and spectacles. They can also get financial assistance for rent and rates (see Chapter 15) and free legal aid. Furthermore, single lump-sum payments are made to meet special needs but, normally, only if the claimant has less than £500 capital. There are also regular weekly payments for exceptional circumstances – for example, if the claimant needs a special diet or his home is difficult to heat, etc.

Regulations which came into force in August 1986, reduced the items for which single payments are made. The amount of money paid out for single payments has considerably increased and the Government wishes to bring their cost down to the 1984 level. It feels that the single payments system in many cases has been abused (see p. 57). But one reason for the upsurge in claims has been the campaigns of certain local authorities and voluntary bodies which made many poor people aware, for the very first time, that they were entitled to claim for certain items under the single payments scheme. Furthermore, the right of the appeal to the social security tribunal if the local DHSS office turned the claim down, resulted in many cases of the appeal being upheld. This gave further publicity to the system of single payments. Supplementary benefit is the name for what was previously called national assistance. National assistance was introduced by the 1948 National Assistance Act and replaced the Poor Law. The 1966 Social Security Act renamed national assistance supplementary benefit, and it is the main Act, as amended, governing the administration of supplementary benefit. Approximately 7 million people, including dependants, relied on supplementary benefit in 1985. It is administered by the DHSS, the ministers of which have now taken over the policy-making functions of the Supplementary Benefits Commission, which used to administer supplementary benefit but which was disbanded on 24 November 1980. The ministers are advised by the Social Security Advisory Committee.

In November 1979 approximately 60 per cent of the supplementary benefit claimants were pensioners, 20 per cent were unemployed and approximately 11 per cent were one parent families. By 1986 the unemployed had overtaken pensioners as the largest group on supplementary benefit.

One important break with the Poor Law is the requirement laid down in the original 1948 Act that officers administering supplementary benefit must 'exercise their functions in such a manner as shall best promote the welfare of the persons assisted and their dependants'. In this connection tramps and similar people are encouraged to lead a more settled life. Temporary board and lodging are provided for them in resettlement units (previously called reception centres). They are now used for single, homeless men and are therefore an addition to the homes provided by local authorities for the homeless. For those who have been out of work for a long time and are on supplementary benefit, or using resettlement units, there are re-establishment centres to help make them fit again for work if suitable work is available.

Able-bodied people of working age must complete a form obtained from an unemployment benefit office and send it to the DHSS before they can receive supplementary benefit, and if suitable work is available supplementary benefit may be refused, though it continues to be paid to the applicant's dependants.

Important changes in the administration of supplementary benefit came into effect as from 24 November 1980. From a system where local officers had a fair degree of discretion to interpret the rules of entitlement laid down by the Supplementary Benefits Commission, the emphasis changed to rules of entitlement laid down by law. In other words, many of the rules which used to be discretionary were given legal backing, i.e. were translated into law. Such a change was recommended by the now defunct Supplementary Benefits Commission in its final annual report (the fifth). Discretionary payments, it argued, sometimes lead to payments being based on moral judgements, to claimants being uncertain of their rights and sometimes to conflict between claimants and officers. Furthermore, discretionary decisions make the scheme more complex and more difficult to administer fairly. On the other hand, benefits based on a legal framework give more publicity to the benefits and make it easier for Parliament to scrutinise the working of the system. But the Commission admitted that, in reducing the amount of discretion, there was the danger that the system would become rigid and certain cases which justified help would not receive it. However, discretion was retained 'for really exceptional cases' under what was known as 'the fall back powers'. Hence some key decisions will still rest on the opinion of the local officers, now called benefit officers. Difficult cases can be referred to regional adjudication officers. There is a chief adjudication officer in Southampton whose job is to ensure that all adjudication officers are interpreting the law in the same way. He sends out guidelines on day-to-day claims. A claimant can, as previously, appeal against a decision to a social security appeal tribunal. If the appeal is turned down, it can be referred to a Social Security Commissioner on a point of law only. As a general rule, where there is an appeals tribunal procedure, ministerial responsibility does not apply. This is to ensure that only judicial considera-

tions, and not political ones, are taken into account when considering an appeal. The Lord Chancellor is responsible for preparing a
list of suitable chairmen for administrative tribunals. There is also a
Council on Tribunals whose job is to keep an eye on how tribunals
are working, particularly in regard to fairness, and make recommendations, where necessary, to the Lord Chancellor for their
improvement – the Lord Chancellor being ultimately responsible
for them.

Other changes in the administration of supplementary benefit
include providing claimants with a form explaining how their
benefit is worked out and much greater publicity to the workings of
the scheme and of the criteria on which decisions are based.

Child Benefit

Child benefit, like family allowance, which it replaced in 1977, is
especially helpful to poorer families, though it is paid to all families
with one child or more and hence is not means-tested. It ceases at 16
unless the child is receiving full-time education. A person's wages is
related to his job and not his needs. Hence an unskilled worker with
a wife and family might find his wage not sufficient to keep his
family above the current poverty level. And because he is working,
he is not normally entitled to supplementary benefit. Unlike the
former family allowances, child benefit is tax-free but, to help make
up the tax loss, child tax allowances for income-tax purposes have
been abolished. Child benefit is the responsibility of the Secretary
of State for Social Services. It is paid for out of taxation. Payments
are made weekly or monthly at the post office or paid monthly into a
bank account.

For one-parent families there is an extra benefit called *one-parent
benefit*. Like the main child benefit it is not means-tested but
anyone on supplementary benefit who receives the one-parent
benefit is no better off because his or her supplementary benefit is
reduced by the amount of the one-parent benefit.

Family Income Supplement

This benefit was introduced by the 1970 Family Income Supplements Act (operative from 1971) to help those families with one

child or more where the breadwinner is on such a low wage that the family income is below supplementary benefit level, yet, because the breadwinner is working full time, supplementary benefit cannot be claimed. It is a means-tested benefit and was being paid to approximately 200,000 families in 1986, just over half of which were single parent families. It can be claimed by the self-employed. The cost of the scheme is paid for out of taxation. The actual benefit is collected at the post office.

Like those on supplementary benefit, families on FIS can obtain free school meals, free milk and vitamins for expectant mothers and children under school age, free prescriptions, free dental treatment, free spectacles and free travel to hospital for any necessary treatment and help with rent or rates.

Miscellaneous Allowances

A *child's special allowance* is paid to a woman whose marriage has been dissolved and who has not remarried. It is paid on the death of her former husband if he was contributing towards the cost of the upbringing of their child or had been instructed to do so by court order.

There is also the *death grant*, which now bears no relation to the cost of funeral expenses.

The above benefits are contributory benefits and part of the national insurance scheme.

The following miscellaneous benefits do not require contributions and are not subject to a means test. They are 'risks' affecting income not covered by the national insurance scheme:

A *guardian's allowance* is paid to a person looking after a child whose parents are dead.

Attendance allowance, which is paid to severely disabled people who need considerable attention either day or night or both.

Severe disablement allowance, which is to help the sick and disabled who do not qualify for contributory sick or invalidity benefit.

Mobility allowance, which helps to pay transport costs for physically disabled people who cannot or are virtually unable to walk.

Invalid care allowance, which is paid to people who cannot go out to work because they are caring for a severely disabled person receiving an attendance allowance. Thanks to a ruling of the European Court of Justice it was extended as from June 1986 to married women, previously excluded from the allowance.
War pensions for the disabled in the forces.

There are also pensions for people who were excluded from the national insurance scheme because they were over pensionable age in 1948. Pensions for people over 80 and the attendance allowance were introduced by the 1970 National Insurance (Old Persons' and Widows' Pensions and Attendance Allowance) Act.

Housing Benefit

The 1966 Rating Act introduced rate rebates for low income households. As rates are a tax on property and related to the income of the household, they could cause hardship, especially to pensioners. The 1972 Housing Finance Act introduced statutory rent rebate for council house tenants on low incomes and rent allowance for low income families in private accommodation. Both now go under the name of housing benefit. Under the 1986 Social Security Act all households, even the poorest, would be expected to pay 20 per cent of their rates, but how this will actually operate must await the Government's proposals for the reform of Local Government finance. Those on income support (a proposed replacement for supplementary benefit – see below) or similar income would, however, have their rent met in full. One reason for all households having to meet at least 20 per cent of their rates might be the concern of the Government that all households should be made aware of financial consequences on family budgets of large rate increases which some local authorities have imposed. Hence there may then be more political pressure on those councils to keep a tighter control on their spending. Another reason is, of course, to reduce public expenditure. There is general agreement that there will be cuts in housing benefit for most people if the 1986 Act comes into operation in 1988. The Government has already made it known that, in its view, people too high up the income scale receive it. (At the present time (1986) one in three households receive housing benefit.) Thus there would be no entitlement to housing benefit for those with capital over £6,000. And between £3,000 and £6,000 'each £250 of capital will be assumed to provide an income of £1 a week', and benefit would be reduced accordingly. Only capital of under £3,000 would be ignored. These rules on capital are the same as for the proposed income support scheme to replace supplementary benefit (see p. 56) and part of the Government's proposals for standardising the rules for all income-related benefits in order to simplify the administration.

Social Security Advisory Committee (SSAC)

This committee gives advice to the Secretary of State on national insurance, supplementary benefit, child benefit and family income supplement. It replaced in November 1980 the former Supplementary Benefits Commission and National Insurance Advisory Committee. The members of the committee represent various interests including trade unions, employers' organisations and friendly societies. It initiates inquiries and makes an annual report with recommendations.

Redundancy Payments

Redundancy payments are lump-sum payments made by employers to employees who are made redundant through no fault of their own – victims, in many cases of technological progress. The amount paid is related to age and years of service. Although strictly compensation payments, they have been included under social security because they often help a worker to keep going until a job is found.

Under the 1965 Redundancy Payments Act, which introduced the scheme, employers pay a surcharge on their weekly national insurance contributions for each of their employees, and this goes to the Central Redundancy Fund. An employer can claim a rebate from the Fund to cover part of the redundancy payment. In this way the cost of the redundancy payments are evenly shared by employers as a whole.

The scheme is administered by the employers themselves, except that the Secretary of State for Employment is responsible for the

Central Redundancy Fund and he authorises payments from it.

At the time of writing in 1986, the following benefits are tax-free – sickness, invalidity, attendance allowance, mobility allowance, child benefit, maternity allowance, disablement benefit, war pension, supplementary benefit (excluding that paid to the registered unemployed), and family income supplement. Other social security benefits including retirement pension, unemployment benefit, supplementary benefit paid to registered unemployed are taken into account for tax purposes.

Summary

The main social security service is national insurance augmented by supplementary benefit and child benefit. Low-wage families who cannot claim supplementary benefit can claim family income supplement.

Assignments

1. Obtain from your DHSS office the latest copy of *Which Benefit?* (FB 2) From reading the pamphlet list the benefits that can be obtained by people on supplementary benefit. Against each benefit give, where available, the number of the leaflet which explains the benefit in more detail.
2. Find out the following benefit rates:

   (a)   The standard rate basic retirement pension (leaflet NP 32).
   (b)   The amount of sickness benefit for a man under 65 and a woman under 60 who are not receiving statutory sick pay (SSP). (leaflet NI 16).
   (c)   The supplementary benefit rate for a pensioner under 80 living in his own home and the rate for husband and wife living in their own home. Also, the rate for a pensioner living with someone else and not paying rent. And the supplementary benefit rate for the following under pension age: (i) a single householder, (ii) husband and wife, (iii) a person not paying rent and living in someone else's household (leaflet SB 1).

   (d)   The amount of maternity allowance (NI 17A).
   (e)   The amount of the invalid care allowance (leaflet NI 212).

   (A very useful leaflet is NI 196 because it gives a comprehensive list of the benefit rates.)
3. Why, in spite of comprehensive national insurance scheme, is there such a large number of people on supplementary benefit? Why has their number increased over the years?

Reading

Ruth Cohen and Beth Lakhani, *National Welfare Benefits Handbook* (Child Poverty Action Group, published annually).

DHSS, explanatory leaflets provided by the Department of Health and Social Security. (DHSS Leaflets Unit, PO Box 21, Stanmore, Middlesex HA7 1AY).

DHSS, *Annual Report* (Department of Health and Social Security).

David Donnison, 'Against Discretion', *New Society* (15 September 1977).

Family Welfare Association, *Guide to the Social Services* (Longmans, published annually).

Finer Report, *One Parent Families*, Cmnd 5629 (HMSO, 1974).

Bill Jordan, 'Against Donnison', *New Society* (13 October 1977).

5 Problems of Social Security (Including the Government's Reform Proposals)

Who are the Poor?

One definition is that the poor are all those people who are dependent on supplementary benefit plus those living below the supplementary benefit level. If we accept this definition, then the number of poor people has considerably increased, particularly in recent years. Thus the number of people receiving supplementary benefit has quadrupled since 1948 from just over 1 million to just over 4½ million. (*Social Trends*, 1986). And if we take into consideration their dependants and those living below supplementary benefit level (approximately 2½ million) the number of poor can be put at around 9 million. Government figures quoted in the *Guardian*, 26 July 1986, show that over 16 million people are living on or just above the poverty line. One reason for the increase in the number of people dependent on supplementary benefit is the increase over the years in its real value so that many people find their income below the supplementary benefit level and can thus claim supplementary benefit. As the nation becomes richer, people's expectations become higher. Other reasons include the increase in the number of one-parent families arising from more married couples separating and more children being born to unmarried mothers; an increasing proportion of retired people in the population many of whom receive only the state pension and, in more recent times, the great increase in the number of unemployed families who have overtaken pensioners as the largest group on

41

supplementary benefit. There are now (1986) approximately 3½ million registered unemployed, well over half of whom are on supplementary benefit. Because of the increase in real terms in the value of supplementary benefit, a person on supplementary benefit today is better off than a person who was on national assistance in 1948. However, if we define poverty in relative terms – not having what most people take for granted – then, even though the poor have been more than protected against inflation, it can be argued they are no longer better off than in 1948 in that their percentage share of the country's wealth is roughly the same as it was then. And since 1979 their percentage share has fallen. Unemployment benefit for a family with two children has fallen as a proportion of the average wage, the gap between poorly paid workers and well paid has widened and pensions are no longer linked with wages – wages having risen faster than prices.

There has been a corresponding increase in expenditure on social security – it now takes up to 30 per cent of all public expenditure. Unemployment is a big factor in this. Unemployment does not just send up the social security bill, the Exchequer also suffers because of reduced taxation receipts including reduced national insurance contributions and there is also the lost production those unemployed would have engendered if they had been working. And it causes ill-health imposing greater demands on the health service and the personal social services.

But why, when supplementary benefit is supposed to be a safety net for all citizens, are there an estimated 2½ million of them living on an income below what those who administer supplementary benefit consider necessary? One reason is that a fair number of people do not claim all the means-tested benefits to which they are entitled due sometimes to pride but more often to ignorance of the benefit system. (There are over forty means-tested benefits apart from supplementary benefit.)

Another reason is low wages, because no supplementary benefit is given to families where the breadwinner is working full time even though his wage plus child benefit and family income supplement may not be sufficient to live on. Furthermore, administrative errors may mean that some claimants are not given all they are entitled to. And it must be remembered that there will always be people who receive sufficient income to keep them above supplementary benefit level but who spend it unwisely.

Policies to Reduce Poverty

Is the Beveridge goal of security against want without a means test still possible? If by *want* is meant anything below the supplementary benefit level of living, then, to avoid means testing, the main national insurance benefits – retirement pension, widows' pension, unemployment benefit, sickness benefit – would have to be considerably increased to bring them up to the supplementary benefit level including the housing allowance. This would necessitate a large increase in contributions and higher taxation, to cover an increased Exchequer contribution, though all benefits could be considered as income for tax purposes so the Exchequer would get some of the money back. In the present economic climate, however, where there is little economic growth to pay for expanding services and where expenditure on social security alone now amounts to about 30 per cent of all public expenditure, it is doubtful if the main political parties would think such an increase politically possible and some among them would think it economically unsound: politically not possible because of the electorate's alleged resistance to higher taxes; and some who support the monetarist views of Milton Friedman would say economically unsound for three reasons – (a) higher taxes inhibit enterprise and encourage higher wage demands which, in turn, stoke inflation, (b) resources are limited so that, if the money supply is to be contained, increased public expenditure means less resources for the private sector and it is upon the private sector that the country mainly depends for its economic growth, and (c) increased public expenditure usually means, as well as higher taxation, increased government borrowing, which increases the money supply and hence inflationary pressures. The Government in its attempt to implement a monetarist economic policy has been doing its best to curb the growth of public expenditure and one aspect of this has been cuts in social security benefits. Thus it has abolished the link retirement pensions had with average earnings. It has abolished earnings related supplements for short-term benefits, it has taxed short-term benefits. Benefit for workers on strike is now only paid to strikers' families. School-leavers now cannot obtain supplementary benefit until after the vacation, i.e. not until September. Child benefit at the interim July 1986 uprating ceased to be linked with the inflation rate. Claims for single payments have been restricted to fewer items. In October 1986 there were cuts in industrial injury benefits.

Denationalisation and privatisation measures are also a means of reducing public expenditure although there are other reasons for these measures. In addition, the Government inaugurated in April 1984 extensive reviews of the social security system which it claimed would provide 'the most substantial examination of the social security system since the Beveridge Report.' There were four reviews covering retirement, benefits for children and young people, supplementary benefit and housing benefit. A Green Paper was published June 1985 and a White Paper setting out the Government's final thoughts on reform of the social security system in December 1985. Legislation was put before Parliament in 1986 and the 1986 Social Security Act embodies most of the White Paper proposals. These proposals are discussed below under the heading to which they refer.

There is, however, an influential body of opinion which would argue that at a time of recession, when there is much unemployed resources, an increase in public expenditure does not necessarily mean less for the private sector. And there are defenders of the Keynesian demand-management policy who argue for increased public expenditure during the present recession (see Thirlwall, 1981). Furthermore, there is still a case for getting back to the Beveridge goal of security against want without a means test (see Meade, 1978, ch. 13; and Parker, 1980). And there are those who, while not going so far as to bring up insurance benefits to the supplementary benefit rates, nevertheless wish to see more generous benefits to help reduce the number of people who have to claim supplementary benefit (see Ruth Lister's chapter on social security in Blake and Ormerod, 1980). Both latter groups envisage cutting out certain tax allowances to help finance the extra costs involved. These tax allowances have been referred to as the hidden welfare state. They mainly help the better off. (The tax system was not in the review teams' term of reference.) There is also support from among those who wish to see more generous benefits for taxing benefits, provided that tax thresholds are raised so that the levels of supplementary benefit and the levels of income at which tax begins to be paid do not overlap.

In spite of the large increase in the number of people who now have to claim supplementary benefit, all governments have, from time to time, aimed at *reducing* their number.

Pensions

The 1975 Social Security (Pensions) Act introduced a new pensions scheme operative from April 1978 aimed to progressively reduce the number of pensioners who have to claim supplementary pension. It provides earnings-related benefits, as well as earnings-related contributions, for everyone except the self-employed. The benefits cover not only retirement but also widowhood and invalidity. It takes claimants twenty years to build up to a full pension so the scheme does nothing to help most of the present pensioners. The pension is based on the claimant's best twenty years of earnings and the average level of earnings nationally at the time of retirement. It is inflation-proof. Contracting out is permitted for those in good occupational pension schemes, though those that do contract out still remain in the flat-rate scheme. They pay reduced contributions to the state scheme. Before this Act there had been three other attempts at pension reform, none of which, unlike this final one, had the support of both the Conservative and Labour parties.

The Thatcher government now argues that the above pension scheme, popularly known as SERPS (State Earnings Related Pension Scheme) was actuarially based on too rosy a picture of the economy and is too costly. Hence, under the 1986 Social Security Act the Government, if it wins the General Election, will introduce a simpler basic pension but eventually it is hoped every employee will be able to contribute to his own additional pension to augment the basic state pension. This would be done by means of an occupational pension provided by the employer but if employees choose to have a personal pension arrangement, they will be able to opt out of the employers' schemes. The advantage of a personal pension scheme is that it is 'portable from job to job'. But the State basic pension would give less money in retirement that SERPS. For example, it would be based on average lifetime earnings rather than the best 20 years and the pension rate would be reduced from 25 per cent to 20 per cent of earnings. And widows, who now inherit the whole of their husbands' pension rights (up to a ceiling) would, under the Act, only inherit half of them. The advantages from the Government point of view are that future generations are relieved of a financial burden. Thus, according to the Government actuary's figures (Cmnd 9711), by the year 2053–4, expenditure on earnings-related pensions would have been reduced from £35.3 billion (the estimated cost of the present scheme) to £16.3 billion. Furthermore, the Government see an advantage in all employees having a private pension as well as a State pension which, today, only applies to the better off. With the money saved there could be more money for the basic pension but, although like the present scheme the new pension plan would be inflation proof, there is no hint that, as prior to 1979, the basic pension would allow for higher living standards for pensioners. Finally, the Government suggests the insurance funds from private schemes would provide capital for investment. The fact that the basic State pension would give less than the present scheme in retirement is fair enough if the private pension schemes make up the difference and everyone is covered by a sound private scheme. But much criticism of the new proposals relates to how far one can trust all employers to provide an adequate pension plan. History shows that in many spheres of social welfare it is the failure of some employers which has necessitated action by the State. It is claimed that few private pension schemes have succeeded in maintaining pensions in line with inflation. Furthermore, it is argued that private pension schemes will increase employers' costs encouraging only modest schemes to keep costs down. Those in a good occupational scheme would be guaranteed a minimum pension. This is one of the conditions for contracting out of the State scheme. But personal pensions would depend on the investment yields and administrative costs of the scheme. However, there would be a 2 per cent special incentive paid by the DHSS on behalf of most personal pension holders into personal pension schemes which would continue until 5 April 1993. Furthermore, the schemes would be subject to tax relief. There would be special provision for those not earning enough to build up full pension rights – those who take time off work to bring up children, disabled people and those not earning because they are looking after the disabled. But these groups would still need a minimum of 20 years earnings to get full pension rights under the State scheme. On the other hand, those not in the above categories – the unemployed for example – would have their State pension based on their lifetime earnings and hence unemployment or low wages would reduce their eventual pension. (Under the present scheme (SERPS) they would earn a full pension based on their best 20 years earnings.) For occupational pension schemes the Government would require a minimum contribution of

4 per cent of salary of which at least 2 per cent would fall on the employer. The proposed changes would not affect anyone retiring before the year 2000 and there would be a transition period until 2010 but, eventually, there would be a system, the Government hopes, in which everybody would be able to contribute either to an occupational pension or to a personal pension as well as the State basic pension.

Child Benefit

All political parties are agreed on the importance of child benefit as a means of combating family poverty. But child benefit, like family allowance which preceded it, has never been large enough to cover the cost of bringing up a child. Increasing the amount of child benefit reduces the number of families dependent on supplementary benefit. Child benefit improved the value of support for families with children by paying benefit for the first child, whereas family allowances were only paid to families with two children or more.

The introduction of one-parent family supplement is a further help in reducing the number of those who have to claim supplementary benefit.

Family allowances used to be taxed. In order to get back the increase in family allowances from those who did not need it, the 1968 Budget introduced what became known as 'claw back'. This was an adjustment of income by which the entire extra payment of an increase in family allowances was recovered from all who paid tax at the standard rate. But because of the low tax threshold the extra family allowances were 'clawed back' from families who needed it. This was one of the reasons for inhibiting the Conservative government (1970–4) from substantially increasing family allowances as promised. But if the tax system could be adjusted so that those on income low enough to justify their being supplemented from public funds did not pay tax, then going back to child tax allowances and taxing child benefit might be the best way of substantially increasing child benefit without making too big an increase in public expenditure. One immediate reform would be to make child benefit equivalent to the supplementary benefit rate for children so that the working poor who cannot claim supplementary benefit are not at a disadvantage with the unemployed poor on supplementary benefit. However, the working poor can claim family income supplement. Child benefit was unaffected by the Government review of social security and the 1986 Social Security Act. Because the increase in child benefit in the June 1986 benefit review was below the inflation rate, there are fears that, over the years, its value will get less and less in real terms.

Sickness

Invalidity benefit was introduced in 1971 and reduced the number of long-term sick and disabled dependent on supplementary benefit but some of them had not been in employment sufficiently long to have the necessary number of contributions to qualify for it. Hence to help these people there was introduced in 1975 the non-contributory invalidity pension, now called severe disablement allowance. Because this benefit is less than the contributory invalidity benefit, its effect on reducing the number of long-term sick dependent on supplementary benefit is much less.

Negative Income Tax

This is a scheme for bringing together personal taxation and social security. Under the scheme a single tax form would be used from which the right to benefit or the liability to tax would be worked out. The tax form would be used, as now, to assess the amount of tax to be paid by people above the taxpaying level, but it would also be a means of giving cash benefits (i.e. a negative tax) to those below the tax level.

The Labour government, when it took office in 1964, hoped to bring in this reform under the name of an *income guarantee scheme* which would deal with the problem of poverty in a comprehensive way. It would replace all the means-tested and universal benefits and guarantee a minimum income at subsistence level for everyone, including an average allowance for housing. But the tax form is normally only submitted once a year, and therefore information about a person's income and expenditure held by the Inland Revenue might be up to a year out of date, and thus, at any time within that twelve months, a person's circumstances might have changed. Hence the government dropped the scheme because it was not sufficiently flexible to adjust benefit quickly enough to meet changing circumstances. The scheme proposed by the Conservative government (1970–4), called a *tax-credit scheme*, avoided this because it was more modest. It would have replaced the main income-tax personal allowances and family allowances and, except for a few outside the scheme, family income supplement. But national insurance and supplementary benefit would have continued, but on a reduced scale. Hence a person receiving a tax credit would be able to claim in addition supplementary benefit, should circumstances worsen, until such time as the Inland Revenue adjusted his or her code in accordance with the worsened circumstances. The scheme would not have covered about 10 per cent of the population and this included the self-employed and those on a very low income.

Advantages of the tax-credit scheme. Based on the current rate of social security benefits at the time the scheme was proposed, those on family income supplement or supplementary benefit would have been better off. It would have reduced means-testing because it would have made family income supplement virtually unnecessary and not as many people would have had to claim supplementary benefit.

Disadvantages of the tax-credit scheme. The estimated cost of the scheme was £1,300 million, yet the late Professor Kaldor of Cambridge University estimated that only £150 million would go to those earning less than £1,000 a year. Hence some people argued that there would have been a greater reduction in the number of people having to claim means-tested benefits if the £1,300 million were spent on increasing the normal social security benefits – pensions, family allowances, etc. But other tax-credit schemes have been put forward which purport to avoid this criticism, notably one by the Young Conservatives (*A Credit to Us All*, 1976). For a number of years little was heard of the tax-credit scheme possibly due to administrative problems of a technical nature which have to be overcome before the scheme can be seriously considered. However, in more recent years there has been a growing awareness in all political parties that some move towards integration of the tax and benefit system is necessary and fresh schemes have been put forward. One put forward by Stephen Davies would give everyone a basic income but all other income would be taxed. There would be supplements for certain categories like the elderly, disabled, one-parent families, but there would have to be a means-tested housing benefit. The existing supplementary benefit scheme would be no longer needed. To pay for the scheme, taxation would have to be considerably increased if, for example, the basic income was equivalent to the supplementary benefit level of income.

Low-wage families

Family income supplement. FIS is paid to low-wage families (see p. 35)

The supplement is half the difference between the family income (i.e. gross income including child benefit) and a prescribed amount approved by Parliament, which varies according to the number of children in the family. But there is a maximum payment.

Does FIS bring poor families, where the breadwinner is working, up to the supplementary benefit level of income? It is difficult to say, as the two forms of benefit are entirely separate. The benefits under FIS are the same for all families with a similar number of children and with similar incomes irrespective of their outgoings, whereas supplementary benefit varies according to the outgoings as well as the income of the family. A rather weak generalisation would be to say that some families will be brought up to or above supplementary benefit level, some will not. Like the Speenhamland system introduced in 1795 in Berkshire (which subsidised farm workers' wages) the scheme might encourage low wages. But, whatever the criticisms, the government could have argued that the scheme was an emergency one until something better was thought out (see the Chancellor's *Budget Statement*, 21 March 1972).

Under the 1986 Social Security Act FIS will be renamed family credit in 1988 assuming the Government wins the next general election. But it would no longer give entitlement to free milk and free school meals. Instead it would include an extra payment to compensate for these items. At present FIS is paid at the same rate for 52 weeks, whether family circumstances have changed or not, but a fresh claim for it can be made for the following 52 weeks. Under Family Credit it would only be paid for 26 weeks at a time. Because of strong opposition, even from many of its own supporters, the Government withdrew its proposal for family credit to be paid by employers which would have meant that in the vast majority of cases it would go to the father and not, as with FIS, to the mother. But the Government saw the paying of family credit by the employer as a small step towards integration of the tax and social security systems. The Government White Paper (Cmnd 9691) gave the assurance that family credit would be set at a level 'which will almost always prove more generous than the FIS which the same family would receive today'. The Government also state that it would be paid to around 400,000 families compared with the 200,000 to whom FIS is paid now (1986). One reason for this is that with FIS, the breadwinner must work at least 30 hours a week, unless a single parent, whereas with Family Credit the minimum working week would be 24 hours. On the other hand, what might reduce the number of claimants is that people with capital of more than £6,000 would not be entitled to Family Credit, whereas with FIS a claimant's capital is not taken into consideration.

Minimum wage. Why not a minimum wage which could be made legally binding by Act of Parliament? Although this would help all low-wage earners whose present wages are below the proposed minimum, it would not raise every low-paid worker and worker's family above the poverty line as there would still be low-wage families with exceptional expenditure (perhaps because there are many children). But the main objections to a minimum wage are based on the reasoning that it would send up labour costs and increase unemployment. But not everyone agrees with this argument. However, about 3 million workers have a legally binding minimum wage fixed by wages councils (successors to the trade boards). These are workers who are in trades or industries with inadequate wage-negotiating machinery. They cover (1986) 2.75 million people, about 80 per cent of them female. Inspectors from the Department of Employment make occasional checks to ensure that employers are not paying below the legal minimum rate. However, many employers still continue to pay below the statutory minimum.

The Government is sympathetic to the view put forward by certain economists of the monetarist school that minimum wage legislation increases unemployment and this it feels is especially so for young people. It considers the wages councils' minimum wages for them are too high so that employers are reluctant to employ young people but would do so if their wages were lower. Hence, under the 1986 Wages Act, wages councils no longer fix minimum wage rates for young people under 21.

The unemployed

At the time of writing in late 1986 the economic recession and the deflationary policy of the Thatcher government make the plight of the unemployed grim indeed. They receive a flat-rate unemployment benefit for twelve months, after which they go on to supplementary benefit. The flat-rate benefit is below the supplementary benefit rate when the additions for rent and rates paid to supplementary benefit claimants are taken into consideration. Therefore, many of those unemployed without any other source of income but the flat-rate benefit have to go on to supplementary benefit. But the unemployed are not entitled to the long-term supplementary benefit rate unless aged 60 or over. The rule was made when there was comparatively little unemployment and it was felt most unemployed would get a job within twelve months. However, nowadays, with over 3¼ million unemployed, many will be unemployed for much longer than twelve months and it does seem an injustice that they do not receive the long-term supplementary benefit rate. As the Social Security Advisory Committee stated in its *First Report* in 1981, 'the growing band of long-term unemployed has to exist on a basic level of personal benefit which is little more then two-thirds of the minimum the Government has established for others in similar circumstances'

From October 1986, under the 1986 Social Security Act, those who leave their jobs without a good reason will have their unemployment benefit stopped for 13 weeks – previously it was 6 weeks. Supplementary benefit, should they claim it, will be cut by 40 per cent for the same period.

Means-testing

So far we have been assuming that means-testing is a bad thing, but there are people, many of them supporters of monetarism, who defend means-testing and would make all benefits means-tested. Apart from strict control of the money supply as one of the chief means of controlling the economy, monetarists would hand all public enterprises over to private enterprise in those cases where they thought private enterprise could do the job as well or better, being more subject to the market mechanism than public enterprise and hence, in their view, more sensitive to needs. And because most people are much better off than they used to be, they could provide for their own welfare in the private market without any help from the state. In other words the welfare state, largely based on the principle of 'universal' provision, should be dismantled and state aid channelled to the minority who are too poor to buy social services. A means test (i.e. based on the 'selective' principle) will reveal who these people are. In any case, the increasing cost of the social services and the limitations on the amount of money available for welfare means that more people will have to provide for themselves – a viewpoint held by many people who are not sympathetic to the monetarists. Furthermore, under the universal principle, when benefits have to be increased to meet rising prices, they can never, because of the cost, be increased sufficiently to eradicate poverty. Selectivity by not giving money to those who do not need it will enable more money to be given to those who really need it. It will allow public expenditure to be reduced, lessen the burden of contributions and taxation and give greater incentives to work harder. Thus the country's wealth will increase at a faster rate. It is true that more means-testing will mean more form-filling, but people today are used to filling in forms and a means test is no longer the humiliating experience it used to be. It is true that more means-testing creates more administrative work, but this will be more than offset by the saving in expenditure on the social services.

On the other hand, the opponents of means-testing argue that selectivity divides the country into two nations when the aim of social policy should be to unite it. Better to retain the universal principle to prevent this division even if means-testing for certain categories of people in need has to be continued. For example, a basic pension is paid to everyone but a supplementary pension which is means-tested is entered in the same book. Thus nobody knows whether a person drawing a pension at the post office is drawing the basic pension or the supplementary as well. Without a universal benefit, those going to the post office to receive their pension would be labelled poor. Hence, providing selective benefits for certain categories of people operate within a universal system, they need not be socially divisive.

The main argument against means-tested benefits is that they are not claimed by many people entitled to them. In 1982 the take-up of certain benefits as a percentage of the total who were entitled to them was as follows: 76 per cent take-up for supplementary pension, 80 per cent for supplementary benefit, 75 per cent for one-parent benefit, 50 per cent for FIS, rent rebate around 72 per cent, and rate rebate 65 per cent (*Social Trends*, 1986). There are, of course, many more means-tested benefits. The 1986 Annual Conference of the Social Democratic Party approved an entirely means-tested system of social security but one which avoided the stigma associated with a means test because the administration of the tax and benefit system would be merged (see p. 48) including the merging of national insurance and income tax so the same means test would be applied to all. Personal allowances would be restructured. Thus, under the scheme universal benefits would be abolished. For example, child benefit, now a universal benefit, would only go to those who did not pay tax. The proposals raise problems of a technical and administrative nature which must be overcome before they can be operative.

The Poverty Trap

This refers to families whose income is just low enough to qualify them for welfare benefits. If they earn more, their net income may not increase because their welfare benefits will be reduced. As an example, take a family receiving FIS. The more the breadwinner earns, the less FIS he receives. In addition he pays more income tax, more national insurance contributions and he could lose his free prescription charges and other benefits. In a House of Commons debate on social security (*Hansard*, vol. 998, no. 39, 3 February 1981) it was stated that a couple with two children on £55 a week would have to get a wage increase of over £20 a week to increase their net income; with four children the rise would have to be £30 to £40 a week. Furthermore, it has been estimated that about 10 per cent of those drawing unemployment benefit or unemployment benefit plus supplementary benefit could be just as well off not working and about 10 per cent could be better off. Again, this is mainly due to the loss of welfare benefits when taking up full-time employment, plus travel expenses getting to work and income tax.

But is all this the fault of the social security system or rather the fault of the low tax threshold and the low wages some employers pay? The Government claims that under family credit 'the worst effects of the poverty trap would be eliminated' because it would be based on net income, i.e. income after tax and national insurance contributions had been deducted.

Government proposals for the replacement of supplementary benefit

Supplementary benefit would be replaced by an income support scheme. With income support there would be a personal allowance. Single claimants under 18 would receive less than those aged 18 to 24; those aged 25 or over would receive more. But all lone parents aged over 18 would get the over 25 rate. There would be one rate for couples over 18, higher than for couples under 18. The present (1986) householder and non-householder categories would be abolished. (The Government has stated that the most important source of help for single householders is, anyway, housing benefit (see p. 37).) In addition to the personal allowance, there would be extra payments called premiums for certain categories of claimants (called client groups). These extra payments would replace the existing weekly additions and single payments now paid under supplementary benefit and would 'reflect the general needs of particular groups' (*Commons Hansard*, 28 January, column 826). This, as the Government states, would certainly make the administration simpler. The categories receiving the premiums would be as follows:

(a) Pensioners aged 60 or over would receive a general premium with a higher premium for pensioners over 80.
(b) Families with children would receive a family premium for each dependent child. Couples with no children would receive only the personal allowance.
(c) Single (lone) parents would receive the family premium plus a lone parent premium.
(d) Disabled people, including the long-term sick, would receive a disablement premium including a disablement premium for each disabled child. For severly disabled people there would be an additional premium. But the Government is to initiate a

review of the various benefits available to the disabled with
special reference to carers (i.e. those who look after disabled
people at home).

Under these proposed new arrangements, long- and short-term
rates would be abolished. As under supplementary benefit, the first
£3,000 of capital would be disregarded for benefit purposes but,
between £3,000 and £6,000 there would be a sliding scale of benefit
– the amount of benefit getting less the nearer to £6,000. Thus
everyone with capital under £6,000 would get some benefit. For the
unemployed and single parents and the disabled, earnings up to a
limit would be disregarded for benefit purposes as now but expenses
involved in going to work would be excluded in calculating benefit.
Like supplementary benefit, income support would not be given to
those in regular work (24 hours per week or more). Furthermore,
the Government intend to exclude students from unemployment
benefit and supplementary benefit during the short term vacations.

The other part of the reformed supplementary benefit system
would be the creation of a social fund out of which payments would
be made to meet special needs not covered by income support. The
payments would be weekly payments or lump sum payments.

Four categories of need would be covered by the fund:

1. *Maternity and funeral costs.* Payments made for these expenses
   would be in the form of a grant starting April 1987. The present
   maternity grant of £25 (1986) paid to all mothers would be
   abolished and so would the present £30 death grant. A new
   maternity grant of around £75 would be introduced for people on
   income support or family credit. In place of the present death
   grant there would be a grant 'to meet the reasonable cost of a
   funeral', again only for people on income support or family
   credit. Entitlement to maternity and funeral costs would be
   based on regulations and there would be a right of appeal should
   the claim be turned down to a social security tribunal and, on a
   point of law, to a social security commission. But in giving help
   to both maternity and funeral costs savings over £500 'will be
   taken into consideration'.
2. *Community care.* Grants would be provided to help, for
   example, handicapped people 're-establish themselves in the
   community, to avoid institutional care, or to ease particular

pressures on families'. Thus money from the social fund could be used to provide home helps and other domiciliary services for the handicapped, or the elderly (see *Guardian*, 20 September 1986). Again savings over £500 will be taken into consideration.
3. *Financial crises*. Payments would be made to help people whose money had been lost or stolen or who needed financial help because of floods or who were stranded away from home. But 'payments would only be made to people who had no resources to draw on and would be recovered when circumstances allow'.
4. *Household expenses*. Help would be given to cover such items as furniture, cookers, etc., but would be in the form of a loan and only provided if the claimant had savings of less than £500. In certain cases, the condition of the loan might be the claimant having to obtain advice on the planning of his or her expenditure. The Government want to involve local authority social workers in helping such claimants with advice on how to manage their financial affairs better but, at the time of writing, social workers are reluctant to be involved because they feel it could eventually lead to social workers giving advice to the DHSS on who should get a loan which might, in some cases, seem to clash with the social worker's aim of doing his or her best for the client.

Income support would be based on a regulatory framework, as supplementary benefit is now, but the social fund would be discretionary except for maternity and funeral payments (see above). However, if help is refused there would be an appeals procedure but those considering the appeal would be DHSS staff, unlike the independent appeals procedure of the social security tribunals. The Government states that having a regulatory framework for special needs, as with the present supplementary benefit system, makes the system very complicated and often it provides 'only a broad approximation of need'. Furthermore, a regulatory system encourages claimants 'to define their needs in terms of what the regulations provide rather than simply explaining their needs as they see them'. In other words, the Government is hinting that, in its view, claims for special needs have been made, irrespective of whether the claimant has such needs, simply because in the regulations it states that such special needs can be claimed for. Thus the Government has emphasised that under the present regulatory system for special needs there has been a big increase in the number of single payments. But the re-introduction of discretion should make the system more flexible and perhaps enable more effective help to be given (see p. 34 for a previous discussion on discretion). Each local DHSS office would have a fixed budget for making payments from the social fund except for maternity and funeral payments, which could possibly inhibit compassion in order to keep within the fund. The Government has, however, stated that there would be a contingency fund 'to meet unexpected demands which put pressure on the allocation of individual offices'. (*Commons Hansard*, 28 January 1986).

As with the Government's proposals for housing benefit, there should be some simplification of the administration as all income related benefits will be calculated in the same way.

Summary

If we take poverty to mean an income below a minimum considered necessary to meet requirements (requirements increasing as the country grows richer) then, in spite of the recession, we should be able to abolish poverty as we have the resources to bring everyone up to this basic minimum. What prevents us doing it? Some people might argue the lack of political will; others might answer the existing economic system makes change difficult – that for capitalism to thrive, poverty for a section of the population must prevail. Others would argue that by retaining some universal benefits too big a proportion of the money spent on welfare goes to people who do not need it. But as a more practical level it is often due to not knowing who are in need and, even if we know who the needy are, ignorance of all the circumstances which give rise to their need. Ignorance of those in need can be reduced by government publicity to encourage those who are entitled to claim benefit to do so. Similar work can be done by local authorities and, in recent years, there has been much publicity on these lines. Some local authorities have appointed welfare rights officers who, like accountants who help the better off not to pay too much tax to the Inland Revenue, help the poor to get all the money they are entitled to from the DHSS. What blunts the effectiveness of this work is that much poverty is among those who are the most apathetic to their rights and are, therefore, least likely to be affected by publicity. Furthermore, we are so concerned not to give money to those who are not entitled to it that we have developed a complex system of checks on claimants' incomes which is off-putting to many people who need help. The large bureaucracy necessitated by this complex system is a further off-putting factor especially when, as under a government anxious to contain public expenditure, attempts to reduce that bureaucracy results in overworked staff in the DHSS with the danger that some claimants perhaps do not get the attention they deserve or a claimant is inadvertently given less money than he or she is entitled to.

A system of universal benefits would make the system much simpler and ensure all receive benefits, reducing means testing to a minimum but it does seem rather absurd to give benefits to everyone in order to ensure that the minority who really need them actually receive them. Even so, for the sake of social unity it may still be better to retain some universal benefits even if all the benefits involving cash payments can not be universal because of the huge government expenditure this would involve or, where insurance contributions formed the basis of entitlement, the contributions would have to be set at an unacceptable high rate. There is the point, however, that if all income were taxed, much of this huge government expenditure would be recouped by the Government. Proposals have been made for everyone to receive a basic tax free income but all income above this would be taxed. There would still have to be additions to meet exceptional circumstances with claimants having to justify exceptional circumstances. The Government does, however, consider its proposed personal allowance, within the proposed income support scheme, as sufficient basic income in itself for most households.

Various negative income tax schemes, called tax credit schemes, have been put forward where everyone completes a form giving details of their income as they do now for the Inland Revenue and would receive a credit if below a basic minimum considered necessary for their needs but taxed if above this basic minimum. Such schemes would substantially reduce the amount of means-testing except for the form all would have to complete. All so far, like the original one put forward under the 1970–74 Conservative Government, have been found to have weaknesses. In any case, all these schemes, like the basic income scheme need an integration of the tax and social security systems that we seem a long way from attaining. But the Government claims that sick pay, now being paid by the employer, and its proposals for maternity benefit to be paid by the employer are small steps towards the integration of the two systems.

And the micro-computers now in each local DHSS office help to bring that integration nearer. The computers should also help claimants by relieving some of the pressure on the officers.

The problem of ensuring that poor people get the best possible help (simply giving money may not abolish the poverty of the claimant) calls for co-operation between supplementary benefit officers in the DHSS and social workers in the local authorities. There is some official contact between them. But how far should DHSS staff play a welfare role in helping claimants with their problems? The pressures on them would seem to suggest that they will have all their time taken up in simply ensuring claimants get the money to which they are entitled and no more. The White Paper (Cmnd 9691) did suggest that officers who administered the proposed social fund should have some liaison with social workers and others and the computerisation of the local offices plus the proposed simpler system of social security by relieving some of that pressure on the staff, may make it possible to increase those contacts, hopefully for the benefit of claimants.

Under the Thatcher government the social security system has been further modified and, if the Government wins the next general election, the system will be modified even more radically. The Government admits that its reforms will mean some people will be worse off (there are gainers and losers in all reform proposals) but it states many people will be better off and, as an example, claims that the change from FIS to family credit will mean 400,000 working families on low incomes will be better off (*Commons Hansard*, 28 January 1986). Critics can point to losers among them – widows, many of next century's pensioners, especially those in insecure employment, most people now receiving housing benefit and young people under 25. One could argue that the Government's proposals attempt to shift more resources on to the very poorest but, within the constraints of its financial policies, the majority of people – and many of them far from affluent – will be worse off. Indeed, hostile critics have argued that the Government's reforms are not really about meeting needs adequately but about cutting expenditure, an accusation strongly denied by the Government. But the original review teams (see p. 44) were told that no extra cash was available.

The Government would argue that we can only do what we can afford. As one of its former ministers said: 'The future of the welfare state and the future of industry are two sides of the same coin' (Patrick Jenkin). But, in spite of the depressing state of British industry, what the Government thinks we can afford falls short of what its critics think we can and should afford.

The undermining of the basic principle of the welfare state continues – the principle that adequate cash benefits would be given as of right under a system of national insurance with means-testing kept to a minimum. But if the tax and benefit system could be effectively merged cash benefits could be given as of right. The form giving details of income would not be considered a means test in the generally accepted sense. But we have waited so long to hear news of the development of such a system that one wonders if it will ever come into operation. In the meantime in 1986, child benefit and insurance benefits (with the possible exception of the retirement pension) buy less than they did in 1979, with a resulting increase in the number of claimants for supplementary benefit. In addition, taxation, except for the rich, has increased, with the poorer sections of the community now paying a greater proportion of their income in taxation.

Assignments

1. List the changes to social security benefits made by the Thatcher government which have added to the number of people claiming supplementary benefit.
2. Discuss how far means-testing should be a necessary part of the social security system.
3. How has our concept of poverty changed since the days of Charles Booth?
4. Give the Government's five reasons for the need to reform the system of social security by referring to its White Paper, 'Reform of Social Security' (Cmnd 9691, December 1985) or 'Social Security Notes', No. 16, February 1986, obtainable free from the DHSS. Discuss any one of these reasons in relation to the 1986 Social Security Act. (Literature critical of the Government's proposals can be obtained from the Child Poverty Action Group, 1 Macklin Street, London WC2B 5NH.)

5. 'A welfare state makes provision for everyone. It fulfils different support functions at different stages throughout life. It recognises a legitimate redistributive role and provides collectively for the common need. The alternative, state welfare, is a system of provision established to cater for the poor. A system which caters only for the poor very quickly degenerates into a poor system' (Archy Kirkwood MP). How far do you think we have travelled the road, if at all, from a welfare state to state welfare since 1945? Give reasons for your answer.

Reading

A. B. Atkinson, *Poverty in Britain and the Reform of Social Security* (Cambridge University Press, 1969).

Michael Beenstock, 'Poverty, Taxation and the Welfare State', *National Westminster Bank Review* (August 1980).

David Blake and Paul Ormerod (eds), *The Economics of Prosperity* (Grant McIntyre, 1980).

Muriel Brown, *Introduction to Social Administration*, 6th edn (Hutchinson, 1985).

Stephen Davies, *Beveridge Revisited* (Centre for Policy Studies, 1986).

Frank Field, *Inequality in Britain* (Fontana, 1981).

Frank Field, *Poverty and Politics* (Heinemann, 1982) chs 1–6.

Howard Glennerster, 'In Praise of Public Expenditure', *New Statesman* (27 February 1976).

HMSO, *Proposals for a Tax-Credit System*, Cmnd 5116 (HMSO, October 1972).

HMSO, *Better Pensions*, Cmnd 5713 (HMSO, September 1974).

HMSO, *Reform of Social Security*, Volume 1, Cmnd 9517 (HMSO, June 1985).

HMSO, *Housing Benefit Review,* Cmnd 9520 (HMSO, June 1985).

HMSO, *Reform of Social Security. Programme for Action*, Cmnd 9691 (HMSO, December 1985).

HMSO, *The Reform of Personal Taxation*, Cmnd 9756 (Green Paper 1986).

House of Commons Select Committee on Tax-Credit, Session 1972–3, *Report*, vol. 1 (HMSO, 1973).

House of Commons, Social Security Bill, 2nd Reading (*Hansard* vol. 90, no. 45, 28 January 1986).

Rudolph Klein, 'Privatisation and the Welfare State' (*Lloyds Bank Review*, January 1984).

Steward Lansley, 'What Hope for the Poor?', *Lloyds Bank Review* (April 1979).

J. E. Meade, *Report on the Structure and Reform of Direct Taxation* (Allen & Unwin, 1978).

John Micklewright, 'Fiction versus Fact: Unemployment Benefits in Britain', *National Westminster Bank Review* (May 1985).

New Society, *How the Poorest Live: New Society Studies Reader* (New Society, 1973).

H. Parker, *Goodbye Beveridge?* (Outer Circle Policy Unit, 1980).

H. Parker, *Action for Welfare* (Social Affairs Unit, 1984).

Social Security Consortium, *Of Little Benefit: a critical guide to the social Security Act 1986* (Child Poverty Action Group, 1986).

SSAC, *First Report of the Social Security Advisory Committee, 1981* (HMSO, 1982).

A. P. Thirlwell, 'Keynesian Employment Theory is not Defunct', *Three Banks Review* (September 1981).

Peter Townsend, 'An Alternative Anti-Poverty Programme', *New Society* (7 October 1982).

Peter Townsend, *Poverty in the United Kingdom* (Penguin, 1979).

6 Health

Development of the Health Services

General

In the nineteenth century the biggest threat to health was contagious diseases. The enormous growth of towns due to rapid population increase and, in the case of the industrial towns in the north, an influx of people seeking work in the developing industries, led in many instances to overcrowded houses, inadequate sanitation and impure water supply, with which the traditional forms of local government could not cope. In spite of the efforts, in certain areas, of *ad hoc* statutory bodies to deal with the problems in the first half of the nineteenth century, deaths from disease continued to rise. Influential reports from doctors and others warned of the dangers of uncollected sewage and contaminated water, but it was not until 1848 that the government acted, and then only after a cholera epidemic in the London area killed over 60,000 people.

The 1848 Public Health Act – the first of its kind – made compulsory the setting up of local boards of health in areas where the death rate was above the national average. In other areas it was left to the local people to decide whether or not to set up a local board. The result was that there was progress in some areas but none in others. The Board of Health, set up under the Act to give central direction and frame general policy, was unpopular and was dissolved in 1854. *The Times* of 1 August 1854 wrote, 'We prefer to take our chance of cholera and the rest than be bullied into health'. Compulsion at last came with the 1866 Sanitary Act, which ordered local authorities to appoint sanitary inspectors with power to take action about water, sewerage and 'nuisances'. The Report of a Royal Commission on Public Health set up in 1869 led to the 1875

Public Health Act, which made compulsory in every area local health authorities under the control of a medical officer of health. In the meantime central direction was restored by making health the responsibility of the Local Government Board, a new government department created in 1871 to be responsible for health and the Poor Law. From this date progress was rapid, so that by the end of the nineteenth century infectious diseases had been greatly reduced. Incidentally this helped the finances of the Poor Law as ill health and poverty are closely related. In the nineteenth century it was the sanitary inspector rather than the doctor who did most to save life. By today's standards medical science was backward. For example, it was not until 1858 that the French chemist Louis Pasteur demonstrated the connection between dirt and disease by discovering the presence of bacteria in the surrounding atmosphere. The discovery led to an emphasis on cleanliness to kill the organisms, or at least to stop them from spreading. Lister pioneered the way by his discovery of antiseptics – he used carbolic acid as a steriliser soon after Pasteur's discovery.

The biggest saver of life in the twentieth century has been the great advances in medical science. While public health is still important, it is the personal health services which are now the biggest factor in keeping people fit. Public health has, however, had to meet fresh problems – atmospheric pollution from motor-cars, pesticides, dumping of toxic wastes, and so on.

Hospitals

Until Lister's day hospitals were dangerous places because of the risk of infection, especially for surgical cases. Surgeons often wore old and dirty coats, nurses were often drunk. It was easy to see that hospitals were for the poor, while the rich were treated in their own homes. Thanks mainly to Florence Nightingale, a middle-class woman who devoted her life to hospital nursing, nursing standards greatly improved.

In the nineteenth century there were three types of hospital. First, there were the voluntary hospitals, the most famous of them, like St Thomas's and St Bartholomew's, being founded in the Middle Ages. Many smaller ones were founded in the nineteenth century by voluntary subscription. Then, as the century progressed, there evolved workhouse hospitals, called infirmaries, out of workhouse sick bays. (See 1867 Metropolitan Poor Act and 1869 Poor Law Amendment Act, p. 13.) Third, there were a few isolation hospitals or fever hospitals run by the local authorities. Free vaccination against cholera was introduced in 1840 and the Poor Law medical officers who worked for the Poor Law Guardians, were responsible for its provision to all categories of people who demanded it – not just paupers.

In 1929 the Poor Law was taken over by local authorities, and they thus took over all the workhouse hospitals as well as retaining the fever hospitals. They could also build new hospitals if they wished. More money was spent by local government on the newly acquired hospitals to eliminate, as far as possible, the atmosphere of the workhouse, and gradually the local authority hospitals began to rival the voluntary hospitals.

The 1946 National Health Service Act nationalised the hospitals and, except for some teaching hospitals, put them under the administration of regional hospital boards.

Doctors

Doctors who worked in voluntary hospitals used to give their services free but obtained their income from treating private patients either in their surgery or in the patient's home.

Working-class people, including the poor, could go to the out-patients' department of a voluntary hospital and, by the end of the century, it was quite respectable for the working class to use the Poor Law hospital. Apart from this there was the local dispensary, public or private, run by a local committee where working-class men, women and children, by the payment of $1d$ to $2d$ a week, could obtain free medical treatment and medicine providing they were not obtaining relief from the Poor Law. Better-off working-class people, and even quite rich people, insured themselves against sickness by joining a friendly society, and receiving medical treatment in return. The very poor had the Poor Law doctor. For those people not covered by these schemes a charge would be made for each visit. In the poor areas the doctor might engage a collector to collect so much from each patient each week, and this would cover visits, treatment and medicine. But in working-class areas most doctors had unpaid bills – a good doctor could not very well cease to treat someone simply because that person had no money.

Doctors and Health Insurance

The biggest stimulus to the development of a comprehensive health service came with the 1911 National Insurance Act, Part 1 of which provided compulsory health insurance for all workers earning £160 a year or less. It covered sickness benefit, disability benefit, maternity benefit, a doctor's services and prescriptions, and free sanatorium treatment for TB. The benefits were administered by friendly societies, insurance companies and trade unions, known collectively as *approved societies*. Doctors and patients still retained their freedom of choice – doctors to choose their patients and patients their doctors – and doctors were represented on all the committees concerned with administration.

Thus there was a doctor on the local insurance committees that supervised the scheme in the local areas and one of the insurance commissioners responsible for the overall management of the scheme was a doctor. Doctors were paid a fixed sum for each insured patient on their 'panel', and this gave them much greater financial security. An extra source of income was private treatment of richer people and others excluded from the insurance scheme.

By 1939 the maximum income for compulsory health insurance had been raised to £420 a year, and this covered virtually all workers. The weakness of the scheme, as the Royal Commission on Health Insurance of 1924–6 pointed out, was that it did not cover the insured person's dependants – wife, children and old parents. Thus about half the population still had to pay fees as private patients or join a sick club where a doctor's services could be obtained by the payment of a regular contribution each week. Furthermore, health insurance did not cover hospital treatment, and a person lucky enough to be in one of the wealthier approved societies received extra benefits from the society.

The Royal Commission anticipated the modern National Health Service by recommending its separation from the insurance scheme, and, instead, its financing from 'the general public funds'.

The setting-up of the Ministry of Health

In 1919 the Local Government Board was abolished and its work given to the newly created Ministry of Health, which also took over the work of the insurance commissioners. It was felt that the Local

Government Board had been too preoccupied with the Poor Law, and the fear of national physical deterioration arising from the Boer war recruitment shock gave support to those who wanted a special department of health to promote actively the nation's health. The new Ministry thus became responsible for public health, national health insurance, local authority housing, health promotion and the Poor law.

The National Health Service

The 1946 National Health Service Act introduced a virtually free health service operative from July 1948, including free specialist treatment in hospitals. Local insurance committees, which previously supervised the doctors, were replaced by executive councils (now called family practitioner committees) which supervised all the personal practitioners – doctors, dentists, opticians and pharmacists. Doctors still retained their clinical freedom and continued to receive, among other payments, so much money for each patient on their list.

The 1946 National Insurance Act (operative from July 1948) abolished the approved societies and sickness benefit was paid by the newly created Ministry of National Insurance, now part of the Department of Health and Social Security.

Local Authority Services

The local authority health services evolved in the latter part of the nineteenth century largely out of concern for children. Between 1850 and 1900, in spite of the big fall in the death rate, the infant mortality rate remained high. As late as 1900 the figure was 156 per, 1,000 live births – roughly the same as in 1850 (today, it is less than 20). This meant that out of every 1,000 babies born alive, 156 died before their first birthday. The main reason for this was ignorance and poverty.

Compulsory education, introduced in 1880, had put all the nation's children on view and the large number suffering from poverty and malnutrition was disturbing.

The fear of national physical deterioration at the beginning of the century was another factor emphasising the importance of the nation's children.

Voluntary action preceded state action. As early as 1859, William Rathbone had started a system of district nursing in Liverpool which provided skilled medical attention in people's homes. Dr Drew Harris, a medical officer, established at St Helens the first infant milk depot, and another medical officer of health, Dr James Kerr, pioneered medical inspection of schoolchildren at Bradford.

The 1902 Midwives Act was aimed at ensuring that midwives were properly qualified. It set up a Central Midwives Board to lay down rules for the training of midwives and to supervise them. The 1936 Midwives Act set up a full-time salaried midwifery service and made local authorities responsible for ensuring there was an adequate number of midwives in their area and that they were competent.

Registration of births had been made compulsory in 1836 but it was only for statistical purposes. The 1907 Notification of Births Act, where adopted by a local authority, required that the local medical officer of health should be notified of any birth within thirty-six hours, to enable him, if necessary, to check on the progress of mother and baby. In 1915 notification was made compulsory in all local authority areas and, at the same time, permission was given to local authorities to look after mother and child. The 1918 Maternity and Child Welfare Act extended this help to children up to the age of 5. Financial assistance was given from the central government to enable this service to be developed. Today the three aspects of child care are (a) notification; (b) a health visitor who is a registered general nurse (RGN) and (c) somewhere the mother can take the baby – a clinic or the family doctor.

In the meantime Education Acts in 1906 and 1907 had brought school meals and school medical inspection.

Other health functions taken on by local authorities were the care of mental defectives in 1913, care and after-care of TB patients in 1914, and treatment of venereal disease in 1917.

The scope of the local health service was considerably extended by the National Health Service Act of 1946.

Under a reorganisation of the NHS in 1974 the local authority health services and the school health services were put under the control of the NHS authorities.

Factors leading to the 1946 National Health Service Act

A comprehensive National Health Service, which started operating in July 1948, was an almost inevitable development after the passing of the 1911 National Insurance Act. There was no logical reason why free medical treatment should be limited to a particular insured group of the population. But more immediate reasons for it were:

(1) Rapid scientific developments in medicine were making the health services increasingly expensive, especially hospital treatment, and it seemed that only the state would have the resources to develop a health service to meet the needs of all the people.

(2) The Emergency Hospital Service set up during the Second World War to meet the anticipated thousands of air-raid casualties highlighted the need to share medical resources more evenly throughout the country, and only some form of central organisation could do this. Thus before 1948 the best specialists worked in voluntary hospitals but drew their income from private fees. Hence they were concentrated in the wealthier areas. By introducing a salaried service for hospital doctors the 1946 National Health Service Act facilitated their more even distribution throughout the country.

(3) It was felt that local authority hospitals could not be given back to local government after the war, as they needed, for efficient management, much larger units of administration than the existing areas of local authorities.

(4) A National Health Service was seen not only as a means of improving the nation's health but also as part of a campaign to abolish want. (The Beveridge Report in 1942 on social security – see Chapter 3 – had stressed the need for a National Health Service and family allowance to supplement the national insurance scheme.)

The Basic Principles of the National Health Service

1. Free access to medical care for all who want it.
2. Freedom for the patient to choose his or her doctor.
3. Professional freedom for the doctor to choose his or her patient and to engage in private practice.
4. The retention of the traditional doctor–patient relationship, with the family doctor as a link between hospital and local services.

Doctors' attitudes to the development of a state medical service have been very much influenced by the fear that it would mean coming under the control of some government department. These fears were the underlying reason for the British Medical Association's wrangle with Lloyd George in the years 1911–13 over the introduction of national health insurance (which came into operation in 1913), and with Aneurin Bevan after the Second World War, when negotiations for the setting up of a National Health Service took place. Permitting private practice was a concession Bevan had to make because he knew many doctors would not accept a full-time salaried service. Hospital consultants were given the option of a full-time or part-time contract. There are charges for prescriptions, spectacles and dental treatment but, until recently, they were considered modest so that the basic principles still stood.

However, under the Thatcher government, the prescription charge has greatly increased and dental charges have increased sharply. There is still, however, financial help with charges for the less well-off and provision for the better off who wish to pay for treatment outside the NHS.

Summary

In the nineteenth century the developments in public health were the biggest single factor in keeping people fit; in the twentieth century advances in medical science have been more important. By the end of the nineteenth century it was realised that the health of individuals was not simply their concern but was also the concern of the nation. National greatness and perhaps even national survival, depended on the nation's health. Furthermore, it had become increasingly realised that poverty was to a great extent caused by ill health.

The first developments were services to protect the health of young mothers and children. The health insurance scheme which became operative in 1913 was perhaps the biggest step towards a health service for everyone. On a limited scale to begin with, its extension to virtually all workers in the interwar years made inevitable the introduction of a National Health Service available to all. But for the bad economic situation in the interwar years, it might have come earlier.

Assignments

1. What factors have led to increasing demands being made on the National Health Service since its inception in 1948?
2. How far has the National Health Service fulfilled its fundamental aims?
3. What were the main deficiencies in the health service between 1918 and 1939?
4. Write a brief biographical account of Edwin Chadwick and explain the importance of his work in improving the nation's health.

Reading

B. Abel-Smith, *A History of the Nursing Profession* (Heinemann, 1960).
W. J. Braithwaite, *Lloyd George's Ambulance Wagon* (Cedric Chivers, 1970).
Maurice Bruce, *The Coming of the Welfare State* (Batsford, 1971).
H. Eckstein, *The English Health Service: Its Origins, Structure and Achievements* (Oxford University Press, 1959).
Ministry of Health, *A National Health Service*, Cmd 6502 (HMSO, 1944).
Brian Watkin, *The National Health Service: The First Phase* (Allen & Unwin, 1978) ch. 1.

7 The National Health Service Today

The Secretary of State for Social Services, the minister in charge of the Department of Health and Social Security, is responsible for the National Health Service. He is aided by junior ministers within the Department, one of whom is the Minister of Health, with responsibility for the NHS under the Secretary of State. Under the National Health Service Act 1946 (amended by the Health Services and Public Health Act 1968) the Secretary has the duty of promoting 'the establishment in England and Wales [there are separate acts for Scotland and Northern Ireland] of a comprehensive health service designed to secure improvement in the physical and mental health of the people of England and Wales and the prevention, diagnosis and treatment of illness'.

The Secretary of State is advised by his civil servants and certain advisory committees dealing with special subjects which he appoints after consultation with interested bodies. Advice is given by a health advisory service which investigates the efficiency of the NHS. The main policy decisions relating to the NHS are initiated in the Health Services Supervisory Board which is chaired by the Minister. *Ad hoc* committees are set up from time to time to investigate special problems. For example, a Royal Commission on the NHS was appointed in 1976 and reported in 1979. Its terms of reference were 'to consider, in the interest of both patients and those who work in the NHS, the best use and management of financial and manpower resources'. It recommended important changes in the structure of the NHS, many of which became operative from April 1982.

The National Health Service has three main divisions:

1. The family (personal) practitioner services (doctors, dentists, opticians, chemists).

2. Hospitals for specialist treatment.
3. Community health services (previously known as personal health services).

Supervising all three divisions is a NHS Management Board. It plans the implementation of decisions taken by the Supervisory Board.

The Personal Practitioner Services

Family practitioner committees (FPCs) are responsible for the provision and general management of the personal practitioner services – services involved in what is now generally called primary health care. This includes entering into contracts of service with the practitioner, preparing lists of them, paying them, and investigating complaints against a practitioner. Since gaining independence from the district health authorities on 1 April 1985, they have expanded their role although still acting within the guide-lines laid down by the DHSS. Unlike the hospital services, the Government does not impose cash limits on family practitioner services and hence FPCs are encouraged to give greater attention to the expenditure of practitioners. The Government's Green Paper, 'Primary Health Care – and Agenda for discussion', published April 1986, states that there is a need for FPCs to develop more systematic means of measuring quality and detecting shortfalls in the provision of services. More detailed information about the services should be given and this would help choice in line with the Government's emphasis on the role of competition, including the competition from private primary health care, in improving efficiency. The Green Paper would like to see the development of patient groups to discuss problems relating to the GP's practice which affect patients. When the group was in consultation with the doctor, it would perhaps help the doctor to see where the practice could be improved. Some patient groups were founded in the 1970s and some included in their activities organising voluntary help where needed to patients within the practice.

Practitioners see themselves as independent practitioners and GPs especially, as history shows, tend to be suspicious of those who want to manage them and hence, for this new relationship between

FPCs and practitioners to develop smoothly, tact and administrative skill will be necessary. On the other hand, FPCs, with their wide experience gained from knowledge of many practices, can be a useful source of advice for some practitioners. Representatives of the practitioners comprise half the membership of a FPC; the other half is made up of representatives of the district health authority, local authorities and some independents chosen by local lay people. The chairman is appointed by the minister. FPCs liaise with other sections of the NHS on matters of joint concern, particularly with regard to community services – services in which local authorities are also interested. Their administrative areas used to follow that of the county councils and the metropolitan district councils. Since the 1982 reorganisation each FPC includes parts of a number of local authorities. Furthermore, each FPC relates to one or more district health authorities.

Doctors, dentists, opticians and chemists each have their own local professional committees which are consulted by the FPC and which are represented on it.

Doctors

The General Medical Council lays down the minimum qualifications a doctor must have and keeps a register of those entitled to practice. The more serious charges against a doctor can be referred to the General Medical Council, and if the charge is proved the doctor can be struck off the register.

There is a Medical Practices Committee charged with the duty, among other things, of trying to ensure an even distribution of doctors throughout the country. It is appointed by the minister and normally consists of seven doctors (five of whom must be in active practice) and two lay people. When a doctor wishes to start a new practice or apply for a vacant practice, he or she must submit an application to the local FPC, which consults the local medical committee and then sends the application with its recommendations to the Medical Practices Committee. If the doctor's application is refused, he or she has the right of appeal to the minister.

This control over the distribution of doctors is only a negative control – the Medical Practices Committee cannot compel a doctor to practice in a certain area, but there are financial inducements to encourage doctors to practice in unpopular areas.

There are in the United Kingdom over 31,000 doctors in general practice and the majority work in partnership or group practice. Doctors can have fee-paying patients if they wish.

Dentists

There are just over 16,000 dental practitioners in the United Kingdom. Their governing body is the General Dental Council. They may practice in any area they choose and have private patients. A patient does not have to register with a dentist. There is a charge for treatment and dentures, but, as with charges for doctor's prescriptions, certain categories of people are declared exempt.

Chemists

There are about 11,000 chemists taking part in the National Health Service in Great Britain. There is a charge for each prescription, but about two-thirds are supplied free to various categories – the poor, the young, the chronically sick, women over 60 and men over 65.

Ophthalmic Services

Ophthalmic services are one of the specialist services provided by hospitals, but there is also a general ophthalmic service under the FPCs. There are about 950 ophthalmic medical practitioners and about 5,200 ophthalmic opticians taking part in the National Health Service in Great Britain. Eye testing and a prescription for lenses are free but there is a charge for spectacles, both for lenses and frames (again subject to exemptions for certain categories of people).

The Hospitals and Community Health

District health authorities (DHAs) are responsible for the hospitals and the community health services. Each district has a district general hospital and a number of other hospitals, some of which may be part of the district general hospital. But a district is not supposed to be so large that members of the authority are 'remote from the service for which they are responsible'. As far as possible the boundaries of the new district authorities follow the boundaries of the old districts, which operated previously under the guidance of the now defunct area health authorities (AHAs). The total membership of a DHA is normally seventeen including the chairman. Members appointed by the regional health authority (RHA) are a hospital consultant, a general practitioner, one nurse, midwife or health visitor. There is a nominee from a university with a medical school, four members appointed by local authorities, plus other members known as 'generalists', one of whom is recommended by the trade-union movement. The chairman is appointed by the Secretary of State. The DHA is advised by a district management team (DMT) led by a general manager supported by professional staff. Its composition and type of organisational structure vary as between one DHA and another. It is a new management structure, only introduced in 1985, and so subject to modifications in the light of experience. The professional chief officers have normally direct access to the DHA on matters relating to their professional speciality but, in matters of administration (now called management), they are responsible to the district general manager. Below the DMT there are 'units of management', each led by a unit general manager and responsible for a particular aspect of the service – for example, a large hospital, or group of smaller hospitals, the community services of the district or the maternity services or mental health etc. These unit managers are also involved in district level management and report direct to the district general manager. In most hospitals there are some private beds which can be used by part-time consultants to treat private fee-paying patients. These private patients pay the full cost of the hospital accommodation and services as well as the consultant's fee.

Many hospitals have small wards or single rooms for those requiring privacy, which NHS patients may use for a daily charge. Treatment is still free.

The DHAs must work with the local authorities on matters of joint concern and hence there are joint consultative committees, as under the previous structure, and which were given statutory authority under the 1973 National Health Reorganisation Act. This joint consultation is particularly important in view of the increasing emphasis placed on the community care. Local authority social workers are the main people involved in working with the health services. Problems which are the concern of the social worker can often cause ill health or, putting it the other way round, ill health in a family can create problems necessitating the help of the social worker. The DHAs are responsible for the School Health Service, so this involves them with the education departments of local authorities. There are also links with the local authority housing department. Not only can bad housing cause ill health but often also medical advice is needed by the local authority to help it decide on the housing needs of elderly people living on their own. There are also strong links between the DHAs and local government because of the responsibility of local authorities for environmental health and the welfare of the physically disabled.

Not only are there joint consultative committees linking the NHS and local government but, since 1976, there has been a system of joint financing. This allows NHS funds to be used on projects of common interest which have in mind the better care of patients. Voluntary bodies also involved in community care can be helped financially from this system of joint financing. The capital costs of the projects are normally met out of the NHS funds and also revenue costs for the first three years, but then revenue costs are met on a reduced scale until eventually, after seven years or so, the local authority bears the revenue costs out of the rates (see DHSS, 1981, p. 5).

Health care planning teams operate at district level and are permanent or *ad hoc*, with the job of reviewing specific health needs. There can be one for the physically handicapped, one for the mentally handicapped, one for the elderly, and so on. The teams comprise representatives of medical, administrative, nursing and social disciplines, as well as representatives from the social services department of the local authority, since health and welfare are closely linked. The DMT uses the reports of the health care planning teams, as necessary, to prepare plans for consideration by the DHA.

The community health physician is a member of the DMT and replaces the old medical officer of health who was formerly employed in local government. Apart from working with other members of the DMT in meeting health needs, this official advises the local authority on environmental health, still the responsibility of the local authorities and previously known as public health.

Regional Health Authorities

These are in England only; in Wales and Scotland there are none. The regional health authorities appointed by the Secretary of State act as his agents, being responsible for the long-term planning of hospital building, regional services and the allocation of resources between the district health authorities. They are also responsible for the design and construction of new buildings and they will undertake the more important building projects. The building directorate in the DHSS has however, overall control. RHAs are advised by professional officers led by a general manager.

Community Health Councils

These represent the views of the consumer and there is one for each of the districts. Half their members are appointed by local government, one-third by voluntary organisations and the remainder by the regional health authority. They comprise from around eighteen to thirty members. The councils have the right to be consulted, the power to secure information, to visit hospitals and other institutions. They have access to the district health authority and to the senior officers administering the district services. They have the duty of issuing an annual report. In general they can look at the adequacy of the health service provided for the community and comment on plans for future development. They can assess how local provision compares with the national picture. In fact, the community health councils can have considerable influence on the development of the health service, but the degree of influence depends on the abilities and enthusiasm of their members.

Community Health Services

One of the main jobs in the field of community health is care and after-care of patients in their own homes in co-operation with the patient's doctor. This is in line with the growing practice of helping people as far as possible in their own home and surroundings (see *Care in the Community*, DHSS, 1981). Thus a patient should go to a hospital for treatment and nursing care if the hospital is the only place where these can be provided.

Home nursing

District nurses provide nursing in the patient's home. In some areas
the nurses work as a team assisted by ancillaries and in close touch
with the doctor and the hospital. The majority of patients are the
elderly and chronically sick, but in certain cases home nursing is
provided for children. Their work includes applying dressings,
giving injections and medicine and generally looking after bed-
ridden patients.

Health visiting

Like district nurses, health visitors are registered general nurses
(formerly called State registered nurses) who have taken post-
registered training. They visit mothers in their own homes (especially mothers who have left hospital after having a baby) and
give advice on the care of the young child. They also advise
expectant mothers. Their visits are not just to help the mothers but
to see that the baby is being properly looked after. Health visitors
also give advice on the prevention of illness and give support to
vulnerable families and to the elderly.

Nursing homes

These are provided by the NHS for people requiring continual care.
These are mainly the elderly. But in many health authorities private
nursing homes provide more beds than provided by the NHS. The
private sector in this field is growing.

Maternity and child health clinics

These clinics give advice on the care of children under 5. (At this age
they come under the care of the School Health Service.) The health
visitors work closely with the clinics.

However, some pregnant women, and mothers with young
children, prefer to get all their help and advice from the family
doctor rather than go to the clinic.

Family planning

This is now part of the National Health Service and includes vasectomy and free contraceptives.

Midwifery service

Midwives attend mothers confined at home and co-operate with the family doctor. They may also visit mothers at home who have had their babies in hospital, until such time as the health visitor takes over.

Ambulance service

Ambulances are provided to convey the sick to and from hospital when they are unable to travel by ordinary transport. They also take those injured in accidents to hospital. In certain areas voluntary organisations organise a hospital car service where owner-drivers take suitable cases to and from hospital. This is an addition to the ambulance service.

Care and after-care

Care and after-care cover persons suffering from tuberculosis and other illneses and those suffering from mental disorder. (Care and after-care of the mentally disordered is the responsibility of the social services department of local government.) It also covers chiropody, especially for the old, and loan of nursing equipment. After-care is important for those leaving hospital.

Prevention of illness

This includes vaccination and immunisation against diphtheria, measles, polio, smallpox, tetanus and whooping cough at clinics or by family doctors. It also includes giving advice on health matters. (The School Health Service also provides vaccination against tuberculosis, diphtheria, polio, etc.)

  The environmental health services run by local government help to prevent illness by keeping the environment clean. These services include controlling atmospheric pollution, ensuring pure water supply, checking on cleanliness in restaurants and food warehouses, and so on.

Health Centres

These were originally built and maintained by local authorities, then built and maintained by the area health authorities and now by the new district health authorities. Some of the services provided in them are general medical, dental, ophthalmic and pharmaceutical services and also specialist services for hospital out-patients. The community health services also operate from health centres. Home nurses, health visitors and midwives in these centres work for a particular group of doctors and only serve the patients of that group. In this way they get to know the patients much better.

When the National Health Service started it was hoped that most doctors would soon be operating from health centres, but for many years very few were built. But since 1965 the building of health centres has accelerated. About one-fifth of all doctors operate from health centres.

General practitioners pay a certain amount for the use of the health centre, but payment is made via the family practitioner committees.

Paying for the National Health Service

About 86 per cent of the cost is paid out of taxation, about 11 per cent out of part of National Insurance contributions and 3 per cent out of charges.

Local Authority Social Services Department Services (linked with Health)

Home helps

Home helps can be provided where a sick person or expectant mother or disabled person cannot be adequately looked after or where help is needed with the housework. Home helps are now mainly involved with the elderly. There is a charge for the service based on the person's income, though a few local authorities have made the service free because of the administrative costs involved in assessing charges.

Care and after-care of the mentally disordered

Mental illness is an acquired condition; mental subnormality (i.e. incomplete development of mind) exists from birth. The local authorities employ psychiatric social workers to visit these people in their own homes. They also provide for them training centres, clubs and residential accommodation.

Residential accommodation

Local authorities provide residential accommodation for persons who require care and attention which is not otherwise available to them. Apart from residential accommodation for certain categories of mentally ill and mentally subnormal people, local authorities provide residential accommodation for the elderly either in homes run by the local authority or private homes run by voluntary organisations. Homes are also provided for the blind and physically handicapped to suit their special needs.

Other services for the elderly

Apart from residential homes and home helps, local authorities can also provide, either themselves or through the agency of voluntary organisations, meals in the homes of the elderly, social clubs, outings and holidays and a laundry service. A charge may be made for these services.

Services for the physically handicapped

These services include practical assistance in the home, recreational facilities outside the home, home adaptations, help in travelling, provisions of meals in the home, reasonable access to public buildings, and finding out who the physically handicapped are and making them aware of the services available to them.

Some handicapped persons are helped by a specialist social worker.

Environmental health

Environmental health officers, previously known as public health inspectors, are employed by local authorities to keep the environment, as far as possible, free from health hazards. This includes such hazards to health as impure air, impure drinking water, bad sanitation, overcrowded housing, contaminated food, excessive noise.

Other services provided by local authorities

Social services departments can arrange for bed linen or clothing to be washed and laundered and can arrange recuperative holidays. For certain of these services a charge may be made. All social workers attached to the NHS are employed by the social services departments of the local authority.

Summary

The National Health Service is under the control of the government. The minister in charge is the Secretary of State for Social Services, who is the political head of the Departmentof Health and Social Security.

The National Health Service has three branches – personal practitioners, hospitals and community health services – which between them provide a comprehensive range of health services available to everyone. It does allow for private fee-paying patients.

The NHS has close links with the local authority welfare services.

Assignments

1. Construct an organisational chart for England of the National Health Service. At the top start with the Secretary of State, the Department of Health and Social Security and the advisory bodies to the minister.
2. Obtain a copy of the annual report of your community health council. Take what you consider to be three of the most important issues discussed and explain why you consider them

important and give the decisions or conclusions arrived at by the
council.
3. Find the address of your district health authority. On a map draw
the boundaries its administration covers. List the local authorities which come within these boundaries.

Reading

DHSS, *Annual Report of the Department of Health and Social Security*
(HMSO).
DHSS, *Patients First*, Consultative Paper on the Structure and Manage-
ment of the National Health Service (DHSS, December 1979).
DHSS, *Care in the Community*, Consultative Document on Moving
Resources for Care in England (DHSS, July 1981).

8 Current Problems in the Health Service

Reorganisation of the National Health Service

A major reorganisation of the NHS took place in 1974 with the main purpose of bringing the community health services, including the School Health Service, which, before 1974, were administered by local government, under the same administrative umbrella as the hospital services. Area health authorities, advised by a team of professional officers, became responsible for the hospitals and community health services including the School Health Service. In most areas of the country, the area health authorities were divided into districts and the day-to-day running of the health service was done by a district management team of professional officers responsible to the area health authority. In the metropolitan areas (i.e. the large conurbations) and one or two other areas the area officers also acted as the district management team. These were single-district areas. Above the area health authorities, but in England only, were the regional health authorities responsible for the allocation of resources to the area health authorities within the region. Statutory joint committees comprising representatives from the local authority and the area health authority (their boundaries coincided) were created, as local authorities still administered services closely related to health.

Under the 1982 reorganisation the regional health authorities remained with very much the same functions. The area health authorities were abolished, and district health authorities, advised by a district management team of professional officers, were set up which, in the main, followed as far as possible the boundaries of the previous districts.

The Report of the Royal Commission on the National Health

86

Service (18 July 1979) criticised the 1974 structure as follows: 'too many tiers, too many administrators in all disciplines, failure to make quick decisions, money wasted' (see DHSS, 1979, p. 4). This is best illustrated by looking at the relationship between the area health authority and the district management team. The district management team of professional officers did the day-to-day work and reported to the area health authority. It was not responsible to the area team of professional officers. The area officers recommended to the area health authority the acceptance, the rejection or the amendment of the district management team's decisions. 'It seems a complete anomaly to have more highly paid and presumably more experienced officers hiding behind their area committee, merely recommending instead of making these decisions' (Coyne, 1976). It was felt by many that area officers had no proper job of work to do. Hence a further reorganisation took place in 1982 and in line with the Royal Commission recommendation, area health authorities, with their team of professional officers, were abolished. The advantages claimed for the new structure are therefore a less complicated administrative structure which, apart from saving money, should speed up decision-making. Furthermore, because in most cases the district health authorities administer a smaller area than the previous area health authorities, the people responsible for the services are closer to the people they serve and hence should be more sensitive to needs. Furthermore, as there is no intermediate team between the district health authority and the regional health authority, the district team of professional officers had the chance to be more creative.

Management

Under the new structure of 1982 there was still consensus management. Each of the chief officers who formed the district team of officers – administrator, treasurer, medical officer and nursing officer, plus a general practitioner and hospital consultant – had to reach decisions, as among equals, by agreement. Each had the power of veto. Often the chairmanship of meetings was taken in rotation. The unfortunate results of consensus management were that it could happen that a decision was made at a meeting but there was nobody to take responsibility for ensuring the decision was implemented as there would have been with a chief executive able to give leadership and keep an eye on how the administrative machine was ticking over. This criticism applied also to the regional health authorities.

Acting on the recommendations of the Griffiths NHS Management Inquiry Report, published in 1983, consensus management has been abolished. General managers have been introduced at regional, district and unit level, with a Supervisory Board, chaired by a minister, deciding broad policy. The Board includes the Permanent Secretary of the DHSS, the Chief Medical Officer and about three other members. The planning of the effective implementation of the Supervisory Board's policy is the job of a Management Board comprising civil servants, business men and members of the Health Service. The Minister of Health, was made chairman of the Management Board in October 1986. As he can make political decisions this should ensure better liaison with the Supervisory Board. Previously, under a non-political chairman, there had been misunderstandings over the interpretation of the Supervisory Board's policy objectives. The Chairman of the Management Board is also a member of the Supervisory Board. It is interesting to note that, although the various management posts within the NHS were open to everyone in and out of the Health Service irrespective of the particular profession of the applicant, the number of appointments from the private sector was comparatively small. Out of a total number of 676 managers at all levels – regional, district and unit – only 81 were made from the private sector. More than 100 managers are doctors and 55 are nurses but the vast majority, around 400, are former administrators. Altogether about 85 per cent of the manager posts went to former NHS staff. Some people think that the new organisational structure can, however, give rise to friction between manager and medical or nursing staff. They point out that nurses and doctors will, in some cases, be subject to managers who know nothing about medical treatment and cannot therefore assess the competence of doctors and nurses. This sort of criticism is found in most large organisations where there are professional officers carrying out the professional work for which the organisation was set up and, on the other hand, administrators (now called managers in the NHS) keeping an eye on broad policy and efficiency. It was voiced particularly in the Civil Service where top people were and in the main still are recruited for their administrative ability rather than for specialised professional expertise. But, of course, managers will not normally make decisions on matters where specialised professional knowledge is necessary without consulting the relevant professional officers. Thus, although nurses are worried that they are no longer, as previously, represented on the district management team, each health authority has been instructed by the minister to designate a senior nurse as its principal nursing adviser with guaranteed access to the health authority. And the manager at unit level must consult with the relevant professional officers, including nurses, and respect their expertise. And 55 former nurses are now unit managers. Thus, although the old-style consensus management has been abolished, managers and professional officers must still work together as a team.

Finance

The real cost of the National Health Service has risen for the following reasons:

(a) the development of medical science has made treatment more expensive
(b) the real wages of its employees have risen
(c) the proportion of older people in the population who need care has been growing
(d) there is an increasing use of drugs to treat depression and stress
(e) there is never enough money for health and thus, as the country grows richer, the real expenditure on the NHS increases.

Problems arising from increasing costs

If about 86 per cent of the NHS is paid for out of taxation, why cannot taxation be raised to meet increasing costs? Even the Labour party admits that to keep on raising taxation to meet rising costs would not be politically feasible even if, which is doubtful, it was economically sound. Alternative sources of income must therefore be found.

About 11 per cent of the cost of the NHS is financed out of part of the National Insurance contribution. Extra income could be found by increasing the contributions.

Charges account for about 3 per cent of the cost of the service. Should they not be increased? Even if charges were considerably increased, the percentage of the income provided would still be comparatively small. And they would defeat one of the main principles of the NHS: that nobody because of lack of money should feel discouraged from making full use of the services available, although many people might feel increases in dental charges have done just that for dental services. Could the cost of drugs supplied to the NHS be reduced by more thoughtful prescribing by doctors? The government has acted on this by limiting the drugs that can be prescribed but it claims that the prescribed drugs are as effective as those that are blacklisted. They are, of course, cheaper and in the first year of the blacklist 1985/86 it has been estimated that there was a £70 million saving on a total drug bill of around £1.5 billion. But some doctors see the blacklist as a 'two-tier health system' as those who can afford and desire a blacklisted drug will obtain a private prescription.

Should private medicine, financed by private insurance, be greatly extended? The more people who take out private health insurance, the more money will be coming into the Health Service as a whole, without the need for extra taxation, increased contributions or increased charges. There are two ways of acquiring private medicine: one is to have a pay bed or be an out-patient of a NHS hospital; the other is to be treated entirely by a private hospital. One can also be a private patient of a general practitioner. Private hospitals, which include nursing homes and clinics, must be registered with the health authorities. Supporters of the extension of private insurance for medical treatment say it will develop competition between the public and private sectors of the NHS, and will improve overall efficiency. It will, for example, show where the NHS is not meeting demand. It will take some of the heavy load off the NHS and reduce its waiting-lists especially for non-urgent, routine surgery. At the present time, they argue, the NHS cannot meet all the demands that are made on it. And supporters of private medicine point out that doctors will still get most of their income from working in the NHS and will therefore still have an interest in making the state system successful. The Conservative government of Mrs Thatcher supports the extension of private medicine. So while it has given as much financial support to the NHS as the previous Labour government, the Conservative government has encouraged private medicine. Under the Conservative government there has been a boom in private hospitals, especially since 1978, half of which are financed by American business. In 1981, for example, 3½ million people were covered for private health insurance and by 1985, 4½ million. In November 1981 there were 32,000 private beds in independent hospitals and nursing homes; 2,500 private beds within the NHS – the NHS had 306,000 beds (*Commons Hansard*, vol. 12, no. 3, 6 November 1981). The opponents of private medicine argue that the use of medical resources should be based on need, not money. Furthermore, under any insurance scheme certain people will be excluded (quite apart from those who cannot afford the premiums) because they are not a business proposition. These are the very people who need most health care – the elderly, the chronically sick, the disabled. These will be left for the NHS to look after. Two services would then eventually develop – a better one for those who pay through private insurance and a poorer state service for the residual poor who cannot afford private insurance and for those who are not insurable. But supporters of private insurance do not see it this way. For example, the then Secretary of State for Social Services, Patrick Jenkin, speaking in Parliament on 3 February 1981 said: 'By relieving the National Health Service of some part of acute in-patient care, that leaves more resources for the National Health Service to spend on those who have not private care, which includes the Cinderella services for the elderly and the handicapped' (*Commons Hansard*, vol. 998, no. 39, 3 February 1981).

Opponents of the extension of private insurance for health care point out that the NHS is controlled by elected ministers and is paid for mainly from taxation, and this leads to a more efficient control over rapidly rising costs than an insurance-based system. This is because taxation is unpopular with the electorate, on which ministers rely for retaining office, while the controllers of private insurance schemes are not elected and can always raise premiums to meet extra costs (see 'The case against extending private insurance', the *Guardian*, 3 September 1980). This same article gives examples of resources used wastefully under an insurance scheme – patients receiving hospital treatment because their insurance only covered hospital treatment but they could have been just as well treated as out-patients; or the case of hospital administrators encouraging patients to stay in hospital longer than they need because they are cheaper to care for than new patients. This had arisen where a hospital is paid a flat rate fee per day for each patient.

At least we would expect private patients using NHS facilities to be charged the full cost of these facilities. In many cases this is not so says the House of Commons Select Committee on Public Accounts (see its 46th report, July 1986).

The most painless way to increase the rate of development of the NHS without increasing the burden of taxation is for the country to grow richer more quickly.

Two more immediate ways of improving the finances of the NHS are:

1. Concentrate more resources on health education and accident prevention so that fewer people have to make use of the NHS. This would save money because, in the long run, preventive medicine is cheaper than treatment.
2. Allocate resources more effectively. In other words, if money is limited, work out better ways of spending the money you have.

This is what the government claims it is now doing. Thus the abolition of consensus management in hospital administration and its replacement by general managers was seen by the Government as a means of improving efficiency and keeping costs down especially if people with managerial ability from private industry with their commercial experience were brought into the NHS. Another important way of saving money, as seen from the Government point of view, was to allow private contractors to tender to carry out ancillary hospital services – cleaning, catering and laundry services for example which had previously been done by employees of the NHS. Domestic staff of the NHS have tendered themselves and, in many cases, won the contract. At the end of March 1986, private contractors had won 148 contracts (the more lucrative ones) and organisations representing domestic staff, 522. At that time the Secretary of State said competitive tendering was saving the NHS £52 million a year, providing extra money for the care of patients. On the other hand, a critic might argue that the Government gave the NHS less money in anticipation of these savings. In general the financial savings have been at the expense of domestic ancillary staff – less of them employed, hours reduced and less pay. There have been cases where the private contractors have been censured by the health authority for inadequate service. But spokesmen for the private contractors state that they are more efficient because they have to keep strictly to the contract which contains penalty clauses for failure to do so. The same discipline they claim, does not apply to domestic staff. On the other hand, in the United States with its very competitive atmosphere, only about one in six hospitals use outside contractors for cleaning and many hospitals use domestic staff for other services. As one American manager, speaking of outside contractors, said:

> It seems to me that you begin to have a collection of people in the hospital who don't have a fundamental loyalty and identity with the hospital. In Lennox Hill all employees are seen as part of an organization which exists to provide a service to patients and their families even though they may not be direct care givers . . . someone who brings in the patient's tray or is cleaning their room has really got to be part of the team that provides the care and the service. That's very hard to sustain if you have a collection of people, all of whom have different employers, some of whom have short-term gains in mind and are not really here for the long haul. (*Health and Social Service Journal*, 13 February 1986).

Allocation of Resources

Geographical allocation

In 1975 a Resource Allocation Working Party (RAWP) was set up and its report in 1976 highlighted the inequalities in respect of resources between areas of the country. Arising from its report richer regions like Thames and Oxford received a smaller proportion of resources than previously, and other regions like the Northern, North-west and Trent regions received a greater proportion. The richer areas did not like it because, even though they were richer, they still did not have enough resources to do all the things they thought should still be done. Until 1982 the gap between richer and poorer areas manouvered but since 1982, although the richer areas have continued to lose resources the poorer areas show little improvement. There has thus been a demand for a revision of the existing RAWP formula. Under the RAWP system money is allocated in England to the regional health authorities but there is then still the problem of distributing the money to the districts and then distributing the district allocation to the various sections of the district.

Social class and resources

A DHSS Working Group chaired by Sir Douglas Black reported in 1980 under the heading *Inequalities in Health*. This pointed out that the health of those in the lower social classes had improved much more slowly than had the health of the more affluent. In some cases it had deteriorated. The lower social classes also use the preventive services – ante-natal care, screening and other GP check-ups – less than the middle and upper classes. In 1986 the findings were still relevant. Why do working-class people on the whole not make use of the NHS as much as middle-class people? Is it because they are not as conversant with the facilities the service offers, are less able to make known their needs than the middle class, or is it because in the poorer working-class areas the facilities are poorer and do not encourage their use as do the services elsewhere? The Black Report did point out that the provision of services was unequal, particularly those concerned with primary care in the inner-city areas.

Priorities in health care

Another aspect of resource allocation is the distribution of re-sources between the different categories of illness. Medical educa-tion quite rightly stresses the curative aspects of medicine, but when resources are limited putting more resources into preventive medicine and less into curative treatment might serve overall health needs better. Governments have been aware of this point and there has been a shift of resources from hospitals to community services with special emphasis on care of the elderly, the handicapped and mentally ill. This shift is to continue (see *Care in Action*, DHSS, 1981). There has also been, as part of the development of community health services, a much greater emphasis on health education. However, health education can make some people develop unnecessary worries about their health so that eventually they go to the doctor for treatment to stop worrying!

Again looking at the question of priorities in health needs, would it not be better for more resources to be allocated for the treatment

of common illnesses which are not fatal but cause much suffering –
arthritis and rheumatism, for example – and less into expensive
high-technology treatment for less common illnesses?

The Family Doctor

The average family doctor's financial position has improved under
the National Health Service and he or she has no longer to limit
treatment according to the financial standing of patients. Nevertheless, many family doctors feel their status has declined. The reason
is that the family doctor has found it increasingly difficult to keep up
with the rapid advance in medical science not only in matters of
treatment but also diagnosis. Hence doctors have had to refer an
increasing proportion of their patients to specialists in hospitals. At
the same time, the prestige and rewards of the specialist consultant
have increased. (The fact that certain illnesses like pneumonia,
which previously needed hospital treatment, can now be dealt with
by the family doctor, thanks to developments in antibiotics, does
not alter the general trend.) However, morale has been restored to
some extent due to the new emphasis on primary care and, since
1966, financial help for improving premises and employing ancilli-
ary staff.

Suggested remedies

(1) Family doctors should concentrate on developing more
effective treatment for those minor illnesses aggravated by strain
and worry. It is this kind of social medicine which the family doctor
is in a unique position to develop because, unlike the specialist in
the hospital, he or she sees patients as a whole in their social
environment, though many doctors would say they do not have the
time to study their patients' backgrounds.

However, because the voluntary and statutory welfare services
may be able to assist some of the doctor's patients to become less
depressed, it is important that the family doctor is aware of these
services. After all, the family doctor is normally the patient's first
contact and the link with all the other services.

(2) Doctors should work in a group, and an increasing proportion
are now doing so. In 1982 only about 15 per cent worked on their

own. If, as seems preferable, the group practice is conducted from a health centre, it will have a purpose-built building, specialised equipment and ancillary staff such as nurses, health visitors, medical social workers and medical secretaries either employed by the district health authority or by the doctors direct. Group practice has the following advantages:

(a) it helps the patient by making it easier for an appointments system to be worked
(b) it helps the doctor to spend more time with the patient, and this time can be used more effectively because of the background information on the patient provided by ancillary staff
(c) by working as a team and exchanging ideas, the doctors have a better chance of keeping abreast with developments in medicine
(d) as a group, the doctors have more resources and cover a much larger number of patients than any one doctor could and therefore it is much more an economic proposition to employ the latest diagnostic aids – they would then have to refer less patients to hospital and this would relieve the junior hospital doctors of some work.

On the other hand, health centres are more impersonal. Most people have to travel much further from their home to see the doctor and are less likely to meet people from their own locality.

All this is not to say that there are not efficient doctors working on their own. After all, what makes a good doctor is not the medical equipment, important as that is, but an interest in and care for the patient.

(3) In the past the training of doctors was criticised for being done mainly in hospitals where the emphasis is on curing disease, with very little of it dealing with the minor ailments that take up most of the time of the family doctor.

The Royal Commission on Medical Education 1965–8 (the Todd Commission) recommended that all medical education should be in two parts. The first part would be an under-graduate general medical education common to all doctors and would last three years. All doctors, including general practitioners, would then undergo postgraduate vocational training in a specialised field. The family doctor's field would be general practice. In this way the family doctor would himself be a specialist and feel no sense of inferiority to other specialists in matters of education and training. This parity with doctors in the specialised fields would also make it easier for the family doctor to work more closely with the specialist in the hospitals and to be brought into hospital work. But, of course, not all doctors wish to do hospital work. Since the Todd Report was published, progress has been made along the lines of its recommendations.

Primary Health Care Services

Community health services plus the family practitioners services are now often referred to as the primary health care services. They were outlined in the previous chapter. The normal concept of a primary health care team is one led by a general practitioner and including a health visitor, a district nurse, a midwife and perhaps a local authority social worker who can help with personal or family problems which may have contributed to the illness the doctor is asked to treat. The social worker can also liaise with the other specialist social workers including those concerned with home helps, psychiatric social workers and the housing officers of the local authority all of whose work has a relevance for health. Sick or disabled people often need a home help and bad housing can be a direct cause of ill health. Thus a wide range of people in local government as well as in the Health Service are involved in primary health care. Three administrative structures are involved – the district health authority, the family practitioner committee and the local authority. One of the weaknesses of a GP led primary health care team is that it only covers the patients on the GP's list. Furthermore, the *Report of the Community Nursing Review* (1986) suggests that some GPs are not aware of the contribution to treatment other disciplines can make. To further improve co-ordination in the provision of primary health care the report recommends the amalgamation of family practitioner committees and district health authorities making one administrative body responsible for primary health care. This is also advocated by the Labour Party. The area covered by this administrative body would be divided into appropriately sized neighbourhood areas each led by a primary health care team led by GPs and nurses in equal partnership. And what of co-ordination with local government?

There are statutory liaison committees representing the district health authorities and the local authorities which consider such things as joint financing of schemes of mutual benefit. The 1979 Royal Commission on the NHS considered that this liaison between the health authorities and local government had been unsatisfactory and put most of the blame on local government. Since then, while the Government can claim it has maintained expenditure on the NHS in real terms, it has reduced financial aid to local government which cannot have improved matters since the Royal Commission reported.

The problem of co-ordination and the need for effective leadership of all the disciplines involved in primary health care will, sooner or later, have to be tackled.

Complaints

The Secretary of State

The Secretary of State for Social Services has the responsibility for ensuring that the NHS is run in the interests of the people. He and his colleagues in the government have the final word on the shaping of its future.

Community Health Councils

The community health councils make representations to the NHS authorities on behalf of patients in general. However, some community health councils encourage individuals to approach them with their complaints. They are then given advice on what to do. And with many CHCs the secretary will, if requested, represent a person appearing before a FPC with a complaint against a practitioner.

Family Practitioner Committees

There is a statutory complaints procedure for the personal practitioner services. For each section of the personal practitioner service there is a local service committee – one each for doctors, dentists, opticians and chemists – appointed by the family practitioner committee. A complaint against a practitioner goes to the appropriate committee and the committee's recommendation goes to the FPC for approval or amendment. If the complaint is found to be justified, part of the personal practitioner's salary may be withheld. An appeal can be made to the minister against the FPC's decision. In more serious cases the FPC may recommend that the practitioner be excluded from the NHS. In this case the matter is dealt with by the National Health Service Tribunal.

Some people feel that the complaints procedure against practitioners is not very satisfactory as the local service committees and FPCs have very strong professional representation and may be over-influenced in the practitioner's favour. The complainant has no professional help and is therefore at a disadvantage to the personal practitioner against whom the complaint is made. The Government Green Paper (Primary Health Care, April 1986) proposes that only the more serious complaints should be dealt with as described above. For lesser complaints FPCs should offer an informed conciliation service between patient and practitioner.

Health Service Commissioner

The Health Service Commissioner investigates complaints in connection with hospital treatment and community care where the complainant feels that he or she has suffered injustice or hardship through maladministration or through a failure to provide the necessary treatment and care. The Commissioner only investigates a complaint if it has already been referred to the responsible authorities but has not been resolved to the complainant's satisfaction. He cannot investigate complaints that challenge the clinical judgement of the doctor, though a special complaints procedure has been introduced for this. If the hospital cannot resolve the complaint, the health authority's regional medical officer seeks a second opinion from two independent consultants. But not all consumer groups are happy with the way the procedure has functioned. The Commissioner will not deal with complaints against personal practitioners as there is already the statutory procedure for referring these to the FPCs previously described. It is in the field of hospital treatment that the lack of an effective complaints procedure has been most felt. This has been particularly true of long-stay mental hospitals where some years ago revelations of cruelty to mental patients came as a great shock.

Hospital Patients' Association

This is a voluntary pressure group which takes up complaints and puts forward its views on the NHS generally to those who run it, including the Secretary of State.

Summary

The National Health Service has ensured that a good standard of medical care is given to everyone irrespective of income. Medical care has therefore greatly expanded. It has enabled medical resources to be more evenly distributed throughout the country, though there is still need for medical resources to be distributed more fairly always bearing in mind that some areas have greater or less health needs than others. Family doctors have been given financial security and yet, at the same time, have retained their clinical freedom. And because the family doctor does not have to worry about the financial standing of patients when prescribing, he or she can perhaps be more of a family doctor than used to be the case, providing he or she is not overloaded.

On the other hand, some family doctors are worried about their status. However, health centres and new training methods have gone some way to remove this worry.

There will never be enough money for the NHS to do all the things one would like it to do, especially as the development of medical science usually makes treatment more expensive. The British Medical Association takes the view that lack of adequate resources has resulted in an 'inadequate and impersonal service' (*The Times*, 12 July 1978). On the other hand, the 1979 Royal Commission on the National Health Service found the NHS was not suffering from a 'mortal disease' but could be improved by better use of resources. It recommended the abolition of prescription charges, to retain it as a virtually free service. And the majority of the public seem happy with the National Health Service (see *Guardian*, 22 December 1981). But it must be remembered that the financial problems of the NHS are partly due to its success. The development of the service has meant more demands being made upon it. This can be illustrated with the example of major hip surgery, which is now more available with the result that more people demand it. This causes longer waiting-lists but, not only that, a hip operation uses the operating theatre all day, delaying other operations. Furthermore, screening campaigns have revealed hidden illness. The problem of financing the NHS will thus be a permanent one and how it will be dealt with will largely depend on the economic policies in fashion at the time. For example, the Thatcher government, influenced by monetarist theory, has attempted to reduce the growth of public expenditure and introduced privatisation of public enterprises (denationalisation). In the NHS privatisation has meant encouraging private medical care and the opening up of domestic and catering services within the hospitals to competitive tendering from outside private contractors, with a view to saving money. The huge increase in the charge for a prescription plus the limited drugs list will also save money and will encourage the buying of medicines outside the NHS. The new organisational structure of general managers is also seen by the Government as a means of improving efficiency and hence making financial savings. But in spite of the Thatcher Government's attitude towards public expenditure it can justly claim that, in real terms, money spent on the NHS is greater than ever before. More patients than ever are being treated and more professional staff employed and new hospitals built. This seems flatly to contradict the reports one reads almost daily of shortages and reduction of services within many health authorities.

In trying to resolve this apparent contradiction demands on the NHS must be taken into consideration and whether the inflation rate of goods and services needed by the NHS corresponds with the inflation rate reflected in the cost of living index. Financial demands on the NHS have risen and are still rising. There is the increasing number of elderly, increasing illness due to large-scale unemployment, there is increased drug abuse and increased alcholism and the high cost of new technology and now the problem of AIDS. In addition, pay increases within the NHS have not been fully met by the Government leaving health authorities to find the rest of the money. And finally, there are no cash limits on family practitioner services yet they have been increasing at a faster rate than hospital services. Hence, in spite of increased resources under the Thatcher government, they might not be sufficient to meet the extra demands on the NHS. The House of Commons Social Services Committee in its 4th Report, 1986 estimates that between 1980/81 and 1985/86 the NHS has been under-funded by £1.3 billion. It states that to keep pace with rising demand real resources should have risen by 2 per cent a year but they only grew by 1 per cent a year. The Government could reply that, apart from expenditure on the NHS being at record levels, the increase in the number of doctors, dentists and nurses between 1979 and 1982 was far greater than the losses suffered since 1982. In addition there was an increase in administrative and technical staff in those years. And as for prescription charges; the elderly and the young and those on supplementary benefit do not have to pay them and the increased income from the charges helps to provide extra services for the NHS. And future expenditure does allow for what are demographic and technological change providing savings are made from increased efficiency. As for the development of the private sector, it helps to reduce waiting lists in the NHS, especially for surgical cases. But, given the philosophy of the Thatcher government, critics might be forgiven for believing (whether true or false) that talk of efficiency is perhaps a disguise for cuts and that the Government wants as much private health care as possible within the limits set by our democratic society even if it means two tiers of health care – one for the better off and one – the NHS – for the less well-off. But it must be remembered that health also depends on factors outside the health services, whether private or NHS – for example, living standards, including housing and working conditions and also nutrition and, most important, the way we live.

Assignments

1. Discuss the ways the work of local government and the National Health Service is linked. Find out what liaison exists between your local authority and the NHS. Suggest ways of improving this liaison. For this last part of the question, chance your arm!
2. Discuss the advantages and disadvantages of group practice among general practitioners for doctors and patients. Where possible make use of your own experience of group practice either located in or separate from a health centre.

3. Write to the British United Provident Association (BUPA), which provides private health insurance, and ask for the cost and benefits of private health insurance to the insured. Then, bearing in mind your other reading, give your assessment of the probable consequences to the National Health Service of the extension of private health insurance and its consequence for health care in general.

4. Given that resources are limited, what would be your priorities in health care? Give your reasons.

5. Discuss the family doctor as the leader of a primary health care team.

Reading

Brian Abel-Smith, *NHS – The First Thirty Years* (HMSO, 1978).

Annual Report of the Health Service in England (HMSO).

R. G. S. Brown, *The Changing National Health Service*, 2nd edn (Routledge & Kegan Paul, 1978).

Anne Marie Coyne, 'Stamping Out the Stamp', *Health and Social Service Journal* (11 September, 1976).

Davies Report, *Report of the Committee on Hospital Complaints Procedure* (HMSO, 1974).

DHSS, *Democracy in the National Health Service* (HMSO, 1974).

DHSS, *Sharing Resources for Health in England,* Report of Resource Allocation Working Party (HMSO, 1976).

DHSS, *Prevention and Health, Everybody's Business*, Consultative Document (HMSO, 1976).

DHSS, *Patients First* (HMSO, December 1979).

DHSS, *Care in the Community* (HMSO, July 1981).

DHSS, *Care in Action: A Handbook of Policies and Priorities for the Health and Personal Social Services in England* (HMSO, 1981).

Leslie Doyal, *The Political Economy of Health* (Pluto Press, 1979).

Green Paper, *Primary Health Care, An Agenda for Discussion* (HMSO, April 1986).

Christopher Ham, *Health Policy in Britain* 2nd edn (Macmillan, 1985).

Health Service Journal (published weekly).

HMSO, Royal Commission on Medical Education, *Report 1965–1968*, Cmnd 3569 (HMSO, 1968).

House of Commons, Debate on NHS management (*Hansard*, vol. 93, No. 78, 14 March 1986).

Rudolf Klein, *The Politics of the National Health Service* (Longman, 1983).

Jeremy Laurence, 'Are We Getting Value for Money from the Health Service?', *New Society* (26 August 1982).

104   *Introduction to the Social Services*

Manchester University Research Team, 'Working on Teamwork', *Housing and Social Service Journal* (19 August 1977).
T. H. Marshall, *Social Policy in the Twentieth Century* (Hutchinson, 1967) ch. 10.
Alan Maynard, 'Privatizing the National Health Service', *Lloyds Bank Review* (*April 1983*).
NHS Management Inquiry Report – Griffiths Report (DHSS, 1983).
Report of the Health Advisory Service (published annually).
Report of the Community Nursing Review: Neighbourhood Nursing, A Focus for Care (HMSO, 1986).
Royal Commission, *Report of the Royal Commission on the National Health Service*, Cmnd 7615 (HMSO), 18 July 1979.
Richard Taylor, *Medicine Out of Control* (Macmillan, 1979).

9 Welfare

The Elderly

The development of services for the elderly

In the last quarter of the nineteenth century there was a growing
public awareness that old age was one important cause of poverty
and, therefore, as part of the growing concern with poverty, there
grew a demand for old-age pensions. The 1908 Old Age Pensions
Act was the first major help to the aged poor outside the Poor Law.
It provided means-tested pensions at 70, paid for out of taxation. A
contributory pension scheme was introduced with the 1925
Widows, Orphans and Old Age Contributory Pensions Act. The
main community services for the elderly were developed after the
Second World War.

Today's services for the elderly (apart from the NHS)

1. There are state pensions for women at 60 and men at 65. The
   pension is not enough to live on by itself and those pensioners
   without other sufficient income can claim supplementary benefit
   (i.e. a supplementary pension).
2. Residential accommodation is provided by local authorities for
   the elderly in need of care and attention. This is a statutory duty
   under the 1948 National Assistance Act. But, there are large
   variations in the availability of homes as between one local
   authority and another. Not every elderly person requiring a
   place in a local authority residential home can get one. In many
   cases, they find a place in private homes and many of these
   elderly receive financial assistance from the DHSS. For example, over a third of those in private homes are on supplementary
   benefit. The cost to the DHSS has escalated considerably over

the years as more and more elderly go into private homes. There is also concern that some private landlords are exploiting the shortage of places by making exorbitant charges for board and accommodation. On the other hand, there are people in residential homes who might still have been living at home if the caring services in the community were more plentiful and better organised.

3. Domestic help and nursing attention are other statutory services which must be provided under the 1948 National Assistance Act. But they apply to all categories of people and not just the elderly.

4. Meals can be provided in their homes to those elderly people who are housebound or who have difficulty in shopping. This 'meals-on-wheels' service is provided either by local authorities or by voluntary organisations.

Local authorities or voluntary organisations, or both, also provide the following services:

5. Day centres for the elderly.

6. Social clubs for the elderly.

7. Friendly visits to the elderly.

8. Social workers' visits to the elderly to give advice on the problems of old age.

9. Independently of the work done by local authorities and voluntary organisations, some doctors make regular visits to their elderly patients.

10. Local authorities provide financial assistance for home adaptations considered necessary for the well-being of elderly people. Some of these adaptations are provided by the NHS. The powers and duties given to local authorities under 1948 National Assistance Act were extended under the 1968 Health Services and Public Health Act.

Three categories of old people

1. Those who are able to live on their own or with relatives.

2. Those needing residential accommodation but not medical care.

3. Those requiring medical care.

Among those requiring medical care are those who can be helped in their own home by relatives or friends aided by a home nurse, those who are sick in residential homes and should, if possible, be kept there among friends, and those who must remain in hospital because they are bed-bound and need long-term nursing care.

Factors which have aggravated the problem of the elderly

1. Normally a society can look after its aged without much trouble because they only constitute a small proportion of the population. But in Britain the proportion of old people in the population has been increasing since the last quarter of the nineteenth century. The proportion of men over 65 and women over 60 in Great Britain today is approximately 16 per cent, whereas in 1911 it was 6.8 per cent. The reason for this increasing proportion of old people in the population is the decline in the birth rate from around 1870 and the increasing expectancy of life during the twentieth century.
2. Since 1945 a greater proportion of young people seek work away from their home area and live well away from their parents when they get married, leading to a greater isolation of the parents.
3. Smaller families result in there being fewer children to share the job of looking after ageing parents.
4. Rapid technological change has undermined tradition so that the opinions of older workers are less respected as their experiences relate to different sets of conditions.
5. Greater affluence since 1945 has increased the gap between living standards of those in work and those in retirement.

What more should be done for the elderly?

We could make them feel more wanted. Should people be allowed to stay on at work longer if they wish to and are still useful? Many people are forced to retire when they are still capable of doing their work effectively, and going out to work gives them an interest among friends and helps to keep them fit. But some people, often trade unionists, object to a later retirement age, even if optional, because they say it would hold up promotions among younger people and would aggravate the unemployment problem.

When people do retire, could not the job centres do much more to find retired people part-time jobs? Some voluntary organisations have been very successful at doing this but there are very few such organisations.

Residential homes which local authorities provide for elderly people are now often the small bungalow type. This allows the elderly to continue to be part of the local community. A group of bungalows is normally under the supervision of a warden, who can be reached by the elderly by simply pressing a bell. Apart from this 'sheltered housing' there are residential homes for the elderly but many of them are of the institutional type, cut off from the local community, and perhaps progress should be made by constructing more non-institutional-type housing.

One interesting development in just a few local authorities is the setting-up of foster homes for the elderly.

Where the elderly are rehoused under development schemes we can ensure (and this is normally done) that if they go into a block of flats as far as possible they are given a flat on the ground floor and are regularly visited, especially in the early days of resettlement, by social workers of the local authority.

Some local authority services for the elderly are optional, and there are wide variations between one local authority and another in the provision of services for the elderly. Perhaps more should be done by central government to spur on the laggards. Even with compulsory services, like residential homes, some local authorities spend a minimum.

The NHS should devote more resources to the old. In 1982 the DHSS imposed greater control over the regional health authorities to ensure more resources were devoted to the elderly (*Guardian*, 21 January 1982). Unfortunately, geriatrics is not popular among young doctors and nurses. As a result, elderly people do not get the medical treatment they should. This often encourages them to put up with illness in the mistaken belief that it is an inevitable part of being old.

Even if the state pension cannot be increased to the point where it is sufficient to live on without any other source of income, everything should be done to encourage the elderly to apply for a supplementary pension if entitled to one. One problem is to find out who the elderly are.

Mothers and Young Children

At the end of the nineteenth century there were, apart from growing sympathy for the poor, three main factors which furthered the introduction of state services to protect the health of mothers and young children (see also Chapter 6):

1. There was concern at the continuing high infant mortality rate.
2. The Boer war recruitment shock led to talk of the physical deterioration of the nation.
3. The introduction of compulsory education in 1880 put all children on show to the authorities for the first time and very many children were seen to be in poor health.

The 1902 Midwives Act ensured that midwives were properly trained, and in 1936 local authorities were made responsible for ensuring an adequate number of them in their areas.

By 1915 local authorities had powers to supervise the progress of a mother and her newly born baby. The 1918 Maternity and Child Welfare Act permitted local authorities, with financial assistance from the central government, to provide services for expectant mothers and their children up to the age of 5. Under the 1946 National Health Service Act it was made obligatory for local authorities to provide this service.

Under the 1946 Act part of the service for mothers and young children was the provision of welfare foods like orange juice, vitamin tablets, cod-liver oil, but in the interwar years those local authorities which ran the service provided milk only.

Today's services for mothers and young children

1. The district health authorities are now responsible for the clinics which provide ante- and post-natal medical and dental care for mothers and for the regular examination of their children. The clinics have the services of doctors, nurses and health visitors, and many have dentists. In quite a number of areas now the clinics are part of a health centre where many more services are found. The clinics give a great deal of advice to the mother. They also provide welfare foods.
2. Health visitors visit mother and child in the home. They see that the baby is being looked after properly, give advice to the

mother and, if they see any strains within the family relationship, they may ask a social worker to call round.
3. A mother with her young child need not necessarily go to the clinic; she could get all the advice and help she requires from her family doctor.

Young mothers who go out to work

Day nurseries are provided by many local authorities and private organisations where a mother can leave her young child under expert guidance while she goes out to work. Places are occasionally offered for children of ill or disabled mothers. There are also childminders who in their own homes look after a group of children. Under the Nurseries and Child Minders Regulation Act 1948 private nurseries and child-minding establishments must be registered with the local authority, which has powers of inspection. In recent years fears have been expressed that some children are being left with unregistered childminders where conditions may be unsatisfactory. But fears have also been voiced at the inadequacy of much child-minding, whether registered or not. To some people the answer is more local authority nurseries. They see day nurseries not only as a means of helping mothers to go out to work but also a means of giving the child a fuller and richer life, of special value to those children who live in urban areas where there are few open spaces. It is claimed that day nurseries will compensate these children to some extent for their poor home background, which puts them at an educational disadvantage when they start school.

Day nurseries expanded during the Second World War when there was a need to employ as many women as possible in war work although many were shut down after the war. There are those now who consider day nurseries an unnecessary luxury because they say they are used by women who simply want to maintain a reasonable level of income by going out to work at the ratepayers' and their children's expense. This criticism does not, of course, apply to one-parent families. The Conservative government view is that it is not its job to provide a free or heavily subsidised day nursery service to enable parents to go out to work. Parents themselves have the main responsibility to see that their young children receive proper care. But the government does provide some financial help to voluntary organisations concerned with the under-5s.

There has been no real proof offered that children whose parents are at work all day suffer in any way even if they have to roam the streets awaiting one of their parent's return. On the other hand, there is no proof that they do not suffer. Some working mothers might argue that the money they earn enables them to provide little extras for the children and some could argue that it keeps the family out of poverty.

The single-parent mother

Because unmarried mothers have tended to be looked on with disapproval, local authority services for them have been slow in developing. Voluntary organisations have been the main providers of help, especially the religious organisations.

Today the unmarried mother makes use of the community health and welfare services and the services of her doctor in the same way as any other mother, but local authorities are encouraged by the government to provide the following extra services for unmarried mothers, though there is no statutory obligation for them to do so:

1. Local authority social workers try to help them.
2. Local authorities co-operate with voluntary organisations in the provision of hostels and homes for pregnant women or unmarried mothers who need residential care. Again, it is the religious organisations who do most in this field.
3. Where an unmarried mother is unable to look after her child, it may be taken into care of the local authority, or the mother can have it adopted. Adoption is governed by the 1958 Adoption Act and the 1975 Children Act.

Arising from the high mortality rate among illegitimate children, there was set up in 1918 the National Council for the Unmarried Mother and Her Child. It is now called the National Council for One-Parent Families. The body co-ordinates the main organisations concerned with illegitimacy. It is a kind of pressure group to protect the interests of children and their parents. Thus it helps not only unmarried mothers and their families but also the growing number of one-parent families, including single parent fathers, arising from divorce and desertion. It is in regular touch with social workers throughout the country and it can refer any woman needing help to the appropriate social worker. There are other voluntary organisations which exist to help one-parent families – e.g. a self-help group called Gingerbread.

Schoolchildren

School meals and school milk

The first state services for schoolchildren were school meals for needy elementary schoolchildren under the 1906 Education (Provision of Meals) Act and medical inspection of elementary schoolchildren under the 1907 Education (Administrative Provisions) Act. They were introduced because of the fear that the nation was deteriorating physically after so many volunteers for the Boer war had been found unfit. Previously some school meals for poor children had been provided by charitable organisations, but their role declined after the 1906 Act. School meals were not obligatory; local authorities could please themselves whether they provided them, and until 1914 their entire cost was borne from the rates. But in 1914 the government gave a 50 per cent grant towards them. This was of particular help to the poorer voluntary schools. During the interwar years school meals were provided in local authority secondary schools and an increasing proportion of children obtained school meals, the local authorities receiving payment from parents who could afford to pay.

In 1921 free milk was provided to needy elementary schoolchildren. The 1934 Milk Act enabled elementary schoolchildren to obtain one-third of a pint of milk a day for a halfpenny. The milk was subsidised by the Milk Marketing Board. School dinners and school milk, even if not universally applied, did a great deal to improve the health of children.

The Second World War necessitated married women going out to work to help the war effort. Mid-day meals for schoolchildren and day nurseries became a patriotic necessity. The 1944 Education Act made it obligatory for local authorities to provide school meals and milk for all children who wanted them. The intention was that both school meals and school milk should be free, but, although the milk was free, school meals were free only to the needy but subsidised for everyone else.

Greater affluence has led to greater selectivity in the social services, and free school milk in secondary education was abolished in 1971. In 1971 it was abolished for the 7 to 11 age group in junior schools. This met with much opposition from those who regarded free milk as a vital factor in maintaining a healthy nation. However, there is the argument that if it is so important then parents can provide it for their children, and those parents who cannot afford it can still get it free. On the other hand, the free school milk supporters say that not all parents who can afford to provide the milk will do so. In other words, to those who say free milk for everyone undermines parental responsibility, they reply that we must protect children from irresponsible parents. Local authorities now have discretion as to what milk, meals and other refreshments to provide and what charges to make. Meals have no longer to meet 'minimal nutritional standards'. Some local authorities have abolished school meals in primary schools and one has abolished them for both primary and secondary schools. At present those on supplementary benefit and Family Income Supplement receive free school meals and local authorities, under discretionary powers, can also provide free school meals to other low income families. Presumably in those schools where school meals have been abolished children whose parents fall in the above categories will receive a packed lunch. Under the 1986 Social Security Act the discretionary power of a local authority to provide free school meals will be withdrawn from April 1988. People on FIS, to be called Family Credit, will also cease to get free school meals from April 1988 but will receive a cash benefit instead.

Originally school meals were to ensure that children received one good meal a day. Fears are now expressed that with many children this will no longer be the case. Many do not receive a satisfactory diet at home and many buy junk food with the money their parents give them for meals. Again as with the earlier issue of school milk, there are those who say it is up to parents to ensure their children are properly fed and not the State. Ideally yes, but circumstances result in many families not doing just that so why should the children suffer? Under the 1944 Education Act part of the object of school meals was to train children in good food habits and table manners, but since the teachers revolted against the supervising of school meals, the social training part has been neglected.

School meals are very useful where the mother goes out to work or the child has a long way to travel to school, but should they be subsidised for everyone, even for those children whose parents can afford to pay for them? This brings us back to the problem of selectivity discussed earlier.

The School Health Service

In spite of the progress made in the health of schoolchildren due to school meals, the School Health Service and improvements in the general standard of health, progress was slowed down because of general malnutrition. Before the introduction of subsidised milk in 1934, about one-quarter to one-third of elementary schoolchildren were undernourished. Evacuation of schoolchildren during the Second World War brought home to the better off the extent of this under-nourishment – they had not realised just how widespread it was. After 1945, with the introduction of the National Health Service, the School Health Service expanded, but the local education authority was still responsible for its administration, though the principal school medical officer was usually the medcial officer of health. Today it is administered by the district health authorities.

Handicapped Children

The first legislation giving help to handicapped children was the 1893 Elementary Education (Blind and Deaf Children) Act which empowered local authorities to pay for the education and mainte-nance of blind and deaf children. The 1899 Education (Defective and Epileptic) Act helped mentally defective children. But compre-hensive legislation to provide for the needs of handicapped children had to await the 1944 Education Act.

How handicapped children of school age are helped today

The local authority must assess the special educational needs of the handicapped child. It first arranges a medical examination in co-operation with the district health authority. In deciding what to do after receiving the medical report, the local authority considers the views not only of the doctor but also of the teacher or educational psychologist and the wishes of the child's parents. If the parents are dissatisfied with the decision of the local authority, they can appeal to a local appeals committee and ultimately to the Secretary of State.

If at all possible, the child is sent to an ordinary school on the principle that a handicapped child should lead as normal a life as possible. But if the disability is too severe, the local authority may send the child to a residential school or special day school where treatment will also be provided. The blind and the deaf must normally be treated in a special school.

Educationally subnormal children are the largest group needing special treatment. These are educationally retarded children and this retardation can be due either to innate causes or to the child's environment. Most of the children in the subnormal group go to an ordinary school; most of the remainder of those in the sub-normal group go to special schools.

But there are children with very severe abnormalities who cannot be educated even in special schools – but they are still the responsibility of the local education authority, even though many of them are in hospital.

Tuition may be given at home in exceptional circumstances.

Maladjusted Children

Under The National Health Service Act of 1946 prevention and treatment is provided in local authority child guidance clinics or in hospital child guidance clinics. Some child guidance is provided by voluntary organisations. One of the jobs of the clinics is to help parents understand their children better and repair any bad relationships between parent and child. In certain cases the clinics may advise that the child lives away from home for a while in a hostel or special school.

Children in Need of Care and Protection

Historical development

Before 1900 children needing care were looked after by the Poor Law or by voluntary organisations like Dr Barnardo's, the NSPCC, and so on. Mainly because of the influence of voluntary organisations, by the end of the nineteenth century laws had been passed against cruelty to and exploitation of children.

A more general concern for children arose, as mentioned earlier, because of the continuing high infant mortality rate, the state's new responsibility for elementary education and concern for the nation's fitness arising from the Boer war recruitment shock. Other factors were revelations of baby-farming (where parents paid unscrupulous people to look after one or more of their children but in reality were ridding themselves of the children), and the concern over the falling birth rate.

1908 Children Act

This Act strengthened the laws on fostering and the inspection procedures of voluntary homes for children, but its chief interest is in what it did for delinquent children. It abolished imprisonment for children under 16, and introduced juvenile courts to keep children away from criminals and remand homes to prevent children from going to prison while awaiting trial. The prison atmosphere was considered likely to further corrupt the child.

1933 Children and Young Persons Act

The main interest in this Act is that it gave powers to the magistrates of juvenile courts to remove children and young persons 'in need of care and protection' from the custody of their parents or guardians and make alternative arrangements for them – mainly in foster homes or in children's homes run by the Poor Law, then administered by the public assistance committees of local authorities.

1948 Children's Act

This Act was based on the *Report of the Interdepartmental Committee on the Care of Children* (Curtis Report) of 1946. Responsibility for the care of the different categories of children needing care, which previously had been shared between different government departments, was centralised in the Home Office. It set up an Advisory Council on Child Care with an Inspectorate. But local authorities administered the Act. Under the Health and Social Services and Social Security Adjudication Act (November 1982), the Advisory Council was abolished. Under the 1948 Act certain categories of children needing care – for example, delinquents, or simply children in need of care – could still be brought before a juvenile court by an authorised body or person as laid down in the 1933 Act and the court could order any of the following for the child depending on the circumstances:

(a) to have the child sent to an approved school
(b) to commit the child to the care of a fit person (normally the local authority)
(c) to place him or her in the care of a probation officer
(d) to order his or her parents or guardian to promise to look after him or her properly.

1969 Children and Young Persons Act

A young person under the Act is someone aged 14 but under 17. A child is someone under 14. The Act abolished approved school orders and fit persons orders, probation and fines for young people under 17. The main orders under the 1969 Act made by the juvenile courts for offenders and those simply needing care are:

(a) an order requiring a parent or guardian to enter into recognisance to take proper care of the child
(b) an order requiring payment of compensation
(c) an order for a stay in hospital in accordance with mental health legislation
(d) a care order committing a child to a local authority (under the 1982 Criminal Justice Act a young offender subject to a care order must be offered legal representation).

It is then for the local authority to decide whether to send the child to a residential community home, to foster parents or to return him or her home. A child with uncontrollable behaviour can be placed by the local authority in secure accommodation, usually located in a community home. The 1982 Criminal Justice Act now lays down stricter criteria for doing this. Where an offender with a care order has committed another offence, no discretion is left to the local authority – the offender under a care order must be removed from home either to foster parents, boarded out or sent to a community home. The order expires when the offender is 18 but may be extended for another year. Then there is:

(e)   a supervision order under which the offender will remian at home under the supervison of the local authority social worker or a probation officer for a specified period up to three years.

Under a supervision order an offender may receive 'intermediate treatment' to give him or her a new interest and environment which may involve living away from home. It normally involves constructive and remedial activities. The 1982 Criminal Justice Act emphasises the importance of the court being involved with the supervisor in laying down what activities the offender should carry out under the supervision order. The assumption must be that supervision in some cases has meant too easy a regime. Unlike a probation order, which it replaced, an offender under a supervision order cannot be brought back to court if he or she breaks the order. Then there are:

(f)   an order requiring an offender to go to an attendance centre (under the 1982 Criminal Justice Act a Crown Court can now give an attendance centre sentence)

(g)   an order committing an offender to a detention centre – it is at a detention centre where the 'short, sharp, shock' treatment for young offenders is given

(h)   a recommendation to the Crown Court that an offender be sent to a borstal for training (the 1969 Act provided for the abolition of borstals and detention centres but they were retained, but youth custody centres have replaced borstals under the 1982 Criminal Justice Act).

It was the intention of the 1969 Act to give greater flexibility in the treatment of juvenile delinquents by increasing the role of local authority social workers in their treatment. Another important aim of the Act was to keep children and young people, as far as possible, out of the juvenile courts. Thus, under the Act, authorised bodies (i.e. the police or the NSPCC) wishing to bring a child or young person before a juvenile court have normally to consult the local authority social services department, and the child or young person should only be brought before the juvenile court if the police or the NSPCC, after consultation with the local authority social workers, are still convinced that nothing less than a court order will do. The local authority has then to provide the court with the details surrounding the child or young person. Even then, the court can make an order only if certain conditions are fulfilled. There is, however, a proviso which allows the police, under certain conditions, to prosecute a young person before receiving the comments of the social worker, but even then the court must normally await the report of the local authority social worker. However, this part of the Act has not been strictly implemented. The degree to which the police consult social workers before making a charge or issuing a summons varies greatly as between one police force and another. Thus the power of the police to prosecute persons between 14 and 17 has not been curtailed, as the 1969 Act intended. It was also the intention of the 1969 Act to phase out custodial treatment for young people under 17. This was not done and in fact custodial treatment in borstals and detention centres greatly increased due, to a great extent, to the rise of juvenile crime. The 1982 Criminal Justice Act reintroduces the provision of custodial treatment for a minority of juveniles. One other provison of the Act has not been implemented. It was intended to raise the minimum age of prosecution to 14; it is still 10.

Another feature of the 1969 Act is that it led to the replacement of former local authority and voluntary homes and hostels, remand homes, reception centres and approved schools by community homes under the control of regional planning committees of neighbouring local authorities. The 1983 Health and Social Services and Social Security Adjudications Act allows community homes to be used for children for whom the local authority has responsibility whether in care or not. And they may not only be in local authority homes but also in homes run by an approved voluntary organisation.

The 1969 Act has been much criticised, especially by magistrates, who felt it has led to too-soft an attitude to a minority of tough juvenile offenders. Another criticism is that by replacing the statutory prescribed action of the courts by informal action out of court often means no effective action at all. Defenders of the Act point out that at a brief court hearing it is not always possible for the magistrates to know what is best for the offender even when the offender's background has been described in a report to the magistrate by the social worker or the probation and after-care officer. The local authority, in deciding what is best for the offender, has the help of social workers, teachers and psychiatrists.

It is true that since the Act juvenile crime has been seen to have soared. Juveniles are now responsible for about a quarter of all serious offences and about half the burglaries and robberies. But the British Association of Social Workers has stated: 'There is a clear correlation between acute delinquent behaviour and social deprivation. Nearly all types of crime have greatly increased since 1969 and the causes are the social and physical environment.'

The dilemma seems to be how to reconcile the welfare of the child or young person, which social workers seem to stress, and the protection of society, which magistrates seem to stress.

The 1982 Criminal Justice Act does not alter the basic principles of the 1969 Children and Young Persons Act, but the 1969 Act has never been implemented as originally intended.

1982 Criminal Justice Act

Among the aims of the 1982 Criminal Justice Act are:

(a) to reduce the number of young people sent into custody by providing the courts with a greater range of non-custodial sentences, though severe custodial sentences will remain for really 'wicked' young people
(b) to give custodial treatment for young people under 21 only if the court feels there is no other way of dealing with them.
(c) shorter sentences.

Where the sentence may be custodial the Act lays down that an offender under 21 must have legal representation and a social inquiry report normally be provided to the court before sentence is passed. Custodial treatment means a detention centre, youth custody centre or residential care order, already referred to.

Non-custodial sentences are supervised activity schemes covered by supervision orders, attendance centre orders and community service orders. Two unusual features of the 1982 Criminal Justice Act are the power given to the courts to impose a curfew requirement with a supervison order, and if a fine is imposed it should normally be imposed on the parents. But the long-term aim of abolishing custodial treatment for juvenile offenders seems as distant as ever.

1980 Child Care Act

This Act replaces the 1948 Children Act. As under the 1948 Act, children and young people up to the age of 17 still come into the care of a local authority when parents or guardians cannot look after them adequately. Thus the parents or guardians may be missing or, due to sickness are unable to take proper care of the children. What is different from the 1948 Act is that the Child Care Act does not cover delinquent children – these come into the care of the local authority via the 1969 Children and Young Persons Act. Thus most of the children who come into the care of the local authority under the Child Care Act have done so at the wish of the parents and no care order by a court is required. A care order issued by a juvenile court would only be necessary if the parents objected. Many of these cases concern physical brutality towards children by parents. In such cases the local authority works with the district health authority, as medical evidence is vital. The voluntary nature of most of the commitals of children to the care of the local authority means that when the parents or guardians consider themselves fit again to look after the children they are normally returned to them. There are a minority of cases where the local authority may refuse the parents'/guardians' request because the authority considers them unfit to look after the children. In such cases the children normally remain in the care of the local authority. However, in such cases parents can appeal and then it is up to the courts to see if the local authority's action was justified. Where there are no parents or guardians to look after the children, the local authority looks after them.

Any authority which has parental rights normally retains them until the young person is 18. Local authorities that receive children into care try to obtain foster parents for them where for various reasons parental care is not possible. Foster homes are inspected by the local authority. Also a local authority has powers to arrange for the adoption of children (see the 1975 Children Act). A child may be placed for adoption by the local authority itself or by an approved voluntary body.

Under the 1948 Act local authorities had to set up a children's department with a children's officer in charge. The children's department is now part of the local authority social services department. In January 1971 responsibility for the child-care services was transferred from the Home Secretary to the Secretary of State for Social Services.

1963 Children and Young Persons Act

This Act was based on the *Report of the Committee on Children and Young Persons*, the Ingleby Report (October 1960). It gave local authorities powers to promote the welfare of children and to take preventative action against family breakdown, even to the extent of giving financial assistance to the family. The 1980 Child Care Act consolidated the 1963 Act in this respect. The Ingleby Report reasoned that in most cases children had to be taken into care because of a breakdown in family life. Hence it was better to try and prevent the breakdown in the first place. Apart from being better from the family point of view if less children did not have to be put into care, it would save the local authorities money, even if it meant employing more social workers to work with problem families.

There is, however, the danger that this emphasis on the family can, where there is the question of whether or not to take a child at risk away from its parents, tips the scales into leaving it with its parents. In just a few cases this has led to disastrous results for the child.

This greater interest in the family was partly due to the apparent increased delinquency after the Second World War and the growing interest in sociology, which then stressed the importance of good family life as the best foundation for a stable, successful society. It was also partly due to the revolt against institutional care and its replacement by the concept of community care (discussed on pp. 128–31).

Physically Handicapped People

Legislation to help the blind, deaf and epileptic goes back to the nineteenth century, but services of a comprehensive nature for the physically handicapped came with the 1946 National Health Service Act and the 1948 National Assistance Act.

Services today for physically handicapped people

1. The family doctor, who is the key link with the various services for the handicapped.
2. Hospital treatment, which can include physiotherapy, remedial

gymnastics, occupational therapy, provision of appliances, the medical social worker's help in resettlement, and so on.

3. Local authority services, most of which are provided under the 1948 National Assistance Act and the 1970 Chronically Sick and Disabled Persons Act. The significance of the latter Act is that it makes mandatory on local authorities much of what had been permissive in earlier legislation. It was hoped that this would bring the bad local authorities up to the standard of the good.

In more detail the main services are:

(a) maintenance of registers of handicapped people in the local authority area, as laid down in the 1948 Act, but emphasised by the 1970 Chronically Sick and Disabled Persons Act, to find out who the disabled are and to let them know what services are available to them (in 1974, 72,000 were so registered with local authorities in England and Wales)
(b) practical assistance in the home
(c) help in getting a radio, television, books or other recreational facilities
(d) provision of recreational facilities outside the home
(e) help in travelling to and from home to take part in the above facilities
(f) adaptation of the handicapped person's home to make it easier to live in or the provision of residential accommodation for the disabled
(g) help in taking a holiday
(h) provision of meals in the home, or elsewhere if needed
(i) help in obtaining a telephone and, if needed, special equipment to use it
(j) under the Disabled Persons (Employment) Act of 1958 local authorities can provide work for the disabled under special conditions. In some cases disabled people have been sent to day centres where they do work for private companies. This has given rise to criticism of exploitation of the disabled.

The following provisions are special to the 1970 Act. In so far as it is 'practicable and reasonable', buildings open to the public either freely or by payment should have facilities in and outside the building for the disabled, and this includes toilets. Such buildings should have a notice stating that provision has been made for the disabled.

Apart from these special services the handicapped have those services which are provided for all who need them whether handicapped or not – domestic help, health visitor, home nursing, ambulance service, and so on.

Social security

Under the National Insurance scheme there are special benefits for disablement including an attendance allowance for certain categories of badly disabled. The disabled can also draw extra supplementary benefit.

Services for special categories of disabled people

These special categories are blind, the deaf, epileptics and those suffering from TB. Local authorities or voluntary organisations supported by local authorities provide special workshops for the blind or provide them with work to do at home. Local authorities and voluntary organisations provide recreational facilities for all the special categories. For deaf children local authorities provide special residential schools and also special schools for epileptics., In certain cases home tuition is provided (see also Chapter 11). There are local authority after-care officers who specialise in TB cases.

Employment services for disabled people

See Chapter 14 (pp. 186–8).

Mentally Disordered People

There are two main types of mentally disordered people. There are those who have a normal intelligence but are mentally ill; there are those who have mental disorder because they are mentally handicapped. Psychopathic disorders may or may not include mental handicap but the patient is capable of abnormal aggressive or seriously irresponsible conduct.

As far back as 1808 local authorities were given powers to set up asylums for criminal and pauper lunatics. The idea was to keep them out of gaols and workhouses where they were a nuisance. But many private asylums existed also. The lack of knowledge concerning either mental illness or mental handicap led to fear and superstition and hence mentally disordered people were isolated from the rest of the community. By the latter half of the nineteenth century, fear of illegal detention led to the 1890 Lunacy Act, which provided for the proper certification, care and control of people with unsound minds. Earlier, under the 1845 Lunatics Act, a permanent Lunacy Commission had been set up .

It was the development of psychology in the twentieth century, pioneered by Freud, which led to much personal treatment outside the asylums and to a more rational attitude to mental disorder. The Royal Commission on Lunacy and Mental Disorder 1924–6 (the Macmillan Commission) stressed the interdependence of mental and physical illness and the need for psychiatric treatment. The 1930 Mental Treatment Act made it possible for mental patients to be treated in mental hospitals without certification, and out-patients clinics for mental illness followed, thus reducing the gap between the general medical services and psychiatric treatment. The 1959 Mental Health Act, based on the Report of the Royal Commission on the Laws relating to Mental Illness and Mental Deficiency of 1957, narrowed the gap even further by stressing the need to integrate mental and physical illness.

The 1959 Act, amended by the 1982 Mental Health (Amendment) Act, consolidated by the 1983 Mental Health Act is the basis of today's services for the mentally disordered and its underlying principle is that mentally disordered people should be treated, as far as possible, in the same way as those who are physically ill. Community care should, wherever possible, take the place of long periods in hospital.

The 1959 Act helped to lessen the stigma attached to mental illness, and thus an increasing number of people have been encouraged to come forward for voluntary treatment. Better methods of treatment have also encouraged this. In the 1960s there developed the policy of treating mentally ill people in psychiatric units of general hospitals rather than sending them to special mental hospitals. In December 1971 the Secretary of State for Social Services forecast that by 1991 there would be no more special mental hospitals. The kind of patients who now go to these hospitals would be receiving treatment in general hospitals, some of them as out-patients. The 1983 Health and Social Services and Social

Security Adjudication Act has financial provisions to help mentally handicapped to leave hospital and be housed in the community.

Today's hospital services for the mentally disordered

According to the seriousness of the mental disorder, there are out-patient facilities, and facilities for short-stay, medium-stay and long-stay patients. For the long-stay elderly patient suffering from chronic mental disorder there is little which can be done except to give kindness. Dangerous psychopaths are sent to special hospitals like Broadmoor, Rampton or Moss Side, which are administered directly by the Department of Health and Social Security. Not so dangerous psychopaths are treated in other hospitals.

Admission to hospital is arranged normally with the family doctor and most go willingly. But there are safeguards for those who have to go compulsorily. An application for compulsory admission must be based on two medical recommendations, one of which must be by a practitioner with approved experience in psychiatry (approved by the district health authority). The other doctor must have personal knowledge of the patient. The consent of the patient's nearest relative must also be obtained, though he or she can be overruled, in which case the relative can appeal to a mental health review tribunal. Compulsory admission may be for assessment – up to twenty-eight days – or for treatment. Compulsory treatment orders are valid for six months, renewable for one year. During this time the patient or someone on his behalf can appeal to the mental health review tribunal against continued detention. There was criticism that compulsory admission should operate within a legal framework so that there would be safeguards at law for the patient. The 1983 Mental Health Act goes a long way to meet this criticism. It provided for the setting up of a Mental Health Commission to keep under review the care and treatment of patients. The Commission has to present a report of its activities to Parliament every two years. It appoints the medical practitioners authorised to give treatment, as well as appointing people to make regular visits to patients and examine their records and listen to their complaints. The Secretary of State has overall responsibility and, from time to time, will issue codes of practice after consultation with interested bodies. In appeals to the mental health review tribunal against continued detention, patients are now entitled to be legally represented at the tribunal. They can now sue the responsible authority for wrongful detention. Any medical practitioner authorised by or on behalf of the patient, approved by the Secretary of State, can examine hospital records in connection with an appeal to the tribunal. Hospital and nursing home managers must keep patients informed of their rights, especially their right to appeal to the tribunal. There is now an automatic referral to the tribunal when three years have elapsed since the last referral. There are stronger controls over treatment, especially that involving psycho-surgery.

The 1983 Act lays down that the district health authorities, the local authorities social services departments and voluntary organisations should be involved where after-care treatment is necessary. The mental welfare officers of local authorities social services departments had the main responsibility for after care and, in 1984, were known as psychiatric social workers.

In line with the principle referred to above of treating mentally disordered people as far as possible in the same way as physically ill people, the 1983 Act gives voluntary (called informal) patients the vote (previously they were disenfranchised).

A person convicted of a criminal offence can be sent to a hospital if the court is satisfied that, on the evidence of two doctors, he or she is mentally ill and hospital treatment is the most suitable way of dealing with the convicted person.

Community services

Local authorities have psychiatric social workers and home helps who visit the homes of the mentally disordered. Social workers have special responsibility in connection with sending a person to hospital. They make the initial assessment of the problem and give advice to the relatives.

Local authorities, by themselves or in conjunction with voluntary organisations, provide day centres and social clubs, and for the mentally handicapped who are able to live at home they provide training centres for the development of skills and aptitudes. Often they can earn a little in sheltered conditions. For those who cannot live at home some local authorities provide residential training centres or hostels. Some of these are used as a kind of halfway house for those who have been in hospital but are not yet ready for community life. Health authority services include health visitors and domiciliary nursing.

Some local authorities provide homes for old people who are mentally infirm, though they may be looked after in normal residential homes for the elderly.

Under the 1984 Registered Homes Act, private nursing homes for the mentally handicapped have to be registered with the district health authority and residential homes, under the 1984 Residential Homes Act, have to be registered with the local authority.

In spite of the official blessing for community care for the mentally handicapped, there are fears that there are still, in many areas, not enough resources to give adequate support to the mentally handicapped transferred from hospital to the community.

The community services are especially important in giving support to parents who have mentally handicapped children.

The family doctor

The doctor plays an important role in that he or she is normally the first contact in the case of mental disorder and is the link with all the other services. Some doctors give psychiatric treatment for the less serious forms of mental illness.

Community Care

This means helping people in their own homes and neighbourhoods rather than in institutions. The Royal Commission on the Law Relating to Mental Illness and Deficiency (1957) began the movement towards community care. By stressing the need for community care in relation to mental disorder, it created interest in the development of community care for other groups – the elderly, children in need of care, and so on.

Community care necessitates close links between local government and the National Health Service.

A great deal of the success of community care, depends on the help that relatives and friends give to the person being cared for. Quite often this help becomes burdensome, so that the helpers themselves are in danger of falling ill. If community care is to be successful, more home helps and nurses are needed to support the relative or friend who is looking after the person needing care.

This raises the question of whether community care means care in the community provided by professionally trained social workers or care by the community (see Alan Walker) where informal cares such as relatives and friends and voluntary organisations are involved as well as professional social workers. Thus the Barclay Report, published 1982, recommended that, where possible, as a means of making their help to those in need more effective, social workers should go out of their way to seek the help of friends, neighbours and relatives of the clients and also work closely with voluntary organisations. The social workers would still have a counselling role but also a managerial role in organising the unofficial carers – organising what Barclay called the 'social network'. Professor Pinker, a dissenting voice in the Report, whilst agreeing that social workers must, where possible, seek the aid of relatives and friends and voluntary organisations, argued that social work had not the resources to organise a social network. Whether it has or not, there is general consensus that more help should be given to informal carers, most of whom are women. It has been estimated that the 'bill for social services would go up 20 per cent if just one per cent of people looking after the elderly gave up' (see Catherine Thompson, 'Carry on Caring'? *New Society*, 22 November 1985).

Community care in relation to children – either delinquents or children whose parents or guardians are not looking after them properly – has led to much greater emphasis on preventive work within the family. Stresses in family relationships can give rise to delinquency and parents' neglect of their children. Instead of waiting for this to happen before action is taken, social workers now try to help beforehand to prevent it happening.

This preventive work and community care generally necessitates the working together of a number of social workers with different specialisms. It thus gives rise to the problem of co-ordination. To help facilitate this co-ordination a new social services department of local government was created under the 1970 Local Authorities Social Services Act. This local authority department is responsible for the care of children previously done by the children's department, the services previously done by the local authority welfare department and some services previously done by the local authority health department (see Chapter 7).

The Act was based on the Report of the Inter-departmental Committee on Local Authority and Allied Personal Social Services, the Seebohm Report (July 1968). The Seebohm Committee itself was set up because of the growing concern with juvenile delinquency and the desire for a family service (see *The Child, the Family and the Young Offender*, HMSO, August 1965).

Social workers and society

Professor Pinker, in dissenting to officially organised social networks, pointed out that should an attempt be made to set them up it could lead to social workers becoming involved in community action of a political nature in order to change the conditions which gave rise to their clients' problems. He argued that social workers should concentrate on personal problems and leave the campaigning to other organisations.

But if many of the problems which affect families and with which social workers have to deal arise from low incomes and a bad social environment, some social workers would argue that unless they campaigned for social reforms, they are simply acting as 'social tranquillisers' by persuading their clients 'to tolerate the intolerable'. On the other hand, taking part in the political battle might make social workers less effective because, already overworked, they would have even less time to help their clients here and now.

The role of social workers

1. To help their clients to understand better the nature of their problems.
2. To give support and to advise their clients on how best to deal with their problems, which involves:

   (a) putting their clients in touch with statutory and voluntary organisations which can help them;
   (b) if need be, themselves making known their clients' needs to these organisations.
   (c) working with clients without undermining the clients' independence.

Among the many points the Seebohm Report made to justify the setting up of a social services department in local government was that of social need cannot be divided up so that each part can be dealt with by a specialist in the part, independently of other social workers. Social need, the Report stated, has many causes and therefore different specialist workers must tackle the problem as a team. This part of the Report caused misgivings in the social services departments. Some interpreted it to mean a social worker must be able to deal with all categoriers of need within the family. In other interpretations the social worker still specialises but co-operates with other social workers where necessary. Thus there are specialist social workers for mentally disordered people and now, because of the increase in child abuse and where, in just a few cases, social workers have failed to take action, there is a growing demand for specialists in child abuse. But social workers still work as a team and have regular consultations among themselves on problem cases and problem families.

There are those who want increased support for the informal carers by giving greatly increasing resources to an enlarged voluntary sector. Some people on the political right support this as a means of reducing the role of the State. Others, usually on the political left, support it as a means, in their opinion, of providing a more flexible, less bureacratic and more democratic service and one likely to be more successful than local government in organising a 'social network' of carers. But the voluntary organisations would still have to be mainly financed by the State and so a bureaucracy would still be necessary to ensure taxpayers' money was being spent effectively. And is there any evidence to suggest that they would be more democratic, in the sense of being accountable to the public, than the State services which are responsible to elected representatives? While the general consensus supports an increasing role for the voluntary sector, there is no consensus that it should be done at the expense of the State sector. The voluntary sector complements the State sector and can best develop by filling the gaps in the State services run by central and local government.

Social workers in hospitals are now employed by the local authority social services department.

Summary

Personal welfare (social) services for the specialised groups – the handicapped, the elderly, mothers with young children, children in need of care, etc. – are provided by local authorities working with voluntary organisations, some of which receive financial assistance from the local authority. The general aim is the prevention and relief of distress. Social workers thus have wide-ranging responsibilities for individual welfare. The services are supposed to be available to all who think they need them. In practice, because of limited resources, some form of rationing is inevitable. This is especially so since 1975 because of cuts in real resources and the worsening of social problems. But in spite of the cuts in real resources in recent years, the greater emphasis on community care has led, over the past decade, to a greater proportion of public expenditue being devoted to the personal social services.

But the demands for the services will increase rather than diminish so that there will never be enough money for them. For example, although the Thatcher government has considerably increased expenditure on the services in real terms there is criticism (as with the NHS) that the planned future growth will not be sufficient to meet demand.

In spite of a comprehensive social services department in local government, it still needs to co-operate with the social services provided by central government, the district health authorities and voluntary organisations and, above all, as the Barclay Report emphasised, with the informal carers – wives, husbands, relatives and friends. The need for this co-operation is very clear in connection with the elderly, where the family doctor, the hospital, the Department of Health and Social Security (for supplementary pensions), voluntary organisations and the housing department of the local authority as well as its social services department are all involved.

Assignments

1. What special problems now face the elderly? What services are available to the elderly? To help answer this question write to Age Concern (National Old People's Welfare Council) and ask for information on the needs of the elderly.
2. 'The 1969 Children and Young Persons Act has worked well for the vast majority of young offenders but not the small minority of persistent offenders.' Give your views on this statement and if

possible get the views of magistrates and social workers.

3. With the growth of 'women's liberation', there is a greater emphasis today than ever on the needs of mothers and young children. Discuss what you consider to be their main needs and how far they are being provided by the state and voluntary bodies.

4. List the duties imposed upon the local authorities by the 1970 Chronically Sick and Disabled Persons Act for helping the disabled. How far do you think local authorities have carried out these duties in full? To help with this write to the Royal Association for Disability and Rehabilitation and ask how far it thinks local authorities have done their statutory duty in connection with the Act. At the same time find out what services your own local authority provides for the disabled.

5. What is meant by *communityy care*? Illustrate by reference to any one category of people needing help in your local authority – for example, the mentally disordered, the physically handi- capped, the elderly, and so on.

Reading

Barclay Report, *Social Workers, Their Role and Tasks* (National Institute of Social Work, 1982).

Michael Bender, 'Crisis of Closure, Analysis of the Effect of the Move from Mental Health Institutions to Community Care', *The Health Service Journal* (17 April 1986).

Britain 1987: An Official Handbook (HMSO).

Paul Cavadino, 'Criminal Justice Act 1982, a Pragmatic Compromise', *Community Care* (11 November 1982).

Curtis Report, *Report of the Inter-departmental Committee on the Care of Children*, Cmnd 6922 (HMSO, 1946).

Growing Older: the White Paper on the Elderly, Cmnd 8173 (HMSO, 1981).

HMSO, *Health and Welfare: The Development of Community Care*, Cmnd 3022 (HMSO, 1966).

HMSO, *Review of the Mental Health Act 1969*, Cmnd 7320 (HMSO, 1978).

House of Commons debate on 1969 Children and Young Persons Act, *Hansard*, vol. 962, no. 53 (9 February 1979).

Ingleby Report, *Report of the Committee on Children and Young Persons*, Cmnd 1191 (HMSO, 1960).

Alan Walker, 'A Caring Community' in Howard Glennerster (ed.) *The Future of the Welfare State* (Heinemann, 1983).

Jeremy Laurence, 'The Selection of Foster Parents', *New Society* (9 May 1986).

Mark Monger, *Casework in Probation*, 2nd edn (Butterworth, 1972) ch. 1.

Second Report from the Commons Social Services Committee, Session 1983–84, *Children in Care*, HC360 (HMSO, 1984).

Second Report from the Commons Social Services Committee, Session 1984–85: *Community Care with Special Reference to Adult Mentally Ill and Mentally Handicapped People*, HC13 (HMSO, 1985).

Seebohm Report, *Report of the Committee on Local Authority and Allied Personal Social Services*, Cmnd 3703 (HMSO, 1968).

Sir Thomas Skyrme, *The Changing Image of the Magistracy*, 2nd edn (Macmillan, 1983) ch. 8 'The Juvenile Courts'.

Eda Topliss and Bryan Gould, *A Charter for the Disabled*, 2nd edn (Basil Blackwell, 1982).

10 Education

History

Before 1870 education was left entirely to private enterprise in accordance with the prevailing theory of *laissez-faire*. The state's role was limited:

1. It provided grants to the Nonconformist and Anglican Church schools called voluntary schools. The first grant was given in 1833.
2. It provided a certain amount of teacher-training which was the responsibility of a committee of the Privy Council originally set up in 1839 to supervise the grants. The committee also employed inspectors to spread knowledge on educational matters.
3. Under the 1833 Factory Act children who worked in textile mills, except lace and silk mills, had to be provided by their employers with two hours' education every working day.
4. Some Boards of Guardians gave education to pauper children in workhouse schools.

The Church schools were the main providers of education for the working class, though dame schools, which were usually schools run by ladies in their own homes, also gave education to a fair number of working-class children. The middle and upper classes were educated in endowed grammar schools and public schools and many went on to university. Education for the working class was limited mainly to reading, writing and arithmetic.

The 1870 Education Act

This Act introduced state schools for the first time. It set up locally elected school boards to provide schools, financed out of local rates, in areas where no voluntary schools existed or where voluntary schools were inadequate to ensure a school place for every child. These schools were to provide an elementary education for children from age 5 to 13. In 1880 attendance was made compulsory in all schools until the age of 10. It was raised to 11 in 1893 and 12 in 1899. But under the 'half-time' system, abolished by the 1918 Education Act, children who had reached a certain level of attainment could attend school for part of the day and work the rest. In spite of the 1918 Act, there were still about 70,000 half-timers as late as 1922.

The 1870 Act provided a reasonable compromise between those who wanted denominational schools and those who wanted secular education.

The reasons for the Act were economic, political and humanitarian.

(1) Although most children received an elementary education under the voluntary system, it was felt there were still too many gaps in it, especially as more and more literate workers with skills were needed for industry and commerce. In fact, economic necessity was perhaps the main reason for the Act. The growing competition after 1870 from the new industrial powers of Germany and the USA underlined this.

(2) The 1867 Reform Act gave the vote to certain categories of working men in the towns. Hence, it was felt there was the need for this new section of the electorate to be reasonably educated to ensure it voted intelligently. When introducing the Bill, the minister, W. E. Forster, underlined the above two points: 'Our industrial prosperity, the safe working of our constitutional system and our national power depended upon it.'

(3) To a great number of people, it was good in itself to give education to anyone who could benefit from it.

In spite of the above, the Act had its opponents who felt it would make the working class discontented with their lowly position in society and less inclined to be obedient to their 'superiors'. And when compulsory education came, some thought it an infringement of personal liberty.

The 1899 Board of Education Act

Before 1899 three bodies were responsible for education: the Education Committee of the Privy Council was responsible for elementary education; the Science and Art Committee of the Privy

Council was responsible for secondary and technical education; and the Charity Commission supervised the endowed schools, which gave a grammar school education. The work of the three bodies needed co-ordinating as there was much overlapping. One of the recommendations of the Royal Commission on Secondary Education of 1895 (the Bryce Report) was that there should be a central authority to stop this overlapping. The Board of Education Act 1899 created the Board of Education to provide this central co-ordinating body. It had a minister at its head responsible to Parliament.

Another recommendation of the Bryce Committee, which was implemented by the 1899 Act, was the setting up of a consultative committee of the Board of Education on which distinguished people could serve and investigate and make reports on different aspects of education. The Bryce Committee felt that education should not be solely the responsibility of the representatives and officials of the central and local government. The consultative committee lasted until 1944, when it was replaced by two central advisory councils – one for England and one for Wales. These, too, have now been abolished.

The 1902 Education Act

This Act introduced a state system of secondary education which benefited brighter working-class children. Previously secondary education could only be obtained at public schools and endowed grammar schools, though the top forms of some board schools had given some secondary education until it was ruled illegal in 1899 as going beyond the powers of the 1870 Act. Under the Act children were to be selected at 11 for the state secondary schools. Some working-class leaders preferred the alternative system of developing the elementary schools so that they provided both elementary and secondary education without selection.

The 1902 Act abolished the school boards, and both elementary and secondary education were put under the control of county councils and county borough councils, created under the 1888 Local Government Act. Boroughs with a population over 10,000 and urban districts with a population over 20,000 were allowed to administer elementary education under delegation from the county councils.

The most controversial part of the Act was the putting of the Church schools (i.e. the voluntary schools) under the administration of the local authorities subject to their managers retaining certain rights over the appointment of teachers. This enabled the Church schools to receive money from the rate fund, and many people objected to this. But the Church schools needed the money as many had fallen behind the board schools because voluntary subscriptions did not equal the money the board schools received from the rates.

The Act also empowered local authorities to provide technical colleges and adult education.

One of the reasons for the Act was again the need for an efficient labour force. Business firms were growing in size and more technicians and managers were wanted.

There was also the desire to help the Church schools financially to help them continue to play a worthy part in the educational system.

There was the desire for a tidier administrative pattern away from *ad hoc* boards to local councils, and this was also in line with democratic trends.

The sort of secondary education the Bryce Report of 1895 had recommended for the working class was of a practical kind, with craftwork in mind. The fact that the local authority secondary schools imitated the endowed grammar schools in the type of education they provided was due mainly to Robert Morant, who drafted the Bill and became Permanent Secretary to the Board of Education in 1903.

The 1918 Education Act

This Act raised the school-leaving age to 14 with no exemptions and recommended it be raised later to 15. It introduced compulsory day release from industry so that young people under 18 could attend school for an equivalent period of three half-days a week, but economic conditions in the interwar years virtually killed this idea.

The day-release scheme under the Act arose from the concern that the juvenile should not be regarded simply as a wage-earner but as a 'workman and citizen in training'. This was the view expressed by the Departmental Committee on Juvenile Employment, which reported in 1917.

Local authorities were required to provide an appropriate

education for older children in elementary schools, and this, in effect, meant giving an education beyond the elementary stage to these children. Since 1911 it has been possible for local authorities to provide separate schools for these older children. They were built in certain areas and became known as central schools but, in most cases, a selection process was applied for entry to these schools. But, even before 1914, some people were suggesting that all children at 11 should go to a separate secondary school.

The 1918 Act provided for more central direction of education. Local authorities now had not only to provide education but report progress to the Board of Education. One reason for more central control was that some local authorities pushed ahead with educational advance but some did not.

Under the Act central government was to bear more of the cost of education – at least not less than 50 per cent.

It abolished fees for elementary schools and extended school medical inspection to secondary schools.

The interwar years

In the interwar years there grew a demand for secondary education for all influenced by a number of factors – the need for greater economic efficiency, the need for a reasonably educated electorate after the 1918 Representation of the People Act extended the vote to all men over 21 and women over 30, and the desire for greater social equality.

The Hadow Report 1926 (Report of the Consultative Committee of the Board of Education on the Education of the Adolescent) recommended secondary education for all, along with the raising of the school-leaving age to 15. It stated: 'Individual and national character would be strengthened through the placing of youth, in the hour of its growth, in a congenial and inspiring environment.' The then existing local authority secondary schools gave a grammar school education and the Report recommended the creation of modern schools to give a secondary education of a more practical nature. It stressed the need for 'parity of esteem' between modern school and grammar school. 'The modern school', it said, 'is not an inferior species and it ought not to be hampered by conditions of accommodation and equipment inferior to those of grammar schools.' Finally, it recommended that secondary education should begin at 11, and thus the separate systems of elementary and secondary education should be replaced by a single education process split into two successive stages.

The Hadow Report had been mainly concerned with children who did not receive a secondary education, but the Report of another Consultative Committee of the Board of Education – the Spens Report of 1938 – was concerned with secondary education with special reference to grammar schools and technical high schools.

The then existing secondary schools, set up by local authorities under the 1902 Education Act, gave a grammar school type of education geared to university entrance. The Spens Report stated that there should also be selective secondary schools for brighter children which would be more vocational, geared to boys and girls 'who desired to enter industry and commerce at 16'. It thus supported three types of secondary education – grammar, technical and the modern (of the Hadow Report). There should be selection at 11, as recommended by Hadow, but with a further review at 13. Both the Hadow and Spens Reports were quite happy with a selective process at 11 because they were much influenced by educational psychologists who believed that children could be reasonably classified by intelligence tests, making the actual selection process reasonably accurate and easy to work. Spens, like Hadow, stressed parity of esteem between all three secondary schools. But the Report recommended the raising of the school-leaving age to 16, as this was the leaving age in grammar schools.

The Hadow and Spens Reports thus pioneered educational advance, but the implementation of their most important recommendations – namely, secondary education for all organised under a tripartite system of grammar, technical and modern with 'parity of esteem' between them plus the raising of the school-leaving age – had to await the 1944 Education Act.

The private sector

By the 1930s most endowed grammar schools were open to all children with ability. The main reason for this was that many schools got into financial difficulties and accepted a grant from the Board of Education and, in return, under a 1907 regulation of the Board, they had to provide free places for 25 per cent of their annual entry 'to scholars from public elementary schools . . . subject to the applicants passing an entrance test'. These became known as direct-grant schools.

The universities

Until the nineteenth century Oxford and Cambridge were the only universities in England and Wales, though Scotland had four (St Andrews, Glasgow, Aberdeen and Edinburgh). Oxford and Cambridge, but not the Scottish universities, were closed to those who were not members of the Church of England. In the eighteenth century many academies for higher education were formed by outstanding dissenters, and these in many cases gave a better education than Oxford or Cambridge. Thus, if you were not a member of the Church of England and wanted a higher education, you could apply for admission to one of the academies or to a Scottish university.

In England and Wales the first universities after Oxford and Cambridge were London and Durham, both founded in 1836. London University had no religious test for admission. On the other hand, Durham University demanded, like Oxford and Cambridge, that its students should subscribe to the Thirty-Nine Articles of the Church of England. It was not until 1871 that religious tests were abolished for Oxford, Cambridge and Durham.

The technical and social problems created by the Industrial Revolution led to an increasing demand for higher education, especially in the physical and social sciences.

Oxford and Cambridge expanded their system of colleges and curriculum in the latter half of the nineteenth century, but the biggest advance came in the provinces, especially in the industrial areas. In 1884 the federal university of Victoria was formed from colleges at Liverpool and Manchester, and in 1887 it was joined by Leeds. In 1903 the federation was replaced by three separate universities of Manchester, Liverpool and Leeds. Mason College, founded in 1880, became Birmingham University in 1900. Sheffield University was founded in 1905 and Bristol University in 1909. Meanwhile, in London the London School of Economics had been founded in 1895 and became part of the University of London in 1900 to form a new faculty of Economics and Political Science. In 1893 the University of Wales was founded, being based on a federation of colleges at Aberystwyth, Cardiff and Bangor.

It will be seen that many of the provincial universities were first preceded by colleges of higher education which, until they received university status, could not grant degrees. In 1926 Reading University was formed after a similar trial period as a college, and so were many universities founded after 1945 when a big expansion of higher education took place. But as late as 1939 only a small proportion of working-class children went to university.

The 1944 Education Act

1. The Act introduced secondary education for all. The schools that provided it were to be 'sufficient in number, character and equipment to afford for all pupils . . . such variety of instruction and training as may be desirable in view of their different ages, abilities and aptitudes'. This Act, therefore, did not preclude comprehensive schools but, in nearly all areas, it was the tripartite system of grammar, secondary technical and secondary modern which developed.
2. It raised the school-leaving age to 15, but this did not come into force until 1947. It also provided for the raising of the school-leaving age to 16 'as soon as it has become practicable'.
3. Local authorities were also made responsible for the provision of part-time and full-time education for all above school-leaving age. This led to a great expansion of day release, full-time further education and day and evening classes, catering for recreational and cultural leisure activities. Part-time day release was to be compulsory for those under 18 and to be provided in county colleges, but this part of the Act has still not been implemented.
4. The Act thus organised 'public education . . . in three successive stages to be known as primary education, secondary education and further education'. The break from primary to secondary at 11 was accepted.
5. The Board of Education became the Ministry of Education with much greater powers given to the Secretary of State. In the last resort the minister was given the power to direct a local authority or the governors or managers of a school when it was thought that they were acting unreasonably.

6. All secondary schools were to have 'parity of esteem', but this has not worked out in practice.
7. The county borough councils and the county councils were made responsible for all stages of education, including nursery schools and special schools for the handicapped, but county councils could, within their areas, delegate educational functions to divisional executives and the larger boroughs and urban districts.
8. Church schools (i.e. the voluntary schools) could choose either to have 'aided' or 'controlled' status. An aided school was to receive grants from the central government to cover teachers' salaries, internal and external repairs, alterations and new construction and maintenance costs. The schools still appointed their own staff and the majority of the governors were appointed by the voluntary body. The governing bodies of controlled schools had to have a majority of local authority representatives, but denominational instruction could continue. The local authority was to be financially responsible for the school.
9. Religious instruction was to be given in all schools.
10. Two central advisory councils on education were set up under the Act – one for England and one for Wales – to advise the minister.
11. All schools, including independent schools, were to be inspected by the Ministry of Education.
12. Fees in state (i.e. maintained) schools were to be abolished.

Summary

Until 1870 education was left to private enterprise. Although under the private enterprise system most people received an elementary education, there were still too many people who remained illiterate – hence the 1870 Education Act was 'to fill the gaps' by providing board schools where no adequate system of voluntary school existed. By 1880 by law all children had to go to school.

In the nineteenth century an elementary education was all that was considered necessary for children of the working class. Only children of middle- and upper-class parents received a secondary education either at endowed grammar schools or public schools. By the end of the First World War there was a growing demand that all children should receive a secondary education. Already the 1902 Education Act had introduced a state system of secondary education administered by local authorities, but the grammar school education it provided was for the brighter working-class children, as there was a selection process at 11. In any case, most working-class parents were apathetic to secondary education. Many felt that it was better for the children to be working at 14 and bringing money into the home than receiving a grammar school education, which, to the parents, seemed irrelevant for the kind of work they expected their children to be taking up. Thus, even as late as 1939, only a comparatively small number of working-class children went to a secondary school. It was not until after the Second World War, as a result of the 1944 Education Act, that the school-leaving age was raised to 15 and all children received a secondary education. It would probably have come earlier but for the economic difficulties of the interwar years.

The ground for the Act had been well prepared in the interwar years with the Hadow and Spens Reports. It is interesting to note that compulsory day release, legislated for under 1918 and 1944 Education Acts, has still not been introduced.

Although there was nothing in the 1944 Act to prevent a local authority giving the three types of secondary education in one comprehensive school, the arguments of the Spens Report against comprehensive schools, plus the emphasis placed on three main student groupings in the Norwood Report of 1943 (Report of the Committee of the Secondary Schools Examination Council on Curriculum and Examinations in Secondary Schools), led to the separate school system being adopted in most areas.

In spite of the development of the state system, the private sector of education, used mainly by the rich, continued to flourish. Not until after 1945 did working-class students start going to the universities in any great numbers.

Two main factors had influenced, and were to continue to influence, the development of education:

(a) the need for more social justice
(b) the need for economic efficiency.

Assignments

1. By making use of reference books in your library, write short biographical notes on the following: Robert Raikes, Robert Owen, Thomas Arnold, Sir James Kay-Shuttleworth, W. E. Forster, Miss Emily Davies, R. H. Tawney, R. A. Butler.
2. Write a brief history of your school or college. For what purpose was it founded? What have been the main developments since its foundation?
3. Discuss the statement that economic necessity, political expediency and higher living standards have all contributed to educational advance in the nineteenth and twentieth centuries.

Reading

Richard Aldrich, *An Introduction to the History of Education* (Hodder & Stoughton, 1982).

Rodney Barker, *Education and Politics 1900–1951: A Study of the Labour Party* (Oxford University Press, 1972).

H. C. Barnard, *A History of English Education from 1760*, 4th impression (University of London Press, 1966).

G. A. N. Lowndes, *The Silent Revolution* (Oxford University Press, 1969).

J. S. Maclure, *Educational Documents: England and Wales, 1816 to the Present Day*, 6th edn (Methuen, 1986).

Frank Smith, *The Life and Work of Sir James Kay-Shuttleworth* (Cedric Chivers, 1974).

11 The Organisation of Education Today

Education is provided by the state via local authorities and private organisations.

Education provided by Local Authorities

1. *Primary education*, which begins at 5 and ends at 11. Some children attend a nursery school, or nursery class which forms part of a primary school, before the age of 5. There are also pre-school playgroups organised by parents and voluntary organisations. Primary education falls into two parts – infant schools for children from 5 to 7 and junior schools for 7 to 11. Both groups are usually housed in the same school building.
2. *Secondary education*, which begins at 11 and is compulsory to 16, but some students voluntarily carry on to 18. There are three main types of secondary school – secondary modern schools, grammar schools, and comprehensive schools. (There are a small number of secondary technical schools, originally intended for a reasonably bright child with a practical bias, but most of them now give a grammar school education.) Some local authorities have established what are called sixth form colleges which provide mainly 'A' level courses. They replace the sixth forms of those secondary schools in particular which had not the number of students in their sixth forms to provide a reasonable range of 'A' level options. Most local authorities have put on a course in their schools called the Technical and Vocational Education Inititiative (TVEI) financed by the Manpower Services Commission (MSC). It is a four-year course of vocational training (see p. 161).

3. *Further education*, either full or part time, is provided for students from 16 onwards in technical colleges, colleges of art and commercial colleges. It covers courses from GCSE level and craft level through to 'A' or intermediate level, on to final degree and final professional level. But before the introduction of TVEI mentioned above there had developed in recent years courses in further education colleges, funded by the Manpower Services Commission (MSC), which it is claimed are more relevant to employment needs. In fact, at the end of 1986, the MSC was financing one quarter of the money spent in England and Wales on work related courses. Both in secondary and further education use will be made of the College of the Air to be set up under the auspices of the MSC and financed mainly by private enterprise which is planned to become operative from 1 September 1987. To provide for a concentration of higher education, with a wide range of courses, both full time and part time in key parts of the country, certain technical colleges or groupings of colleges have been designated *polytechnics*, and they, too, are administered by the local authorities. Local authorities also provide courses of a recreational nature at day and evening classes. Most colleges of education (for teacher-training) in England and Wales are under the financial and administrative control of local authorities, but many have merged with polytechnics.

Private Education

For primary and secondary education there are three main types of private school:
1. *Independent schools*, which include private and public schools and which receive all their funds from fees and endowments.
2. *Private schools*, known as direct-grant schools because they received a grant direct from the Department of Education and Science providing they allocated 25 per cent of their places in the secondary sphere to pupils from local authority schools, but they were phased out. Some joined the state system; some became completely independent. It was the Labour government which began the phasing out of direct-grant schools because the schools

were selective, contrary to the comprehensive principle that government supported. The 1980 Education Act of a Conservative government introduced what is called the 'Assisted Places Scheme' under which local authorities have discretion to give financial help, where considered necessary, to parents whose children are bright enough to qualify for a place at an independent school.

3. *Voluntary schools*, which, normally, are Church schools. There are three main types of voluntary schools:

(a)   *aided schools*, where the voluntary body appoints two-thirds of the governors of the school – the local authority appointing the other third; they receive financial help from the central government for all external repairs and improvements; the local authority pays the maintenance costs of the interior of the buildings; aided schools appoint their own teachers and control religious instruction, but the local authority pays the teachers' salaries and must be satisfied with their qualifications

(b)   *controlled schools*, where the local authority is financially responsible for the school, though the property still belongs to the voluntary body and where the local authority representatives comprise the majority of the governors; the local authority appoints the teachers but the governors must be consulted about the appointment of the head-teacher and any teacher appointed to give denominational religious instruction

(c)   *special arrangement schools* still exist in a few areas where the local authority, by special arrangement, contributes to the cost of building the school and its maintenance; it also appoints the teachers and one-third of the governors, but the governors control religious instruction and are consulted on the appointment of teachers giving denominational religious instruction.

Private higher education

Universities are part of the private sector but all, except Buckingham University College, receive a great deal of money from the government, which is distributed through the University Grants Committee. The universities are free to use the money as they wish, but their accounts are subject to inspection by the House of Commons Select Committee on Public Accounts. They provide education beyond the secondary sphere (i.e. higher education) with their own degrees and postgraduate courses, and extra-mural courses.

There are, apart from the universities, privately run colleges providing art and commercial courses.

Handicapped Children

These are mainly the responsibility of the local authorities. Where possible the child remains at a normal school and only goes to a special school if absolutely necessary. Local authorities run special schools for different categories of handicapped children. Some children are so handicapped that they cannot even go to a special school, but their education is still the responsibility of the local education department.

Finance of Education

The cost of the state system of primary, secondary and further education is shared by central and local government. The central government grant to local authorities for education is part of the rate support grant. The rate support grant for 1982–3 covered 56.1 per cent of local government expenditure, of which about half was education expenditure. Government financial assistance for local authority higher education in England is allocated to the colleges via the National Advisory Body for Public Sector Higher Education (NAB) created in 1982. There is a similar body for Wales. In Scotland money is still channelled direct. There are extra grants for local authorities with special social needs, for example those local authorities with a large immigrant school population. Local authorities contribute to an education pool to help share the cost of higher education between them.

Primary and secondary education are free, school meals are subsidised and there is financial help to parents of children who cannot afford school meals and other school expenses.

In further education, students pay a nominal fee for tuition.

Nearly 90 per cent of university expenditure is financed by the Central Government. It is allocated via the University Grants Committee. The Central Government also gives financial assistance to private colleges of education which train teachers.

Church schools receive financial help from the central government and local authorities.

Students taking courses at universities or other establishments of further education can receive grants from their local authorities to cover tuition fees and maintenance allowances. This includes Buckingham University.

Awards and financial assistance are given, at the discretion of the local authority, for other exceptional circumstances.

Administration

The Secretary of State's responsibilities

Under the 1944 Education Act the Secretary of State is required to 'secure the effective execution, by local authorities under his control and direction, of the national policy for providing a varied and comprehensive educational service in every area'. The minister makes known his or her wishes for the organisation and administration of education by means of statutory instruments and circulars. The minister can overrule a local authority or the managers or governors of any school in the state system if he or she thinks they have acted, or propose to act, unreasonably, but what is considered 'unreasonable' can be challenged in the courts. In practice the minister rarely uses the power of direction. Persuasion by negotiation is the usual method. Hence there is much consultation between the Department of Education and Science (DES) and the local education authorities. All the chief education officers are known to the DES. Informal contact is therefore very important and, in this connection, note the importance of the minister's inspectors, whose task it is to see that the schools and colleges are being run properly and who are available for consultation and advice.

The DES is not only responsible for the schools and further education run by the local authorities but it also has links with the universities by its supervision of the University Grants Committee, which was previously supervised by the Treasury.

The DES is responsible for promoting civil research via five research councils – the Science and Engineering Research Council, the Medical Research Council, the Agricultural Research Council, the Natural Environment Research Council and the Social Science Research Council.

Advisory bodies

Under the 1944 Education Act the Minister had to appoint a central advisory council for England and one for Wales. These replaced the consultative committee of the Board of Education set up under the Board of Education Act of 1899. (Note some of the famous reports produced by the central advisory council for England – Crowther, Newsom, Plowden.) But these councils no longer function. There remain specialised advisory committees.

For example, the National Advisory Body for Public Sector Higher Education, the University Grants Committee, and in 1983 the Secondary Examinations Council (SEC) was set up 'to advise the Government on the ways in which the national system of secondary education may best meet the needs of the education service and its clients'. Apart from supervising 'the operations of examinations' in secondary schools, it also covers examinations after the end of the compulsory school period (see Cmnd 9469).

However, the Secretary of State relies mainly on the civil servants in the DES for advice and assistance. These include Her Majesty's Inspectors (HMIs)

The local authorities' responsibilities

The local authorities execute and administer state education under the DES's control and direction. They employ the teachers and build and maintain the schools and colleges. The local education authorities are the county councils and the metropolitan district councils which must, by law, appoint an education committee to administer education advised by the chief education officer of the local authority. The education committee must have co-opted members, usually one or two teachers and two or three representatives from the churches, It works through a number of sub-committees.

Pressure groups

A number of bodies have access to the Secretary of State for Education and Science and are usually consulted when new matters of policy arise. The local authorities not only act as independent units but act together through their associations which put their views to the government on matters of common interest to all the authorities in their association. They also circulate information to their members.

There are the teachers' unions – the National Union of Teachers, the National Association of Schoolmasters, four associations representing headmasters, headmistresses, assistant masters and assistant mistresses in grammar schools, the National Association of Teachers in Further and Higher Education and the Association of University Teachers, all of which not only protect their members' interests with regards to pay and conditions of work, but, as professional organisations, put forward their views on education. There are also pressure groups representing parents.

Parliament

Parliament obviously influences education policy because the Secretary of State must ultimately seek its approval for the policies pursued.

Summary

There are three main stages in education – primary, secondary and tertiary. Tertiary is sometimes called higher education and is part of further education in that it is undertaken beyond the official school-leaving age.

There is a state system of education administered by local authorities under the supervision of the Department of Education and Science and a private system which includes the universities. Large sections of the private sector receive financial assistance from the government; virtually all the universities do. Working closely with the state schools are Church schools, some of which receive financial help from both local government and central government; some are financed entirely by local government.

Assignments

1. Explain the relationships between the following: the principal of the college, the academic board, the board of governors, the

local authority, the Department of Education and Science, the Secretary of State for Education and Science.

2. Do you think the education service would be better run if it were taken out of the hands of local government and administered directly by cental government? Give reasons for your answer.

3. In July 1982 Customs and Excise were demanding that VAT (Value-Added Tax) should be paid on adult education courses which are non-vocational, i.e. taken for purely recreational purposes. Vocational courses would not be affected. Discuss how far it is possible to differentiate between the two types of course.

Reading

Britain 1987, An Official Handbook (HMSO).
H. C. Dent, *The Educational System of England and Wales* (University of London Press, 1969).
HMSO, *Report of the Working Party on Management of Higher Education*, Cmnd 7130 (HMSO, 1978).

12 Developments in Education since 1945 and Current Problems

Higher Education

(1) There has been a great expansion of higher education. (By higher education is meant not only degree courses but professional courses at final level.)

(2) The number of universities has increased. There are now forty-six in Britain and, in addition, the Open University – the 'University of the Air'. In its first academic year, 1970–1, places were available for 25,000 students, which, at that time, was about half the intake of all other universities in England and Wales. In 1945 Britain had seventeen universities.

(3) Teacher-training colleges, later known as colleges of education, and still under the control of local authorities, have been reorganised – some merging with polytechnics, some with universities, some continuing as separate colleges but providing other courses apart from teaching courses, while some have closed down. But a small number remain primarily for teacher-training. The government justified the closing down of some colleges of education with the argument that the falling birth-rate will mean fewer teachers will be needed.

(4) Universities are no longer the only institutions awarding degrees. In the public sector some colleges and groupings of colleges in certain key areas have been designated polytechnics (there are 30 of them) and, along with certain other colleges, run their own degree courses outside the university system. The degrees are awarded by the Council for National Academic Awards, which also supervises the courses. This dual system of degree awards is known as the binary system. Apart from degree courses, polytechnics, as their name indicates, put on a wide variety of high-level

courses. In fact, more than half the students in higher education are in polytechnics and other colleges administered by local authorities.

(5) The Ministry of Education was renamed the Department of Education and Science in 1964 after its merger with the Ministry of Science and divided into two main administrative units – one is concerned with the schools of England and Wales and further education, and the other with the universities and civil science.

(6) The *Report of the Committee of Higher Education* was published in 1963. The Committee was set up in 1961 because the opportunities for higher education did not appear to be expanding fast enough. Chaired by Lord Robbins, it was to report on higher education 'in the light of national needs and resources'.

The Report accepted the need for an expansion of higher education and thought it could be achieved without a lowering of academic standards. There were 'large reservoirs of untapped ability in the population, especially among girls', the Report stated. It estimated that 560,000 places for full-time higher education would be needed in Britain in the academic year 1980–1, i.e. 17 per cent of the age group, compared with 8 per cent at the time of the Report. In the academic year 1984–85 there were 566,000 full-time students in higher education in Britain excluding overseas students. In 1985 there were 120,000 students following Open University courses, more than half of which were at degree level.

It was the Robbins Report which recommended most of the main developments listed above – the creation of new universities, the granting of university status to the colleges of advanced technology, the improved status of teacher-training colleges and the setting up of the Council for National Academic Awards.

The merging of the Ministry of Education with the Ministry of Science in 1964 to form the Department of Education and Science, with one division responsible for higher education and the other for the schools system, was a compromise solution to the proposal of the Robbins Committee that there should be a separate Ministry for Higher Education called the Ministry of Arts and Sciences. The schools did not want a separate ministry; the universities did.

Reasons for the big advance of higher education

(1) The big expansion of secondary education, arising from the 1944 Education Act, meant that the proportion of young people in

the secondary field capable of benefiting from higher education increased.

(2) There was a large increase in the number of schoolchildren arising from increased births after the Second World War. In recent years there has been a fall in the number of children starting at primary school.

(3) Economic necessity has been a big factor in the development of higher education. The Robbins Report stated:

> We do not believe that modern societies can achieve their aims of economic growth and higher cultural standards without making the most of the talents of their citizens. This is obviously necessary if we are to compete with the other highly developed countries in an area of rapid technological and social advance.

Almost twenty years earlier two other reports had made the same point. These were the Report of the Social Committee on Higher Technological Education of 1945 (the Percy Report) and the report of a committee appointed by the Lord President of the Council on Scientific Manpower (the Barlow Report), published in 1946. The Barlow Report stated what the Robbins Report later confirmed, that many more young people were capable of taking advantage of a university education. It concluded 'that only about one in five boys and girls, who have intelligence equal to that of the best half of the university students, actually reach universities'.

(4) In line with more egalitarian and democratic trends, accelerated by two world wars and higher living standards, the expansion of higher education was considered right in order that citizens should, as the Robbins Report put it, develop their 'capacity to understand, to contemplate and to create'. Or, to quote Robbins again, 'the good society desires equality of opportunity for its citizens to become not merely good producers but also good men and women'.

(5) The greatly increased financial assistance to students and higher living standards have meant that the more ordinary families can afford to let their children take advantage of higher education.

Current problems in higher education

The cost of education is rising. Each year it has taken an increasing proportion of the gross national product – 3.1 per cent in 1951, 7.7

per cent in 1976. But since 1976 the proportion has declined. In 1979 it was 5.4 per cent, in 1984 5.2 per cent. No matter how desirable it may be, can we continue to afford, in view of rising costs and economic difficulties, to provide a place in higher eduaction for all those who are 'qualified by ability and attainment and who wish to have a place' (the Robbins criteria?). By higher education is meant not only university education but different levels of education beyond the secondary sphere. The Government in its Green Paper (Cmnd 9524) has accepted that we can and has even accepted the wider criteria of the UGC and NAB that higher education courses should be available 'to all those who can benefit from them and who wish to do so'. But with its eye on the cost the Government makes its acceptance dependent on the benefit justifying the cost and a vigorous selection procedure.

The Robbins Report reflected the optimism of the Keynesian era of economics when the economy was expanding at a faster rate than at any previous period. But, starting in the early 1970s, the world economy has moved into recession and economic growth has slowed down. Instead of prices falling, as in the previous recessions, prices have risen. Hence the Government in its Green Paper (Cmnd 9524) admits a reduction in real terms of about 3.5 per cent in the financial year 1984–5 in the resources provided for higher education compared with 1980–81 while 'student numbers rose substantially'. In the universities, the cuts have necessitated a cut in student intake and the easing of some lecturers into early retirement. The 'substantial increase' in student numbers has taken place in the public sector – in the polytechnics and other colleges – an actual increase of around 30 per cent. This has worsened staff–student ratios. The Green Paper admits that the 'financial restraints' have limited spending on books, journals, the development of information systems, building maintenance and running costs generally. But it goes on to say that expenditure plans for 1985–6 to 1987–8 should provide sufficient resources. However, the assumption is that there will only be sufficient resources if additional money comes from the private sector and, as with the NHS, extra resources are released from greater efficiency. The Government argues that, in view of the recession cuts have been made to help save the economy. If the economy does not recover, there will be even less money for higher education. In addition, the 1960s saw a rapid and uncontrolled expansion in education. Hence, in the Government's view, the cuts are useful in getting rid of flab. One mitigating factor is that because of the drop in the birth-rate in the mid-1960s, between 1984 and 1986, the number of 18- and 19-year-olds will fall by one-third. Even so, around 40,000 young people (the estimate varies) since 1981 will have been denied a university education which they would have received if the cuts had not been made. Many of them, however, will have gone to a higher education college in the public sector. And, in spite of the cuts the Government can rightly claim that there are more students in higher education than ever before. Units costs have thus been substantially reduced and, with future cuts, are expected to fall even further.

In its green paper the Government argues that the education system in general as well as higher education should be more geared to the needs of the economy. Thus, while humanities and social studies are still important, greater emphasis should be given to science and technology. Furthermore, higher education needs to generate a positive attitude to work; it should encourage the entrepreneurial spirit; it should beware of anti-business snobbery; it should have links with industry and commerce and the local community. Most, if not all the institutions of higher education do carry out these recommendations – the Government is asking them to do more. In the Green Paper the Government reveals its concern about the quality of teaching in higher education institutions. It intends to give universities the power to sack lecturers or, to put it more politely, limit academic tenure. (Lecturers normally have security of tenure to protect academic freedom.) The Government is also concerned about the lack of accountability of universities to its staff, students and the public. A hard-hitting Green Paper by Sir Keith Joseph, the then Secretary of State who initiated it, did admit later that its tone could have been better.

The emphasis the Government places on the role of education serving the economy and with it the vocational aspects of education has given rise to the fear that within the universities the independent and critical spirit upon which human progress so much depends will be weakened. As the Robbins report put it education is to help people to develop their 'capacity to understand, to contemplate and to create'. The Government might reply that higher education has always had a vocational element providing doctors, lawyers, administrators, engineers, etc., and all it is trying to do is get a better balance between the humanities and the more vocational orientated subjects. To further this better balance, part of the formula for assessing how much money each university is to receive from the UGC is the quality and relevance of the research carried out by the university. This could be one way of taking money away from the humanities if by reference is meant relevance to the present market place.

What should be the structure of higher education?

The present binary system of universities with their own degrees, and polytechnics and certain other colleges awarding degrees under the auspices of the Council for National Academic Awards, has been criticised. The critics quite rightly point out that universities have the greatest prestige and receive a much higher proportion of resources than the polytechnics and others. They particularly resent what they consider to be the inadequate resources allotted to the polytechnics because they feel that, given adequate resources, the polytechnics, in certain fields, could provide a better education than the universities because they would be orientated to the more practical needs of society.

Other critics see the binary system as acceptance of first- and second-class institutions in higher education similar to grammar and secondary modern schools in secondary education. As in secondary education, the grammar/secondary modern system has been virtually replaced by a comprehensive system, so these critics would like to see a comprehensive system for higher education. Thus there would be 'polyversities' covering work of existing universities, polytechnics, colleges of education and certain technical colleges. Two main arguments are put forward for the changes. First, all forms of higher education would get their fair share of resources and this would mean that higher education would be better adapted than it is now to meet the needs of the modern technological society. Second, polyversities, like comprehensive schools in secondary education, would further the development of a more homogeneous and egalitarian society.

Those who defend the special position of the existing universities usually believe in the necessity for an educated elite to provide the leadership of the required calibre. Such an elite is best nurtured in the existing type of university, which zealously upholds the liberal tradition of ensuring that a subject is studied in depth from all points of view.

On the other hand, there are those who think that, in view of our limited resources, the binary system is the most practical line of advance.

The reorganisation of the colleges of education is in line with the recommendation of the Committee of Inquiry Report 1972 (James Report) on *Teacher Education and Training* that future teachers would benefit from closer association with students in other fields of higher education. Some critics argue that the quality of teacher-training has been adversely affected by being part of one large institution concerned with so many other things. In any case, for many people, experience has shown that most students do not normally mix and interchange ideas with students in other disciplines.

Secondary Education

(1) There has been a big expansion of secondary education due to the 1944 Education Act and the increased number of school-children, with more students staying on at the different types of schools after school-leaving age. But in spite of great progress in the secondary sphere the Report of the Minister of Education's central advisory council, *Half Our Future*, in 1963 (the Newsome Report), which considered the education of children between the ages of 13 and 16 with average and less than average ability, found that 80 per cent of the schools which these children attended (mainly secondary modern schools) were deficient from the accommodation point of view.

(2) There has been a great expansion of all forms of secondary education, not just that provided in secondary schools. Hence there has been a great expansion of the work of technical colleges which provide craft courses and intermediate professional courses including business and technical education courses for those students who have finished compulsory schooling. But in spite of the development of courses at technical colleges of further education the Report of the Minister of Education's central advisory council in 1959 (the Crowther Report), entitled *15–18*, stated that the

majority of young people between 15 and 18 received no full-time or part-time education.

In 1981 about a third of school-leavers had some form of further education, either part or full time. But the great increase in unemployment has resulted in training schemes for unemployed school-leavers under 18 which are a form of vocational education (see Chapter 14). A new and very unusual development is a four-year technical and vocational course of training under the control of the Manpower Services Commission for young people commencing at the age of 14. It is called the Technical and Vocational Education Initiative (TVEI). Pilot schemes began in 1983. Some authorities and teachers are upset that a big slice of education is not under the control of local government (the traditional providers of education), as the Manpower Services Commission provides the money as well as the overall supervision, and this at a time when cuts have been made in local government funding.

A White Paper (Cmnd 9823) published in 1986 outlines the Government's plans to expand the TVEI scheme by providing new courses. Local authorities have discretion as to whether or not to provide a TVEI course in their schools but, by July 1986, only 18 authorities had not. By the autumn of 1987 it is expected that the scheme will be a truly national one. The money provided for courses by the MSC is a big inducement to participate. Critics of TVEI say the money should have been put into education as a whole so all students could benefit. They also argue that the course revives the old division between the academic – the bright ones who eventually do 'A' levels – and the not so bright who do practical subjects. However, if in teaching the practical subjects they are related to their social and environmental background, they can be educational in the true sense of the word and not simply vocational. The Secretary of State for Education has said (2 July 1986) that the biggest constraint of the scheme's expansion was 'shortages of teachers in the appropriate subjects, not money'. The fact that such a scheme has been introduced could be taken by some people as criticism of our educational system for not providing enough students with sufficient skills for the world of work and the shortsightedness of our commercial and industrial leaders for not sufficiently involving themselves in the education process. A College of the Air is to be set up under the auspices of the MSC, financed mainly by private enterprise, which is planned to be operative from 1 September 1987.

A new body, the National Council for Vocational Qualifications (NCVQ) is to be created to co-ordinate and rationalise the various vocational courses. It will be responsible to the Secretary of State for Employment.

A further stage in the by-passing of local authorities in educational provision was the Government announcement (October 1986) to build twenty City Technology Colleges (CTCs), some to be located in deprived inner city areas, for 11- to 18-year-olds; to be financed jointly by Central Government and, hopefully, private enterprise and run by independent trustees.

The 1964 Industrial Training Act did something to encourage employers to provide day-release facilities for the training of their young employees by setting up industrial training boards each for a particular industry. Each board has the power to make a levy on the employers within the industry (small firms are exempt). But employers receive back a percentage of the levy for each employee they release for training. Hence there is some financial incentive to provide day-release facilities. Much of the teaching is done by technical college teachers – the purely vocational teaching is done by teachers appointed by the appropriate training board. Boards can also provide their own training courses.

The 1981 Employment and Training Act abolished all but seven of the 23 boards (see p. 186).

(3) The most interesting development has been the swing to comprehensive schools. Just a few local authorities introduced comprehensive schools soon after the 1944 Education Act but the majority kept to the tripartite system. The Labour administrations of 1945–51 did not encourage comprehensive schools and the Conservative administrators of 1951–64 discouraged them except in rural areas. But when the Labour party was returned to power in 1964 its official policy was to abolish the 11-plus examination. In 1965 the DES issued *Circular 10/65*, requesting local authorities to prepare schemes for the reorganisation of secondary education on comprehensive lines.

In 1965, 8 per cent of secondary schoolchildren in England and Wales in state schools were in comprehensive schools – and in 1984, over 84 per cent. Under Conservative governments local authorities can please themselves whether or not to plan their secondary education on comprehensive lines.

Why has there been a swing towards Comprehensive Schools?

It was due to a weaknesses in the selection system and the tripartite structure:

1. The selection process at 11 was not as efficient as originally anticipated. A fair percentage of children (the estimate varies) went to the wrong school, judging by their performances later on.
2. Although it was possible for a child at 13 to be transferred to another type of school where the selection procedure had obviously been wrong, in practice, because of administrative difficulties, the transfer system did not work satisfactorily in most areas.
3. The selection procedure works against children from working-class families where the home background is not conducive to study. The proportion of children selected for grammar schools in the middle-class areas was very much higher than the proportion in working-class areas. Hence, a great deal of potential talent was wasted. For evidence of the influence of social class on school performance see the 1954 Report of the Minister of Education's central advisory council, entitled *Early Leaving*.
4. Selection and the tripartite system is seen by some as a form of educational apartheid conducive to an elitist and authoritarian society. On the other hand, they consider comprehensive schools as conducive to a more homogeneous, democratic and egalitarian society.
5. In rural areas it is not an economic proposition to have a small grammar school and a small secondary modern school, and thus most people agree that in rural areas comprehensives are what are needed.

What are the arguments against comprehensive schools?

1. If a grammar and comnprehensive school existed in the same area, the grammar school would probably cream off the brighter pupils and the comprehensive school would cease to be a comprehensive. Hence comprehensive schools necessitate the destruction of good grammar schools.

2. The less academic pupil, for his or her own sake, needs a different kind of educational environment than the academic type. In any case, as the Spens Report stated (1938), 'It would be difficult . . . to find Heads who would be competent to control and inspire both developments as to control and inspire one or the other.'

3. The brighter children develop the best with other bright children in the more academic atmosphere of a grammar school, and we need to develop brighter children to the utmost to have leaders of industry and commerce and the professions in sufficient numbers and of sufficient calibre.

Some general points on the comprehensive debate

There seems no reason why, given the right sort of school buildings, similar equipment and quality of teachers, as good an education cannot be provided for a bright child in a comprehensive school as in a grammar school. Indeed, some supporters of comprehensives would say they give a better education because a comprehensive school is a better reflection of society then a grammar school.

The main criticism of comprehensive schemes of education arises from a desire to retain the grammar school, or at least it would appear so. But does this go deep enough? Is not our attitude to comprehensive schools in secondary education and polyversities in higher education determined to a great extent by our political faith? The people who support comprehensive schools are usually the same sort of people who support the polyversities, and they tend to be more radical, while more conservative people tend to oppose them. This is because the radical has much more faith than the conservative in the power of the environment to change an individual's way of life: hence his greater faith in blue-prints for a better world and a greater willingness to accept change. The radical sees the environment of a comprehensive school, because it embraces children of all abilities and social backgrounds, as being more conducive than the tripartite system to creating the more democratic and homgeneous society which he desires. The conservative, on the other hand, is more inclined than the radical to believe in Original Sin, has less faith in the power of the environment to change individual personality and hence is more distrustful of blue-prints and new ideas, tending to see the advantages of the status quo. The grammar schools have served the country well –

why destroy them? In any case all this talk of egalitarianism is so much romantic nonsense!

The comprehensive debate, like the polyversities debate, when we get down to it, is a political debate about the kind of society we want.

Comprehensives and the independent sector

While it is possible to abolish the state grammar schools and have a state comprehensive system, what of schools in the private sector? The government might ask them to become comprehensive and integrate into the state system, but it could hardly force them to join in the comprehensive system. Yet the state system will never be truly comprehensive if private schools cream off the brighter children for themselves. Very few are likely to join voluntarily – the majority would argue that to bring in a much wider range of ability into the schools would be to change their nature.

General Certificate of Secondary Education

Much criticism is levelled at our educational system. At the secondary level 90 per cent of students leave school with a qualification in at least one subject at 'O' level or CSE. If, however, a low pass in CSE in only one or two subjects is considered a poor result, then roughly 40 per cent of the children leave secondary school with inadequate and sometimes no paper qualifications. Some employers have complained that young people come to them hardly literate or numerate. On the other hand, a far larger proportion of students now obtain 'O' level and 'A' level passes than in previous years. In 1985 the Government published a White Paper (Cmnd 9469) outlining its proposals for improving the system of primary and secondary education with its thoughts mainly centred on the 40 per cent of students for whom the normal 'O' level and CSE courses did not appear appropriate. As part of its policy for improving the educational system at secondary level the White Paper outlined the Government's policy for replacing the GCE 'O' level courses and the CSE by the General Certificate of Secondary Education (GCSE) which became operative from September 1986. The first GCSE examinations will be held in 1988. Thus, instead of two separate systems there is one single system. One of the aims is to try and find out what candidates know and hence, although a single system, there are to be 'differentiated papers or differentiated questions within papers in all subjects'. So all candidates should be able to answer all the required number of questions although some questions will require greater skills than others and higher grades will be given to those candidates who correctly answer the questions requiring higher skills. Although a single system, most schools will divide pupils, after two, three or four years of their school career into different classes according to their supposed abilities. Thus pupils of similar abilities in a particular subject will be eventually taught together (see letter from the Deputy Chief Executive, Secondary Examinations Council, *The Listener*, 2 October 1986). This is similar to the streaming which took place in most comprehensive schools where a pupil could be in a low stream for one subject but in a high stream for another subject. The comprehensive school made it possible for the system to be more flexible and it is hoped that the GCSE will increase this flexibility. With the 40 per cent low achievers in mind, the Government in its White Paper emphasises the importance of 'craft and practical skills'. Presumably GCSE courses will be developed with that in mind. Some schools do provide courses leading to vocational qualifications which the Government wishes to encourage and, apart from these courses, there is the TVEI four-year course. In the development of courses and their curriculum, the Government is anxious to have the co-operation of local authorities, teachers, parents and employers. The aim of the curriculum (i.e. the educational content) is to ensure it is in keeping with broad educational objectives. The Government obviously feels an important part of the educational objective is training pupils for the world of work and, in its opinion, in the past not enough attention has been paid to this. Other Government aims outlined in the White Paper are to improve the quality of teaching and to encourage parents to become involved in the activities of the school to which they send their children. In 'harnessing the energies' of parents the Government hopes educational standards will be improved. Thus the 1986 Education Act gives parents greatly increased representation on the governing bodies of schools.

The GCSE does not affect GCE 'A' level. That will be retained as 'A' level courses 'provide a foundation for degree courses and play an important role in selection for higher education'. The Government is, however, 'taking action to promote greater breadth for those engaged in 'A' level studies, without reducing standards'.

Primary Education

There has been a revolutionary change in teaching methods. Children now learn by doing rather than being lectured at. The teaching methods developed in the primary schools might have relevance for secondary and further education. Educational research is perhaps mainly responsible for them, but two reports in the interwar years by the Consultative Committee of the Board of Education may have had some influence. These were the 1931 Report on *The Primary School* and the 1933 Report on *Infant and Nursery Schools*. There are critics, however, who argue that the large number of school-leavers who cannot do simple arithmetic or write clearly goes back to the 'new-fangled' teaching methods. The White Paper, on the other hand, did state that literacy and numeracy would be improved if their teaching was related to the context in which they were needed. Another criticism in the White Paper was that pupils' abilities were often underestimated and that 'they were not given enough responsibility to pursue their own inquiries'. This criticism is relevant to all forms of education.

Many new primary schools have been built, but the 1967 Report of the Central Council for Education (the Plowden Report), *Children and their Primary Schools*, stated that there were still too many old and inferior buildings being used for primary education; classes were still too big (most still around the forty mark) and the committee felt 'that a higher priority in the total educational budget ought now to be given to primary education . . . Nobody ought to be satisfied with the conditions under which our four million primary schoolchildren are educated'. A greater proportion of the eduction budget has since be allotted for primary education. In 1984 only one primary class in one hundred had over 40 pupils and one in five over 30.

Independent Schools since 1945

Here we are concerned mainly with possible developments. The main concern has been how to integrate the independent (i.e. private) sector of education into the public sector (about 6 per cent of the school age population go to independent schools). The 1944 Report of the Committee on Public Schools (the Fleming Report) expressed concern at 'the unreality of an educational system which segregates so thoroughly the boys of one class from those of another in a world where, much more than in the past, they will meet in later life as equals'. It recommended that a minimum of 25 per cent of places should be reserved at day schools and boarding schools for pupils from local authority schools. Arising from this report, more independent schools (mainly the day schools) opened their doors to pupils from local authority schools. Arising from this, the Report, more independent schools accepted financial help from the central government and became direct-grant schools, having to reserve at least 25 per cent of their places free for children from local authority schools. (The local authority paid the direct-grant school for the children's tuition.) In recent years some local authorities with a comprehensive system of education refused to take up places at direct-grant schools for children in local authority schools because the direct-grant schools refused to become comprehensive. Starting in September 1976, direct-grant schools began to be phased out. They had either to join the maintained system (i.e. be financially supported, either wholly or partly, by the local authorities) and become part of the comprehensive system, or they had to become completely independent. In January 1976 fifty-one had opted to join the maintained sector.

Those direct-grant schools that chose to become independent felt that if they became comprehensive their special qualities would be lost. The phasing out of direct-grant schools was recommended by the Report of the Public Schools Commission of March 1970 (the Donnison Report). It also recommended that independent schools should be integrated into the state system. The 1980 Education Act with its assisted places scheme halted this trend.

Education for Leisure

There have always been people who take up educational courses in their leisure time simply for the fun of it. Higher living standards since 1945 and, more recently, high unemployment and the growth of active retired people have greatly increased their numbers. Such courses range from pottery to philosophy. Their needs are catered for by the Workers' Educational Association, the extra-mural departments of universities, evening classes (including some day classes) in state schools and colleges, radio and television.

Value for Money?

The more we spend on education, the less we can afford other things. Hence it is important that the money is well spent. In other words, the money invested in education should give an adequate return. In business it is possible to express the return on a sum invested as a percentage of that sum of money. This is what is meant by the percentage return on capital and it can be compared with the money return on other investments. It is one way of finding out how to allocate the country's resources between different uses. But how can the return on any given sum spent on education be measured? Education to those who receive it provides a great deal of individual satisfaction, but this cannot be measured in money terms. Education helps economic growth by providing skills but just how much nobody knows, though attempts have been made to measure it. But even if education did not help economic growth, it would still be worth while because, by making citizens more knowledgeable, it creates a more understanding society, and therefore a pleasanter society to live in.

Although it might be almost impossible to assess the return on the overall investment in education, perhaps in specific spheres money could be spent more productively.

The Government has emphasised this for both higher and secondary education. In its expenditure plans to 1987–8 (Cmnd 9428) it stresses the need 'for continuing gains in efficiency if standards are to be maintained'. Thus the Government is hoping that one spin-off from its policy of restricting the growth of expenditure on education will be greater efficiency in education, the savings from which will partly compensate for the shortfall in money provided.

Equality of Opportunity

Does our education system provide equality of opportunity?

It did in that all students using the state or private system of education had the opportunity to get to a university to pursue their studies at the highest level. Thanks to government financial assistance in the form of student grants, no student needed to discontinue his or her education because of lack of money.

But the recent financial cuts in education and, in addition, the reduction in the real value of student grants (all part of the expenditure cuts of the Thatcher government) have made this no longer true. Some qualified students will not get the place they want in higher education and some students will be discouraged from doing so because of the financial strait-jacket the present grant puts them in.

But even if students who are qualified can find a place in higher education, it does not mean there is equal opportunity for all students to pursue their studies to the highest stage commensurate with their abilities. Thus two young people might have equal intelligence, yet one might gain a university degree and the other leave school at 15 without an 'O' level. The following are some of the factors that might be responsible for this and thus stand in the way of equal opportunity.

(1) Home background is of vital importance in educational attainment. Some children have a home conducive to happy study; some have not. Evidence reveals that a much higher proportion of students in higher education come from middle- and upper-class homes than from working-class homes. Some suggested reasons for this are:

(a) the majority of working-class parents have more modest aspirations for their children's careers than middle- and upper-class parents

(b) a higher proportion of working-class homes are less conducive to study than middle- and upper-class homes

(c) many working-class parents cannot afford to buy books which would aid their children's education

(d) some people argue that schools have a middle-class outlook or ethos which working-class children find more difficult to attune themselves to than middle- and upper-class children.

(2) Some schools are better than others – they have better teachers, smaller classes, or both; or the students who go to them come from homes where study is encouraged, so the teacher–student relationship is a good one. Hence a student going to one of these schools is more likely to do well than if he went to a school where the teachers were poor, the classes large and fellow-students not so keen on study because of parental indifference. In general, within the state system, middle-class areas have better schools than

working-class areas. This is not because of any difference in the size of classes but because of the other two factors: the teacher–student relationship and the quality of the teacher. The teacher–student relationship is usually better in middle-class areas than in working-class areas, because, in general, middle-class parents encourage their children to study more than working-class parents do. There are usually, on average, better teachers in schools in middle-class areas because more teachers apply to teach in these schools and therefore the local authority can be more selective.

This criticism also applies to comprehensive schools. Although, on the whole, they help to further educational opportunity, comprehensive schools in middle-class areas will tend to be more 'successful' than those in poorer areas.

Some local authorities spend more money than others on education. How successful a child is can therefore depend, to some extent, on where he or she lives.

Private schools often have better facilities and gain more 'O' and 'A' level credits than state schools because they have more money to employ more teachers to keep class sizes down and can pay teachers above the normal pay scale in order to obtain well-qualified staff.

Can anything be done to weaken the forces working against equality of opportunity? Only parents themselves can provide a home environment conducive to study, but what already has influenced parents to encourage their children's studies and will continue to do so in the future are higher living standards and the widening of educational opportunity. Higher living standards increase material satisfaction and whet the appetite for more. At the same time, widening educational opportunity makes more parents appreciate that education can be a means of obtaining a higher income and increased material satisfactions because it qualifies, in principle, a young person for a better job. But however enlightened parents become, there will always be inequalities of opportunity because of differences in home background and differences between schools – a good school can compensate for a poor home background. To help reduce the difference between areas, there developed the concept of Educational Priority Areas (EPAs), which means channelling a greater proportion of resources to the schools in the deprived areas. Extra resources have been made available to some areas but not on the scale as originally envisaged. But the long-term solution is to increase the standard of living of the working class and rebuild deprived environments. This is already taking place, but too slowly. The problem is particularly acute in the inner-city areas of the older industrial towns.

Should perhaps private schools be abolished to equalise opportunity between the most affluent sections of the population and the rest? This, to some people, would be an attack on personal liberty. Why should parents be forced to send their children to a state school if they want to send them to a good private school? Furthermore, there are a great variety of private schools (although admittedly not all are good) and some educational advance has been due to the experimental nature of some of these private schools. On the other hand, there are those who say the state system of education will never be as good as it should be while those in positions of power and influence can opt out of it by using the private system. If they had to use the state system for their own children, they would soon see to it that the state system was very much improved.

The answer here is perhaps not to abolish the private system but to devote more resources to the state system so that differences between two sectors are diminished. In this century much progress has been made in this direction, but much more still needs to be done. The cutting back of teacher-training may prove a backward step. The average class size in the state primary schools varies between local authorities but is now around twenty-two, which is perhaps still too many to ensure that all are properly taught. And it is in the primary school where the foundations of the basic skills – reading, writing and arithmetic – are learnt. About 25 per cent of primary classes have thirty children or more. Even in secondary schools the average class size is sixteen. We should perhaps work for more equality of income so that all parents have a more equal chance of sending their children to a good private school if they wish to.

Because of the recession and monetarist policies leading to cuts in public expenditure the expansion in education has been halted. With the idea of improving the quality of schools by encouraging competition between them and, at the same time, giving parents greater freedom in choosing a school for their children, consideration has been given to a voucher system. The basic idea of such a system is that the state would still be responsible for education but parents would be given a voucher which would be given to the school of their choice and which could then be exchanged by the school for state money. Parents could choose the school they wished their children to go to. As the vouchers would be a school's main source of income, schools would compete for custom and poor schools would go out of business. Private schools would still be run for profit. The supporters of this scheme argue that it would improve the quality of schools and give more parental choice. Opponents argue that because of the greater demand for the better schools, they will charge more and poorer parents would not be able to pay the extra above that allowed for in the voucher and would have to send their children to the poorer schools. In any case it is very difficult for a parent to judge the quality of education schools provide and many teachers fear the voucher system would result in the overstressing of the cash value of education.

Summary

Secondary education for all has inevitably led to a big expansion of higher education, an expansion also encouraged by greatly increased financial assistance to students and higher living standards in general. Because of economic recession that expansion has been halted. Furthermore, partly due to the recession, more emphasis has been placed on gearing higher and secondary education to the needs of commerce and industry. The MSC now plays an important role developing courses in the secondary sphere with this in mind.

Side by side with the state system, the private enterprise system of primary and secondary education for the richer members of the community has continued to flourish, though, as the state system has advanced, the private system is not as important as it used to be but is still very influential and a voucher system would strengthen it. In recent years more thought has been devoted to finding ways of integrating the private system and the state system. How far you think this should be done and how far you think the parallel development of comprehensive schools is a good thing depends, to a great extent, on the sort of society you think we should be aiming for.

The two main factors in the development of education have been (a) the need for an efficient labour force, and (b) the need, as the franchise was extended, pushed by democratic and egalitarian pressures, to consider the aspirations of the working class.

Assignments

1. Make a list of the independent schools in your district or county local authority. How far do you think independent schools should be an essential part of our education system?
2. What do you understand by 'equality of educational opportunity'? To what extent is there equality of educational opportunity in Britain? What factors have contributed to greater equality of educational opportunity since 1945?
3. If possible, obtain from your local authority the average class size in its primary schools and secondary schools. Also, what percentage of its primary schoolchildren are in classes of thirty or more?
4. Discuss how the student intake at your college has been affected (if at all) by government policies in the last few years.

Reading

Rodney Barker, *Education and Politics 1900–1951: A Study of the Labour Party* (Oxford University Press, 1972).
M. Blaug, *Introduction to the Economics of Education* (Penguin, 1972).
Tessa Bridgeman and Irene Fox, 'Why People Choose Private Schools' *New Society* (29 June 1978).
Central Advisory Council for Education (England) *Reports:*
    Crowther Report, *15–18* (HMSO, 1959).
    Newsome Report, *Half Our Future* (HMSO, 1963).
    Plowden Report, *Children and Their Primary Schools* (HMSO, 1967).
John Clare, 'Schools of Scandal: the Failure of Britain's Education System (*The Listener*, 31 July 1986).
C. B. Cox and A. E. Dyson, *Black Paper 2: The Crisis in Education* (Critical Quarterly Society, 1969).
DES, *Education: A Framework for Expansion*, Cmnd 5174 (HMSO, December 1972).
DES, *Departmental Circular 7/73, Development of Higher Education in the Non-University Sector* (Department of Education and Science, 26 March 1973).
Hazlegrave Report, *Report of the Committee on Technical Courses and Examinations* (HMSO, 1969).

HMSO, *Better Schools*, Cmnd 9469 (HMSO, 1985).

HMSO, *Working Together – Education & Training*, Cmnd 9823 (HMSO, July 1968).

HMSO, *The Development of Higher Education into the 1990s*, Cmnd 9524 (HMSO, 1985).

HMSO, *Education for All: a Brief Guide to the Main Issues of the Swann Report* (Cmnd 9453) *on the Education of Children from Ethnic Minority Groups* (HMSO, 1985).

HMSO, *Review of Vocational Qualifications in England and Wales: a Report* (HMSO, 1986).

HMSO, *Primary Education in England: A Survey of HM Inspectors of Schools* (HMSO, 1978).

HMSO, *The Curriculum Reform 5–16* (HMSO, 1985).

House of Commons, Higher and Continuing Education (*Hansard*, vol. 100, no. 136, 25 June 1986).

James Report, *Teacher Education and Training: A Report by a Committee of Inquiry* (HMSO, 1972).

William Letwin (ed.), *Against Equality* (Macmillan, 1983).

Robin Pedley, *The Comprehensive School*, 3rd edn (Penguin, 1978).

Maurice Preston, 'Higher Education: Financial and Economic Aspects', *Royal Bank of Scotland Review* (December 1985).

Public Schools Commission Second Report, *Report on Independent Day Schools and Direct Grant Grammar Schools* (HMSO, 1979).

Robbins Report, *Report of the Committee on Higher Education*, Cmnd 2154 (HMSO, 1963).

Eric Robinson, *The New Polytechnics* (Cornmarket, 1968).

David Rubenstein (ed.), *Education and Equality* (Penguin, 1979).

Russell Report, *Adult Education: A Plan for Development* (HMSO, 1973).

Michael Rutter, Barabara Maughan, Peter Mortimore and Janet Ouston, *Fifteen Thousand Hours: Secondary Schools and their Effects on Children* (Open Books, 1979).

Stuart Simon, 'Higher Education Solely a Means to an Economic End?' (*The Listener*, 6 June 1985).

13 Youth Service

Definition

By 'youth service' is meant the many local authorities and voluntary organisations which provide informal educational and social activities for young people. The official title under which they all operate is the 'Service of Youth'.

History

During the First World War the government encouraged local authorities to set up juvenile organisation committees comprising representatives from the local education authorities, voluntary organisation and interested individuals to encourage youth activities. These committees continued to function in many areas in the interwar years – the vast majority of the services were provided by voluntary organisations like the YMCA, the YWCA, Girl Guides, Boy Scouts, etc.

During the Second World War the Board of Education (which became the Ministry of Education in 1944) became responsible for youth welfare, and local education authorities were again reminded of the need to co-operate with voluntary bodies by means of a co-ordinating committee in order to promote youth activities. A National Youth Committee was created and later replaced by the Youth Advisory Council, which made reports on youth activities on the assumption that they were an essential part of the education service. During the war the opportunities for helping the war effort stirred the imagination of many young people and the Youth Service expanded rapidly. Under the 1944 Education Act it became an integral part of further education. This means that local authorities have not only to provide full-time and part-time education for persons over school-leaving age, but also 'leisure-

176

time occupations in such organised cultural, training and recreational activities as are suited to their requirements'.

In the mid-1950s criticisms were made that the Youth Service
received inadequate funds from central and local government, and
it is true that interest in it had waned. Perhaps one reason for this
was that there were all sorts of important developments requiring a
great deal of government money. Thus resources were limited, and
the Youth Service suffered when economies had to be made. In
1958 the Albermarle Committee was appointed.

> to review the contribution which the Youth Service of England
> and Wales can make in assisting young people to play their part in
> the life of the community . . . and to advise according to what
> priorities best value can be obtained for the money spent.

Its report, *The Youth Service in England and Wales*, came out in
1960. Arising from its main recommendations, local authorities
gave more help to youth organisations both in money terms and in
providing more adequate premises. A Youth Service Development
Council was set up to advise the Minister of Education and a
national college for the training of youth leaders was founded.
Certain colleges and universities also provide courses for youth
leaders to help them gain professional status and thus qualify for
better pay. Qualified youth leaders are assisted by part-time
workers, some of whom may have appropriate qualifications.
Qualified teachers are recognised as qualified youth workers. The
Youth Service Development Council was disbanded in 1971. The
present advisory body to the DES is the Youth Service Review
Group.

Administration Today

Broad policy is laid down by the DES within which local authorities
and voluntary organisations must work. Apart from helping voluntary organisations by providing premises, equipment and financial
assistance, many local education authorities supplement the work
of the voluntary organisation by providing youth centres and clubs
of their own. Most local authorities have youth councils, advised by
full-time, paid youth officers, which comprise representatives of the
voluntary organisations as well as the local authority. In spite of

local authority financial assistance, the voluntary organisations provide most of the money they need themselves. In England most of them are members of the National Council for Voluntary Youth Services.

There are two main types of youth organisation – those that are linked with a local parent organisation like church youth clubs and those which are not attached to a local parent body. The Boy Scouts and Girl Guides can belong to either type, though they are linked to a national parent body.

Among other bodies representing youth is the British Youth Council which represents all the main voluntary youth organisations and is the main forum of the Youth Service. It also acts as a pressure group. Some other organisations are the Community and Youth Workers Union, the National Association of Youth and Community Education Officers, the National Association of Youth Clubs, the National Association of Boys' Clubs, the Youth Hostels Association, and so on. Acting as an umbrella and helper for them all is the National Youth Bureau, founded in 1973, financed mainly by the Central Government.

Some of the Problems of the Youth Service

There is still the immediate practical problem of the shortage of good youth leaders. Since the Albermarle Report more money has been devoted to the Youth Service but, in spite of that, in some areas premises are still inadequate and some local authorities are still ungenerous in their financial asssistance. However, there has been some progress. In 1957 there were only 700 full-time staff; in 1982 there were 3,500 full-time youth leaders and about 500,000 part-time staff. Closely connected with the shortage of good youth leaders is the criticism made, arising from an inquiry by the DES, that the activities of the Youth Service are not sufficiently adventuresome (see Bone and Ross, 1972).

The problems of the Youth Service cannot be isolated from the problems of the wider society. We want the Youth Service, apart from providing games and dances and adventure pursuits, to help make good citizens with a sense of community service. But if the society within which the young find themselves exalts material success, and aggressive competition to obtain it, is it any wonder

that many young people think of a youth group in terms of what they
can get out of it rather than in terms of what they can contribute? It
is significant that, during the Second World War, when Britain had
a cause worth fighting for and fought for it, the Youth Service had
its most rapid expansion. However, a hopeful trend in recent years,
both within and outside the Youth Service, has been the growing
number of young people who give up their spare time to help the
elderly, the sick and the handicapped. The young people doing such
voluntary work in the community are often members of such
organisations as the International Voluntary Service, Task Force
and Community Service Volunteers which receive financial help
from the DES. At the same time, schemes like the Duke of
Edinburgh's Award Scheme, which operate through various organisations and firms, help to develop in young people a sense of
challenge and purpose in life. A DES discussion paper produced in
1975, *Provision for Youth*, is relevant. It raises the question as to
how far the Youth Service should keep to its primary educational
function of developing activities for leisure time, or how far it
should co-operate with workers in other social services in helping
the disadvantaged. This also applies to delinquents. For example,
young delinquents under the supervision of a social worker or
probation officer may be given 'intermediate treatment' when,
under a supervisor, they are given constructive activities to help
them become good citizens. Various sections of the Youth Service
have been encouraged to accept people on 'intermediate treatment'
into their midst. Unfortunately youth groups have not always co-
operated and, in certain areas, the probation and after-care service
has had to expand its own 'intermediate treatment' activities.

The underlying assumption of the Youth Service is that it helps to
develop in a beneficial way young people's characters. But some
people see a danger here. Thus a youth club might become an end in
itself. It may actually segregate the young people from the
community around them and, within it, young people might
develop their own code of right and wrong which may not be the
community's code and may be harmful to a young person's
development. This is especially true in the inner-city areas, where a
shabby environment and an exceptionally high rate of unemployment results in many young people feeling cut off from the
mainstream of society. While young people need to work things out
for themselves in their own groupings, they also need the experi-

ence and guidance of adults. One has to strike a balance between the two. The youth organisation should be separate from and yet part of the larger community.

The Report of the Committee of Inquiry on the Youth Service, which was published in October 1982, saw its first duty 'to help all young people who have need of it'. This help takes three main forms: (i) providing pleasurable recreation; (ii) providing a rescue service for young people who are unhappy and near despair; (iii) providing social education. Social education involves joint activity with other young people which gives greater confidence in personal relationships; participation in decision-making within the group which develops responsibility; community service, which in turn can lead to participation in community affairs and political activities on issues which affect young people, and this can provide greater knowledge of the workings of society and of democratic processes.

The Report was very critical of the Youth Service for 'not meeting the social education of young people as fully as it should'. Shortage of money may be a 'contributory factor' but the main reasons are underestimating the importance of social education and not making clear what is meant by it. The Youth Service has failed to take relations with the local community seriously. People do not know 'what the Youth Service is about'. It has failed to co-operate with other organisations and there is 'inadequate provision to meet the needs of the over-16s'. The committee is not just blaming Youth Service workers for these shortcomings – local authorities and central government must also share the blame. Of its many recommendations, one is that staff training should be 'monitored' by a 'national supervisory panel' and that a minister within the DES should co-ordinate the work of all departments with an interest in youth affairs and that he should speak for the Youth Service within the administration. The Government eventually responded to this critical report by issuing DES, *Circular 1/85*. It stated the Youth Service 'is of immense value to the Nation' and it also praised the voluntary sector – the main provider of the Youth Service. The Government accepted the need for greater co-ordination of the various organisations involved with youth. Hence, arising from the Report, the Government has set up a national advisory council for the Youth Service on which sit representatives of youth organisations, including young people themselves. The Government has also set up a youth unit within the DES which should go some way to meet the Review's recommendation for a minister within the DES to co-ordinate the work of departments with an interest in youth affairs. It urged local authorities to improve their links with youth organisations to help improve co-ordination of activities and, with the aim of improving training, 'all concerned' should co-operate with the Council for Education and Training in Youth and Community Work, established in December 1982. Local authorities are asked to report to the Secretary of State for the DES their existing arrangements for co-ordination, planning and management of the youth organisations in their area and give their views on how these arrangements contribute to effective training. Voluntary organisations should be encouraged to improve their management techniques and 'grant aid is available for voluntary organisations for short-term experimental projects in managerial innovation'. The youth organisations responded to the DES circular in a joint statement in March 1986. They stressed the need for close links with local authorities which 'have the duty to secure the provision of services for young people'. But they also stressed that 'an effective Youth Service is . . . dependent upon it having adequate finance'. The implication must be that in their opinion youth organisations are not adequately financed and that some local authorities do not have close enough links with the Youth Service. On the question of finance, the Youth Service is not likely to get any extra cash from central and local government. In its opening paragraphs to its circular, in keeping with its economic philosophy, the Government warned of the limited amount of money available. 'Local authorities will need, in future, to continue to appraise carefully their funding of the Youth Service relative to other claims on their total expenditure.'

Summary

The Youth Service effectively dates from the Second World War. It comprises mainly voluntary organisations assisted by local authorities who often supplement the work of the voluntary organisations by running youth clubs of their own. All are linked together under the umbrella of a local authority youth council, advised by full-time youth officers operating within a framework of regulations laid down by the DES. The aim of the Youth Service is to help young people broaden their interests and become good citizens. To some extent, therefore, it complements the work of schools. But the Youth Service can only marginally affect the good-citizenship aim; the main influence in this connection is the total environment in which the young person finds himself, and the Youth Service is only a small part of this environment. In recent years greater recognition has been given to this; and while the Youth Service still has an important role in catering for the individual needs of the young, it is much more concerned today than it used to be with social and political issues, though the 1982 Report of the Committee of Inquiry into the Youth Service found its involvement in such issues not very widespread. It should, however, be remembered that the Youth Service is responsible for only a relatively small proportion of youth provision.

Assignments

1. If you were running a youth club, what sort of activities would you organise? Give reasons for your choice.
2. If the Youth Service only provides a relatively small proportion of youth provision, list as many as possible of the other bodies or institutions concerned with young people. Discuss the role of one of them in relation to young people.
3. Go to the reference library and ask for the *Report of the Review Group on the Youth Service in England*, Cmnd 8686. After studying it, choose what you consider are two of its more important recommendations. Then discuss their significance.
4. Find the names of five organisations in your area which cater for young people. Give the name and address of their secretaries and write a short paragraph on each, outlining their main activities.

Reading

A Joint Statement on DES Circular 1/85 (National Youth Bureau, March 1986).
Albermarle Report, *The Youth Service in England and Wales*, Cmnd 929 (HMSO, 1960).

Annual Report of the Duke of Edinburgh's Award Scheme.

Margaret Bone and Elizabeth Ross, *The Youth Service and Similar Provisions for Young People* (HMSO, 1972).

DES, *Circular 1/85*.

DES, *Provision for Youth*, Discussion Paper (Department of Education and Science, 1975).

HMSO, *Experience and Participation: Report of the Review Group on the Youth Service in England*, Cmnd 8686 (HMSO, October 1982).

National Youth Bureau, *Year Book of the Youth Service in England and Wales*.

14 Employment Services

Employment Offices

The 1909 Labour Exchanges Act created the first national system of labour (now called employment) exchanges. They were the first government offices to be built to provide a service for the people. Their purpose was to reduce unemployment. They could not create work, but unemployment was often due to lack of knowledge – workers not being aware of jobs available perhaps only a few miles away and employers not being aware of the labour available locally. At first the trade unions were suspicious of the labour exchanges, fearing they would supply workers willing to accept less than the trade-union rate. Originally run by the Board of Trade, they became the responsibility of the newly created Ministry of Labour (now called the Department of Employment), in 1917.

Employment services today

The 1973 Employment and Training Act removed responsibility for employment and vocational training services from the Department of Employment to a newly created Manpower Services Commission (MSC) which operated through two bodies – the Employment Services Agency and the Training Services Agency – but are now run directly by similar divisions of the MSC. But the employees of the MSC remain civil servants. The Department of Employment still has overall responsibility for manpower strategy and industrial relations. Thus the government employment services are now run directly by the Employment Services Division of the MSC operating through jobcentres. There are, of course, private employment exchanges. Employment services provided by jobcentres include information on jobs available, advice on job opportunities and, in the main centres, there are occupational guidance units which help people with special problems and needs.

Since the 1940s there has been a separate service, with its own management structure, for professional, executive, managerial, technical and scientific appointments. It is now known as Professional and Executive Recruitment and it is located on its own premises in certain key centres and its operations are based on a nationwide register of jobs and job-seekers. Employers are charged a fee for this service.

Unemployment benefit offices of the Department of Employment pay unemployment benefit through the post on behalf of the DHSS. Advice and assistance are also given to redundant workers by the Employment Services Division, but the Department of Employment still has responsbility for the Redundancy Fund and redundancy payments.

Vocational Training

Technological progress means that at any given time some industries are declining and some expanding, and the problem is to move workers from the declining industries into those that are expanding. This often necessitates a worker undergoing a course of retraining to learn new skills. In many cases, particularly if the workers seeking a new occupation are young, the employer will arrange for training to be given. In cases where retraining is not given by employers the government may arrange training by means of vocational training schemes. As indicated above, this vocational training is the responsibility of the Training Service Division of the MSC. The training is carried out in skillcentres (previously known as government training centres) and now administered by the Skill Centre Training Agency of the MSC, but it can be provided in colleges of further or higher education and employers' establishments.

Both employed and unemployed workers aged 18 or over are accepted for training and are paid by the government a training allowance which, in order to encourage people to take up training, is markedly above the rate of unemployment benefit or supplementary benefit.

The first government training centres were established in 1925, but it is only within the last fifteen or so years that any significant expansion in retraining has taken place. The range and levels of the courses are now much greater than they used to be, and continue to be extended. The vocational training scheme was known as TOPS (training opportunities scheme), but is now called the job training scheme. Employers who allow their premises to be used for training receive a payment from the MSC.

About a third of the skillcentres have been closed, mainly those underused but a mobile instructor force is being developed. Furthermore, employers will probably have to pay higher fees for training specially geared to their needs. The aim is for the Skill Centre Training Agency to recover its costs.

Industrial Training Boards

Virtually all industries had their own industrial training board to encourage training within the industry, and the Manpower Services Commission had the job of co-ordinating the work of these industrial training boards on matters of common concern and helping the boards with their training responsibilities.

The MSC gave financial support to industrial training boards which carried out training schemes. Other bodies providing suitable training and, sponsored by industry, could also receive financial support from the MSC. However, the 1981 Employment and Training Act has resulted in the abolition of sixteen of the twenty-three boards, and the remaining boards must finance training themselves from a levy on employers. But, with some boards, employers, whose training is satisfactory, are exempt from payment of most of the levy.

Services for Disabled People

The shortage of manpower during the Second World War underlined the importance of getting servicemen and factory workers back to work after injury and was one of the main factors in the development of services for the disabled. The first major scheme for training and resettlement of the disabled started in 1941 under the auspices of the then Ministry of Labour working in co-operation with the then Ministry of Health. Its object was the rehabilitation of war casualties.

The present services to help disabled people find jobs are based on the Disabled Persons (Employment) Acts of 1944 and 1958, and these Acts are based on the findings of two committees – the Tomlinson Committee which reported in 1943, and the Piercy Committee which reported in 1956. A register of disabled people in the area is kept at the employment office, but registration is voluntary. (Under the 1970 Chronically Sick and Disabled Persons Act local authorities must seek out the disabled and make known to them the services available.)

Disablement Resettlement Officers

Each large employment office or jobcentre, now administered by the Employment Services Division of the MSC, has a disablement resettlement officer (DRO) who gives advice to disabled people on jobs and, when necessary, on rehabilitation and training. He or she is advised by a local disablement advisory committee now known as the committee for the employment of disabled people (CEDP), and others including the disabled person's family doctor. The Secretary of State for Employment is advised by the National Advisory Council on Employment of the Disabled.

Employment Rehabilitation Centres

Some disabled people can be found jobs alongside ablebodied people without special training. Others need rehabilitating and the Employment Services Division runs rehabilitation centres where disabled people can adjust themselves gradually to normal working conditions. They are not taught new skills but given confidence and vocational guidance. The staff includes doctors, occupational psychologists, social workers, disablement resettlement officers and workshop supervisors with a knowledge of industry. The DRO at the centre and the DRO at the employment office or jobcentre co-operate when the time comes to find the disabled person a job. In recent years mentally disabled people have been accepted at the centres. A few rehabilitation centres are run by voluntary organisations and receive financial assistance from the Manpower Services Commission.

Sheltered workshops

For those disabled people who will not be able to work under normal conditions there are sheltered workshops run by Remploy Limited, a non-profit-making company mainly financed by the Manpower Services Commission. Its board is appointed by the Secretary of State for Employment, who is the minister responsible for it. Some local authorities and voluntary bodies also run sheltered workshops with the help of grants from the MSC.

Blind people

There are special services for blind people and some employment offices have blind persons resettlement officers. The Manpower Services Commission gives financial assistance to those local authorities and voluntary organisations which provide sheltered employment for blind workers.

Additional training for disabled people

Where possible disabled people make use of the training facilities that the non-disabled use, the Job Training Scheme for example and for young disabled people the Youth Training Scheme. Some go to skillcentres, some to technical and commercial colleges for training, some are trained for a professional career. Some employers are prepared to give training in skilled or semi-skilled work; and some voluntary organisations give training aided by grants from the Training Services Division.

Employers and disabled people

Under the 1944 Disabled Persons (Employment) Act employers of twenty or more persons must normally employ a quota of disabled people.

The Unemployed

Helping the young unemployed

Unemployment in the United Kingdom has risen from 2.9 per cent of the work-force in 1974 to 13.4 per cent in July 1985, when it was still rising. If those unemployed who are not registered and those on temporary work schemes are included, the number of unemployed (December 1986) is around 4 million. If there were no temporary work schemes, half the young people under 18 would be unemployed.

A twelve-month voluntary youth training scheme (YTS) was introduced in 1983 for all school-leavers aged 16. By 1986 it had been extended to two years for 16-year-olds and one year for 17-year-olds. It gives job related training leading to a recognised vocational qualification. There is a training allowance. Training is provided by private employers, nationalised industries and local authorities. The scheme is financed by the government, the employers and the European Social Fund. The MSC is advised on the work of the programmes by a special programmes board comprising representatives from the CBI and the TUC and also education and careers services of local government and youth and voluntary organisations. Local area boards give more detailed supervision. Most of the young people who finish the youth training course will not get a job, but the course should improve their job prospects in the long term. There is a danger that unscrupulous employers will use the scheme as a source of cheap labour.

The MSC administers a community industry scheme which provides disadvantaged young people with temporary practical work of benefit to the local community. A weekly wage is paid. The scheme is run under the auspices of the National Association of Youth Clubs and managed by a board on which sit representatives of interested bodies. Payments are paid to employers who take on young people full-time in their first year of employment.

The long-term unemployed

Private firms and nationalised industries have been encouraged to sponsor work schemes for the adult unemployed. These schemes are part of a programme launched by the MSC and which began on 1 April 1981 under the title *community enterprise programme* and now known as the *community programme*. It provides up to a year's paid employment. As the title suggests, the work provided is mainly concerned with improving the local environment. But there are other types of project. A district health authority in Merseyside has sponsored a variety of health schemes (see *Health Service Journal*, 26 June 1986). Other measures to help adult unemployment include encouragement of short-time working and early retirement and job splitting to reduce redundancies. Financial help is provided by the MSC to help unemployed people and those under the threat of redundancy in their search for a job in another part of the country.

The Voluntary Projects Programme enables unemployed people to do unpaid voluntary work without losing benefit. And for those who wish to start their own business there is an Enterprise Allowance Scheme (EAS) which gives them £40 a week for a year providing they raise £1,000 to start the business. Other schemes to mitigate the evil of unemployment are the Wider Opportunities Training Programme which provides courses to help people get a job; a Job Restart Programme whereby the long-term unemployed are given counselling interviews to help them find work. In this connexion, a network of jobclubs are to be opened at jobcentres which will not only provide counselling but also free use of stationery equipment – typewriter, photocopier, etc. A job training scheme – a successor to the Training Opportunities Scheme (TOPS) launched in 1978 – has been introduced to teach new skills needed by employers and add to skills a person already has. And what is called the Job Start Allowance pays £20 a week for six months to anyone over 18 who has been out of work for 12 months or more and who takes a full-time job paying less than £80 a week. The £20 is, however, taxable but does not affect FIS or Housing Benefit.

Ethnic Minorities

Some of the ethnic minority groups (e.g. Asian peoples) have difficulty with the English language. For these there are special courses in literacy.

Women

In 1951 women comprised 31 per cent of the labour force. In 1986 they comprised 40 per cent. Approximately 3.4 million work part time and 5.4 million full time. On the other hand, 12.4 million men work full time and 0.7 million part time. About a quarter of a million workers work at home and do not bother to go on the unemployment register.

While many women are in secure full-time jobs with pay and conditions comparable with men's (in central and local government, for example) most women workers are found in low-paid jobs – distribution, textiles, clothing and footwear; for example, 44 per cent of these low paid are clerical workers. The 1975 Sex Discrimination Act and the 1975 Equal Pay Act have helped women to gain more employment opportunities. However, when a woman is interviewed for a job along with men and a man gets the job, it may be a case of sex discrimination, but how can it be proved? But the law is helping to change attitudes, albeit slowly. (In the same way it is difficult to prove racial discrimination, but, again, since the 1976 Race Relations Act, there seems to be less racial prejudice.)

Health and Safety at Work

Concern for the health and safety of workers began with the Factory Acts in the nineteenth century to protect workers in the textile trade and was extended in the latter half of the century to workers in other industries. The first legislation to protect miners was the 1842 Mines Act. Under Public Health Acts, local authorities can enforce sanitary standards in places of work. The 1961 Factories Act is the last in a long line of Factory Acts. The 1963 Offices, Shops and Railway Premises Act at last gave some protection to office workers. The 1954 Mines and Quarries Act protects underground workers and there are special Acts to protect farm workers, railway workers and seamen.

The 1974 Health and Safety at Work Act (operative from 1 April 1975) strengthened the enforcement procedures of previous Acts and extended their scope. Eventually it is intended to provide one comprehensive set of rules covering health and safety at work which will mean the gradual replacement of existing Acts covering health and safety. Under the 1974 Act responsibility for health and safety at work has been hived off from the Department of Employment and given to a Health and Safety Commission responsible to Parliament via the Secretary of State for Employment. It has six advisory committees on toxic substances. The 1974 Act set up a Health and Safety Executive responsible for enforcement, though working in co-operation with local authorities. In 1973 the Employment Medical Advisory Service was set up with the job of identifying health risks at work. Since 1975 it has operated within the Health and Safety Executive. It took over from the Medical Services Division of the Department of Employment. General practitioners and the advisory service must work closely together. Many employers, of course, voluntarily maintain a medical service for their employees.

Employment Protection

The 1975 Employment Protection Act, operative from November 1975, set up an Advisory, Conciliation and Arbitration Service (ACAS) to improve industrial relations, protect and extend the rights of employees, including the requirement that firms should consult appropriate trade unions about proposed redundancies. More detailed protection of employees was provided in the 1978 Employment Protection (Consolidation) Act.

The 1975 Sex Discrimination Act and the 1975 Equal Pay Act can be included under employment protection, and protect mainly women. The 1976 Race Relations Act makes it illegal to discriminate on the ground of colour or race when considering someone for a job or for training. Arising from all the above Acts, mainly geared to protect employees, there has been a big increase in the number of cases referred to industrial tribunals set up under the 1964 Industrial Training Act. Employees are making much more use of them to remedy what they consider injustices at work. But it is suggested that the tribunals have aggravated unemployment because small firms are unwillimg to take on workers in case they are taken before a tribunal when trade recession necessitates dismissals. But only 4 per cent of dismissals are referred to a tribunal. Appeals can be made from a tribunal to an employment appeal tribunal.

Careers Service

History

As far back as 1910 the Education (Choice of Employment) Act empowered local authorities to give advice on careers to young people under 17. The 1909 Labour Exchanges Act set up the first state labour exchanges, many of which had juvenile departments to help young people find a job. In the interwar years some local authorities ran a juvenile employment service; some left it to the Ministry of Labour to provide.

The 1948 Employment and Training Act unified the service centrally by setting up a central youth employment executive to deal with central administration consisting of representatives from the Department of Labour, the Department of Education and the Scottish Education Department. But the dual system of local authority youth employment in some areas and Department of Employment services for youth employment in other areas continued. The 1973 Employment and Training Act ended the dual system and, since April 1974, all local authorities in England and Wales have to provide a careers service. Today the Secretary of State for Employment is in charge of the central administration, advised by a careers service advisory council. Most local authorities have a careers service committee.

What the careers service provides

It provides young people attending school or college with information and advice to help them choose a career, and help in finding employment when they have completed their full-time education. Special attention is given to disabled and disadvantaged young people. But the service can be extended to include all young people in their early years of employment. If necessary, it follows up the careers of young people who have started work to see how they are getting on and gives further advice if required. But its value is not simply finding young people jobs but in helping them to make the best use of their talents. It works closely with the Manpower Services Commission.

Some Problems

A high level of employment is important for social welfare. It provides income and reduces claims on the social services. On the other hand, unemployment leads to a greater demand on the social services because it may lead to illness, poverty, and housing neglect, family breakdown, crime and suicide. In addition there is the financial cost to the nation arising from benefits paid to the unemployed, taxes foregone and output lost as well as the extra financial burden placed on the social services, both statutory and voluntary. But the number of people in work depends to a great extent on government economic policy – the employment services can only marginally affect the employment situation. At the present time (1986) there are about 3¼ million registered unemployed.

The success of the employment services depends on the degree to which they are used, both by employers and those seeking work. In the past the local employent exchanges were thought of as places of last resort for those who could not find a job – there was a feeling of humiliation at having to use one. They needed to get a new image, to develop as an expert agency on careers guidance for everyone (even the retired) so that it would be quite natural even for a person in a good job, seeking a change, to consult the local employment office. Progress had been made in this direction by the development of sections which deal with special categories of workers, especially the Professional and Executive Recruitment Service and, more recently, the Occupational Guidance Service and the Training Opportunities Service.

But the biggest single factor in providing a new image has been the creation of jobcentres. These are bright and attractively furnished and easily located. They have a better placement record than the old exchanges. Another factor was giving the work of finding employment to an Employment Services Agency, now the Employment Services Division of the MSC, and leaving the payment of unemployment benefit to the Department of Employment. This separation of the two functions means that the image of the employment service is not dulled by its association with unemployment and the 'dole' even if 'dole' is now paid by Giro cheque. (While the unemployed must register for work to qualify for state benefits, there is no obligation on employers to notify vacancies.)

The current lack of job opportunities has led to the organisation of temporary work schemes and training already referred to. Without them the unemployment figures would be higher.

The expansion of vocational training is necessary and requires much greater co-operation than there is at the moment between employers, teachers and the Training Services Division. Employers may expect only skills to be taught that they consider strictly relevant to the job. Teachers, while accepting the importance of these skills, are also concerned with the all-round development of students and their role not just in the firm but in the wider society. This applies to retraining courses for older people, but especially to 16–19-year-olds, many of whom go on day-release courses to further education colleges. But it is not only a matter of training – it is very important that much greater knowledge of the needs of the labour market should be developed so that those who are trained can get a job for which their training qualifies them. Work on this is still done by the Department of Employment.

Many workers are reluctant to volunteer for retraining, but this may be partly due to the limited number of skills that have been taught, and for some it is hard to get training. If greater use is made of technical colleges, a much wider variety of courses should become available.

The main responsibility for training rests with employers. The scrapping of so many industrial training boards (first introduced in 1964) by the government, because the boards had done little to increase the number of trained people, does perhaps suggest that many employers show little enthusiasm for training. This may be one of the reasons for Britain's lack of competitiveness in certain industries. In 1981 two-thirds of British workers had no vocational qualifications (*National Institute Economic Review*, 26 November 1981).

What may go some way towards remedying this are two programmes on which planning began in 1982. One is the Open Tech programme 'to widen training opportunities for adults in technician and supervisory skills'. Both unemployed people and employed people are eligible. The other is a four-year technical and vocational course of training for young people commencing at the age of 14 referred to in Chapter 12. The Manpower Services Commission has overall responsibility for them but works closely with the Department of Education and Science and teachers in schools and colleges.

The 1970 Chronically Sick and Disabled Persons Act has led to greater co-operation between local authorities and the Department of Employment. But the employment services for disabled people can only be successful if employers are willing to employ them and provide jobs commensurate with their abilities. Many firms do not take the quota of disabled people they are legally supposed to, though annual awards are made by the MSC to firms who go out of their way to make employment available. The comparatively recent legislation aimed at giving the employee greater security and job satisfaction is an indication of the growing awareness that employment is a partnership between employer and employee, and an equal partnership at that. How fast it will lessen industrial conflict will depend largely on Britain's ability to succeed in economic terms.

However, two developments will be seen by some people as backward steps in the development of good industrial relations. One is that young people under 21 are no longer protected by wages council regulations. This means they will have to accept lower wages but the Government argue this is a good thing because young people will then have a better chance of getting a job. And wages councils for those over 21 can no longer make regulations relating to holiday pay and holiday entitlements. In this connexion it is important to remember that wages councils were set up to protect workers in those trades and industries subject to low wages and where trade union organisation was weak. Secondly, the Government agrees with certain economists that to be more competitive and to provide more job opportunities wage settlements must be much lower. Some people see the trade union legislation introduced by the Thatcher government and the experience of the miners' strike as part of a deliberate government attempt to weaken the trade union movement's bargaining position. On the other hand, there are those, and the Government is one, who think that certain trade unions had become too powerful.

With regard to the careers service, the careers officers of a local authority must co-operate with schools and colleges, particularly with the teachers who give careers advice. They must co-operate with employers and know the job opportunities in all fields of employment, which necessitates not only contacting employers but working closely with employment officers at jobcentres or employment offices. In some local areas liaison committees have been set up comprising representatives of the careers service, the Employment Services Division and Training Services Division. At the same time careers officers must interview and keep in contact with the young people and also with their parents. This is asking a great deal of careers officers: hence the importance of training and staffing. The Piercy Committee, set up in 1951 to consider the recruitment and training of careers officers (then called youth employment officers), recommended a full-time training course of one year for new recruits. For many years little progress was made with this recommendation. It is only in recent years that much greater attention has been paid to training, and most careers officers are qualified in some way. But in view of the recent cuts in public expenditure adequate staffing may not be possible.

Summary

The employment training services and the employment services, including employment services for disabled people, have been hived off from the Department of Employment and are the responsibility of the Manpower Services Commission operating through its Training Services Division and Employment Services Division, but the Secretary of State for Employment still has general repsonsibility for them. The Manpower Services Commission comprises representatives from the employers, the trade unions, local government and the professions, plus nominees of the minister. Similarly, responsibility for health and safety at work has been hived off from the Department of Employment to a health and safety executive.

The Department of Employment, among other things, has direct responsibility for industrial relations, the Redundancy Fund and the payment of unemployment benefit.

The new structure has helped to improve the image of the employment services.

It has also improved the relationship between staff and clients, as the staff can concentrate on employment problems without the risk of possible friction with clients associated sometimes in the past with telling clients how much unemployment benefit they were entitled to. But with unemployment now over 3 million, staff in the employment service must feel very discouraged. However, the employment service is not only concerned with helping people to find a job, it is also concerned with their training, protecting their health and safety while at work and helping them as employees in their relationship with employers. The MSC has launched a number of work and training programmes to help soften the blow of unemployment and improve the quality of the existing work-force.

To reduce unemployment, two schools of thought – one incom-

patible with the other – are currently (1986) competing for
Government favour. One is for tax cuts; the other is for increased
investment on what is known as the infrastructure – roads, sewers,
hospitals, schools and housing – necessitating increased public
expenditure. On the causes of the present unemployment there are
economists who think it is due to wages being too high (aggravated
by too-generous welfare benefits) which make our exports less
competitive. Another school of economists says unemployment is
due to lack of demand aggravated by monetarist economic policies.
To the layman it must seem odd that we spend millions of pounds on
training and temporary work schemes to keep the unemployed from
despairing and yet we cannot provide them with a regular job of
work essential to the well-being of the country.

Assignments

1. Obtain the latest *Annual Report* of the Manpower Services
   Commission (which will normally send you a copy on request)
   and, after reading it, make your own summary of the main
   developments during the past year. Discuss what, in your
   opinion, is one of the most interesting developments, explaining
   why you think it is interesting.
2. Outline the purpose of two of the services or schemes discussed
   in the *Annual Report* of the MSC. Discuss how far they are, in
   your opinion, realising the purpose for which they were introduced.
3. What services are there to help disabled people to find employment? The Manpower Services Commission, the local employment exchange or jobcentre, certain voluntary bodies and
   perhaps your local authority can provide material to help you
   with this question.
4. Why do you think most women workers are found in low-paid
   jobs? The National Advisory Committee on Careers for Women
   might help you with this one.
5. When you are working, either for a private firm or in the public
   service, what laws are there to try to ensure that you are treated
   fairly by your employer and that you come to no physical harm?
6. Show the connection between employment and the cost of the
   social services.

Reading

Action for Jobs (Central Office of Information 1986).
Albermarle Report *The Future Development of the Youth Employment Service: Report of a Working Party* (HMSO, 1965).
W. H. Beveridge, *Full Employment in a Free Society*, 2nd edn (Allen & Unwin, 1960).
DE News (Department of Employment).
Health and Safety at Work Commission, *Occupational Health Services: The Way Ahead: A Discussion Document*, 2nd edn (1978).
Health and Safety at Work Commission, *Report 1980–1* (HMSO, January 1982).
Local Government Training Board, *A Career as a Careers Officer* (Local Government Training Board, n.d.).
MSC, *Annual Report* (Manpower Services Commission).
Robens Report, *Safety and Health at Work*, Cmnd 5034 (HMSO, 1974).
Jim Tomlinson, *Monetarism: Is There an Alternative?* (Basil Blackwell, 1986) Ch. 2 Reducing Unemployment.

15 Housing

History

It was the danger to public health from slums which led the state to take an interest in housing. Acts of Parliament in 1868 and 1875, and strengthened in 1879 and 1882, gave local authorities powers to deal with insanitary property and areas, even if they were privately owned. But they were permissive acts; compensation had to be paid, so little was done, except in Birmingham under the leadership of Joseph Chamberlain. The 1875 Public Health Act permitted local authorities to make bye-laws laying down minimum standards for new housing. The 1980 Housing Act consolidated previous legislation, made it mandatory for local authorities to deal with insanitary property and areas, and strengthened the laws relating to minimum standards for new housing. It also made it clear that local authorities could build new houses themselves, but, before 1914, only a few did – the vast majority of new houses before 1914 were built by private enterprise and some private-enterprise housing bodies had built homes for working-class tenants. Local authorities concentrated on demolishing insanitary houses, but progress was slow because of the opposition of vested interests. But, by 1914, new housing was sanitary, some progress had been made on slum clearance, there was a little local authority housing and, of interest for the future, housing schemes, deliberately planned to be aesthetically pleasing, had been completed by private enterprise – Bourneville (1879), Port Sunlight (1888) and Letchworth Garden City (1903).

It was not until after the First World War that a housing shortage was officially acknowledged. One reason for this was the growing acceptance in government circles that decent housing was a basic human need and leaving its provision to the free play of supply and demand had left many people without decent housing.

The core of the housing problem was and still is this: if housing is a basic human need, what can be done for people who cannot afford to buy a house or rent a decent dwelling? The first attempt to tackle this problem was the coalition government's 1919 Housing and Town Planning Act (Addison Act). It mandated local authorities, with the aid of a government subsidy, to build houses for letting below the economic rent. Rent control, introduced during the war on certain private houses to stop profiteering, was continued.

In 1923 the Conservative government introduced a new policy. Both local authority and private-enterprise housing was subsidised by the government, but local authorities were only permitted to build for rent if private enterprise could not do so. But under the first Labour government, which came to office in 1924, the Wheatley Act once again allowed local authorities to build houses for letting at subsidised rents irrespective of what private enterprise was doing. The Wheatley Act also increased the government subsidy but, for the first time, the rate fund had to share part of the subsidy. Under this policy many local authority housing estates were built. Unfortunately, low-income-group families could not afford even the subsidised rents so the council houses benefited mainly the better-off working-class people. Differential rent schemes were made permissible by the central government but few local authorities operated them. Even under the Wheatley Act the vast majority of houses were built by private enterprise mainly for sale.

A new housing policy was inaugurated by the National government in 1933. Local authorities were to concentrate on slum clearance (started by the Labour government's 1930 Housing Act) aided by government subsidy, while private enterprise was to build, without subsidy, houses for rent and for sale for all classes. This policy inaugurated a great era of slum clearance and house-building which helped Britain to get out of the inter-war slump.

By 1939 many working-class people had local authority rented houses and a fair number had become owner-occupiers. But the vast majority of working-class people lived in private rented accommodation built before 1914 and much of it sub-standard.

Housing Policy since 1945

Subsidised local authority housing has provided rented housing. Until 1949 local authority housing had been for working-class families, but in that year the Labour government, in order to encourage mixed social groupings on council estates, abolished the rule.

Unsubsidised private enterprise housing has provided houses for sale and some rented accommodation, mainly flats.

Rent control was abolished in 1957 on all houses except those with very low rateable values, the assumption being that there was enough accommodation for everyone. The abolition of rent control would, it was claimed, cause a shake-out and all would eventually be in accommodation suited to their pocket, if not their needs. Rented accommodation, which since 1945 had disappeared, would again be on the market as landlords would be able to increase rents and make enough money to keep their property in good repair. But it did not work out that way mainly because the supply of houses in relation to demand was overestimated. As a result, the 1965 Rent Act reintroduced rent control for all furnished and unfurnished accommodation, except that at the luxury end of the market. Part of the 1980 Housing Act provided a much more modest step to help bring more rented accommodation on to the market. It allows 'shorthold' lettings whereby tenants have security of tenure at a 'fair' rent for an agreed period of between one and five years. This does not affect existing regulated tenancies. Furthermore, in England and Wales, under a system of 'assured tenancies', houses can be built and let by approved bodies at rents outside the provisions of the Rent Acts. At the Conservative Party Annual Conference, October 1986, the Housing Minister committed the Party to relaxing rent controls in the private sector should it win the next general election. Rent control would be abolished for new tenancies.

Slum clearance has continued but on a diminishing scale (see below).

Improvement grants to encourage home improvements were introduced in the 1949 Housing Act.

There are three types of statutory assistance to poorer people to help them pay their rents: (a) rent rebate for council tenants; (b) rent allowance for private tenants; (c) supplementary benefit. Since 22 November 1982 under the 1982 Social Security and Housing Benefits Act, people on supplementary benefit living in council houses have had their rents and rates paid by the local authority instead of receiving an allowance for housing in their supplementary benefit. Similarly, from April 1983, those on supplementary benefit living in private accommodation have had their rent and rates paid by the local authority and, if owner-occupiers, their rates paid. The cost to the local authority is refunded by the DHSS. The new scheme should be of great benefit to those local authorities who are owed millions of pounds in rent arrears.

However, under the 1986 Social Security Act, operative from 1988, if the Government wins the next General Election, all households, even the poorest, will have to pay a percentage of their rates.

There is a rate-rebate scheme for owner-occupiers and those who pay rent which include rates if their income is below a certain level. Owner-occupiers of less expensive properties receive tax relief on mortagage repayments.

Under the 1980 Housing Act it is now obligatory for local authorities to sell their houses at a discount on the market price to sitting tenants who wish to become owners. The percentage discount depend on the length of tenancy.

A housing corporation has been set up to promote the growth of housing associations and give them financial help and guidance in the building of homes. Housing associations are non-profit making.

The 1977 Housing (Homeless Persons) Act made it obligatory for local authorities to provide accommodation for defined groups of homeless people.

The 1980 Housing Act had given tenants of council houses security of tenure and more freedom in the planning of their homes including subletting and taking in lodgers. No tenant can be evicted without a court order. Tenants of private accommodation already had a high degree of security of tenure.

Some comparative statistics

In England and Wales between 1919 and 1923 about 65,000 houses a year were built, between 1923 and 1932 about 200,000 a year, and between 1932 and 1939 about 300,000 a year. The 300,000 mark was not reached again until 1964. Over 400,000 a year were built in 1967 and 1968 but the number has declined since those peak years. In 1974, for example, only 278,000 dwellings were completed in Great Britain, and in 1984 198,400.

In 1914 there were 8 million dwellings in England and Wales

while in 1982 there were over 18 million. The number of dwellings has more than doubled, yet the population has only increased by just over a quarter. In fact there is actually a surplus of homes over households, but because they are unevenly distributed there are towns where there is an acute housing shortage.

In the interwar years most houses were built by private enterprise. Since 1945 about two-thirds have been built by public enterprise, mainly by local authorities and new town development corporations. With higher living standards house ownership has greatly increased. In 1914, 90 per cent of the houses were rented from private landlords; in 1980 just over 50 per cent were owner-occupied. Less than 3 million houses are now rented from private landlords and 75 per cent of these are over fifty years old.

In 1984 the total housing stock for Great Britain was divided as follows:

Owner-occupied	61 per cent
Public rented	28 per cent
Private rented	11 per cent

In December 1979 for Great Britain the age of housing was as follows:

Constructed since 1944	46 per cent
Constructed 1919–44	23 per cent
Constructed pre-1919	31 per cent

The Administration of Housing

Housing policy is the responsibility of the Secretary of State for the Environment. He is advised by the civil servants in his department.

The minister has no direct control over private builders except in the matter of minimum standards of building construction for new houses and their location. Such controls are enforced by local authorities. But he may influnece private builders during the course of normal contact with their representatives on the advisory committees and elsewhere. The private builders themselves have set up the National House Building Council in an attempt to set standards and controls by inspection and certification. It has government support but many private builders have not joined it.

The minister exercises a great deal of control over local authorities' housing policies. To build houses, local authorities must borrow money but first must get the minister's approval for doing so and, at the same time, submit their housing plan to his department for approval. Although rents and rates help to finance local authority housing, the central government gives substantial financial help. Local authorities therefore have a certain degree of discretion but must work within a fairly tight framework of regulations laid down by central government. The 1957 Housing Act imposes a duty on local authorities to assess not only housing conditions but also housing *needs*. It permits local authorities to build, convert, acquire, enlarge or improve property to meet housing needs.

Substandard Housing

In spite of much slum clearance there are in England and Wales roughly 2½ million dwellings (nearly one-sixth of the housing stock) that are below standard. They lack some standard amenity such as a bath or are in need of some essential repair.

What is being done about sub-standard housing?

Local authorities can provide grants to private owners for home improvements, such as putting in a bath or inside toilet, and for necessary repairs. Local authorities can also provide grants for general improvements to large houses or for converting them into flats.

Under the 1969 Housing Act local authorities can also designate 'general improvement areas' and improve the environment and encourage house-owners to improve their homes with the aid of grants. Under the 1974 Housing Act local authorities can declare 'housing action areas', where they have powers to compel landlords to make improvements to their property to enable a whole area to be improved. At the same time there are government grants to local authorities towards the improvements to a particular area.

Under legislation going back to the nineteenth century, landlords can be compelled by the local authority to do repairs necessary for the health of the occupant.

Under the 1968 Rent Act a local authority can issue a certificate of disrepair on a house, and this entitles the tenant to a reduced rent until the repairs have been carried out.

A tenant can request a local authority to make the landlord install standard amenities, but improvements would normally mean an increase in rent which some tenants may feel unable to meet.

Finally, slum clearance continues but now on a much reduced scale as there is more emphasis on repairs and modernisation. The central government gives a great deal of financial support to local authorities for all aspects of their housing activities. Relatively more money is given to those authorities with greater housing needs.

Although good progress has been made in slum clearance, high-rise flats, in which many people from the slums were housed, have been found unsatisfactory for families with children. But improvement to 'twilight' housing is slow, especially in the inner-city areas. Many owner-occupiers are too poor to improve their homes even with the aid of grants. Some landlords do not care, being quite content with the income they are receiving from their property as it is.

Because of cuts in the central government grant for housing, local authorities have found it difficult to keep their housing stock in good repair. One attempt to mitigate this problem is the 1986 Housing and Planning Act which makes it easier for local authorities to sell off housing estates to private developers or private trusts. This is of particular interest to local authorities in the conurbations where the unpopularity of certain housing estates and, in some cases, faults in their construction, have led to their general deterioration aggravated by vandalism. The act also provides for a bigger discount on the market price for local authority tenants wishing to buy their rented house.

The 1972 Housing Finance Act laid down a fair-rents procedure to enable landlords to obtain bigger rents and thus have a greater inducement to keep their houses in good repair.

Summary

The housing shortage, officially recognised after the First World War, is still with us, for, despite much housebuilding and slum clearance, one-sixth of our dwellings are sub-standard and therefore we still have a long way to go before everyone is in an adequate home. Even worse there are still people without a home. The big drop in the number of houses built in recent years and the financial difficulties in maintaining the housing stock, both private and public might well result in a serious worsening of the housing situation in the future.

Private rented housing is still scarce, though housing associations do meet some of the need for rented housing. In recent years housing has suffered greatly from public expenditure cuts.

More investment in housing is obviously needed but, in view of the constraints on public expenditure arising from the Thatcher government's economic theory, how to do it? One suggestion is to abolish mortgage tax relief and use the money saved for housing investment. But when the numbers who benefit from such a subsidy outnumber those in need of adequate accommodation, will a political party risk losing votes by supporting such a policy? On the other hand there are those, even in the Conservative Party, who believe that public expenditure should be increased, even at the expense of tax cuts, and invested on the infrastructure, including housing.

In the past great emphasis was placed on new housing. Not only were slums demolished but so was older property that was still adequate and often substantially built. In recent years the knocking-down policy has been modified and much more emphasis had ben placed on rehabilitation of older property, aided by the concept of 'housing action areas'. This change in official policy is due to a number of reasons: it is cheaper (in the short run at any rate); it retains housing variety; and, most important, it preserves community life. Older properties are now in much better shape than they were about twenty years ago. Another reason for this is the big rise in house prices leading to a bigger demand for the older but, initially, cheaper houses.

But even if we have enough adequate houses we have to ensure that everyone can afford to move into one. In this connection the rent rebates introduced by the 1972 Housing Finance Act should have helped many poor families to take advantage of local authority housing or move into more adequate private accommodation. But we must be cautious – with housing, what you expect does not always happen, as the abolition of rent control in 1957 illustrated and, in any case, in certain urban areas there is an actual housing shortage in that there are less dwellings than families.

By law, local authorities have to borrow the money to build their houses but they also receive financial help from the government. But the loan charges are a great burden in view of continuing high interest rates. In addition, there is the cost of repairs and management, so that despite higher rents local authorities suffer a big financial loss on council housing, whereas before 1940, when loan charges were small, they actually made a surplus on council housing. This had led to the sale of council houses to sitting tenants. It is argued that not only will this save money for the local authority but it will also give the former tenant a new pride in his home, and greater mobility. On the other hand, some people argue that to reduce the housing stock of a local authority where there is a waiting-list for council houses will only make it more difficult for some families to get a home.

Under-use of housing is another problem. There are houses standing empty, there are large houses with few people living in them and there is homelessness.

There are those who say that council housing should be only for those who cannot afford to buy a house and the aim of housing policy should be to have as many owner-occupiers as possible. Owner-occupation is seen as a means of fostering individuality and self-reliance and as something people would prefer anyway. The Conservative Party is the supporter of this viewpoint; and the Labour government in 1977 issued a Green Paper which came out in support of owner-occupation – however, the Labour Party, in line with its support for a more equal homogeneous society, has at the same time supported council housing for all who want it.

One problem with owner-occupation arises when the owners have not the money to pay for necessary repairs, resulting in some districts, in a whole neighbourhood looking shabby.

Another problem which has been given publicity of late is the growing concern at the high cost to those local authorities which house homeless families in hotels, hostels and other private accommodation. Much of this accommodation is in a very run down condition and it would seem that some tenants and some local authorities are being exploited by unscrupulous landlords. And, finally the high cost of houses in the south of England compared with the north is hindering the movement of labour to the south where there are more job opportunities.

Assignments

1. Discuss the view that council houses should only be available to those who cannot afford to buy a house.
2. Find out from your local authority the following:
   (a) the number of council houses it has
   (b) the number of council flats it has
   (c) what proportion of its housing stock it has sold to tenants.
   How far do you agree with the sale of council houses?
3. What policies have been developed to help low-income families obtain and retain adequate housing? How effective do you think these policies have been?
4. Why, when there has been so much house-building in the last sixty years, are there still people without a home? The organisation Shelter might provide you with material for tackling this question.

Reading

Fred Berry, 'New Homes for Old Houses – Does it make Sense?', *Municipal Review* (March 1975).
Christopher Booker and Bennie Gray, 'How Subsidised Housing is Threatening to Bring Local Government to Financial Disaster', *The Observer* (11 May 1975).
Marian Bowley, *Housing and the State 1919–1944* (Allen & Unwin, 1945).
Britain, 1987: An Official Handbook (HMSO).
John Burnett, *Social History of Housing*, 2nd edn (Methuen, 1986).
Catholic Housing Aid Society, *The Housing Poor: A New Appraisal* (1976).
Cullingworth Report, *Council Housing: Purposes, Procedures and Priorities* (HMSO, 1969).
D. Donnison and C. Ungerson, *Housing Policy* (Penguin, 1982).
Duke of Edinburgh Report, *Inquiry into British Housing* (National Federation of Housing Associations, July 1985).
Michael Fleming and Joseph Nellis, 'A New Housing Crisis?', *Lloyds Bank Review* (April 1982).
House of Commons, Housing debate (*Hansard*, vol. 102, no. 158, 25 July 1986).
Chris Holmes, 'Public Money and Private Space', *New Society* (13 February 1975).
Peter Malpass and Alan Murie, *Housing Policy and Practice*, 2nd edn (Macmillan, 1987).

210   *Introduction to the Social Services*

New Society, Special Housing Issue (25 July 1986).
H. Rose, *The Housing Problem* (Heinemann, 1968).
Various pamphlets from 'Shelter', 86 The Strand, London WC2.
David Webster, 'A "Social Market" Answer on Housing', *New Society* (12 November 1981).

16 Planning

History

Town and country planning had its origins in the public health legislation of the nineteenth century. From legislation to create sanitary conditions, it was a logical development to legislation on the layout of towns. The first Housing Town Planning Act was in 1909, and permitted local authorities to prepare schemes for land under development or likely to be developed. The 1932 Town and Country Planning Act extended local authority planning powers to all land, but local authorities could please themselves whether they used them or not, and, for those that did, parliamentary approval was necessary, which often took over three years to obtain and, in the meantime, it was difficult to prevent unwanted development in the planning area. By 1939 only 3 per cent of Britain had official planning schemes. Thus planning in the interwar years was, in practice, limited to public health and house-building standards.

The main planning of the interwar years was the attempt, made under the 1934 Special Areas Act, to attract new industry into those areas of the country worse hit by the Great Depression and known as 'depressed areas'.

The 1945 Distribution of Industry Act changed their name to 'development areas' and enlarged them, but the policy remained the same and is still in operation, though modified by the 1960 Local Employment Act and the 1972 Industry Act.

The depressed areas gave rise to the Barlow Committee Report, published in January 1940, on the geographical distribution of population. It criticised the concentration of population in the London area and supported greater diversification of industry to the regions. To apply this policy it recommended a central planning authority. In 1941 the Uthwatt Committee on Compensation and Betterment and the Scott Committee on Land Utilisation were set

211

up. The three reports of Barlow, Uthwatt and Scott, plus the interest in rebuilding towns arising from bomb destruction during the war, were mainly responsible for the 1947 Town and Country Planning Act, which laid the foundations of the modern planning system.

Planning Administration

The 1947 Act set up a central authority – the Ministry of Town and Country Planning. All land development had to be officially approved to try to ensure the best use of the land, bearing in mind all its various uses – for industry, agriculture, roads, houses, parks, airports, and so on. The ministry laid down the broad planning framework, but the actual planning authorities to whom one wrote for permission to build were the local authorities – county councils and county borough councils, though county councils could delegate planning to the larger district authorities. If planning permission were not granted, or if planning permission had been given for a project to which there were objections, an appeal could be made to the minister and, if need be, a public inquiry could be set up conducted by one of his inspectors to hear all viewpoints and then a report would be made with recommendations for the minister to consider. Furthermore, all planning authorities had to submit development plans to the central government for approval and all building had to conform to the development plan. From time to time development plans were brought up to date. The 1947 Act thus brought in compulsory, creative planning and the administrative procedure it created is more or less the same today, but the Department of the Environment is now the central authority.

The 1968 Planning Act replaced the development plan system of the 1947 Act. Local planning authorities now submit structure plans to the Department of the Environment for approval which set out the principles on which a whole planning area is to be planned, and include possible transport developments and the plan's possible economic consequences. Within the broad policy laid down by the structure plan, local plans are drawn up. The minister is not normally concerned with the local plans, and planning appeals in connection with them are decided by independent inspectors who report to the local authority and who can in fact be appointed by the local authority. Plans may be altered from time to time.

The 1968 Act also provides for public participation in planning in line with the Skeffington Report of 1969, *People and Planning*. Thus individual members of the public and representatives of voluntary organisations can give their views in the formative stage of the structure and local plans. County councils are responsible for the structure (i.e. strategic) planning and district councils for the local plans. Local authorities have wide powers for undertaking development, including compulsory purchase. The Town and Country Planning Acts of 1971 for England and Wales and 1972 for Scotland have consolidated the 1947 Act but have retained its essential features.

One of the problems of planning is that it changes the pattern of an area. Some landowners gain because new development enhances the value of their land, while other landowners suffer compulsory purchase and often feel unfairly compensated. Town and Country Planning Acts of 1953, 1954, 1959 and the 1976 Development Land Tax Act were mainly concerned with this problem of compensation and betterment.

New Towns

The 1946 New Towns Act, consolidated by Acts of 1965 and 1968, provided for the building of new towns after consultation with local authorities and objectors. One of the aims of new towns is to stop the outward sprawl of existing towns, particularly London. Certain areas outside towns are designated as 'green belts' and no development is allowed on these except in special circumstances. The first new towns were built on land beyond the designated green belts.

In more recent years new towns have been seen as growth-points for the economy and some new towns have been built around existing towns – the first was Peterborough in 1968. One of the advantages of building a new town around an existing one is that an established administrative structure already exists.

The building of new towns was entrusted to development corporations financed by the government. Originally the intention was to hand the new towns, when completed, to local government, but the New Towns Act 1959 ruled the development corporations should be dissolved and the new towns be handed over to a

Commission for New Towns. In Wales a new town has been taken over by the Development Board for Rural Wales. Local authorities, however, provide the normal local authority services. The 1976 New Towns (Amendment) Act provides for the transfer of housing and some other assets of the more 'mature' new towns to the local authorities. But, taking Britain as a whole, the Commission has responsibility for the industrial and commercial assets of most of the new towns. There are now in Britain thirty-two new towns completed or still being developed, and financially they have been a success.

The experiment in mixing the social classes in certain of the new towns by having houses for professional people next to houses for, say, factory workers failed due to the class consciousness of British people.

The expansion of new towns has been challenged on the grounds that they help to speed the decline of older towns which are within their sphere of influence. It is true that many of the older towns, including London, are declining in population, due partly to demolition in the inner city areas and due partly to firms moving to less congested areas. This, of course, is not all due to new towns – it is mainly due to the great exodus to surburbia which has been going on for decades encouraged by conventional thinking and government policy.

Urban Renewal

This is a comparatively new concept which embraces the total environment of a town. In some towns slum clearance is still an aspect of urban renewal but there are others – rehabilitating derelict land (witness the 1982 Derelict Land Act), clean air, control of traffic, shopping centres, preservation of interesting areas and buildings, etc. – all those things which help to make a town a pleasanter place in which to live.

The 1952 Town Development Act encouraged local authorities to co-operate on such problems as congestion and overpopulation. For example, one authority may have little or no land for houses, while a neighbouring local authority may have a surplus. Many housing sites have developed from such co-operation. And local authorities may co-operate on building plans because planning in one local authority may affect the build-up of traffic in another local authority.

Special attention is given to traffic, especially since the 1963 Buchanan Report (*Traffic in Towns*) – the first report to emphasise the need, when planning buildings, to take into consideration their possible effect on traffic patterns.

The Clean Air Acts of 1956 and 1968, consolidated by the 1974 Control of Pollution Act, permit local authorities to establish smoke-control areas where the emission of smoke from chimneys (except in special circumstances) is an offence.

Planning Acts lay down that lists of buildings of architectural or historical interest should be compiled by the Secreatry of State for the Environment and the Secretaries of State for Scotland and Wales. To demolish such a building requires special consent from the local planning authority or appropriate Secretary of State. The Secretaries of State also give financial assistance for the repair and maintenance of buildings of outstanding interest.

The 1967 Civic Amenities Act requires local planning authorities to designate 'conservation areas' of special architectural or histori-cal interest, and buildings within such an area may not be demolished without permission. The Historic Buildings and Monu-ments Commission for England, known as English Heritage (there are similar bodies for Scotland and Wales) manages ancient monuments and gives grants to local authorities for the mainten-ance of historic buildings in conservation areas. (Local authorities can make grants or loans for any building of architectural or historical interest.) Voluntary organisations also play an important role in campaigning for the protection of buildings of historic and architectural interest.

Much housing development has gone on in the inner cities and in the outer suburbs but much of it – the tower block type of development – has not been successful because it does not suit family life. Planners and architects have been blamed for not being in close enough contact with the human problems inherent in housing policy. In many cases the new building technology for this type of development has been applied in such a way that faulty constructions have been erected causing much inconvenience to residents and local authority housing departments. Unemployment is aggravated in the inner cities, especially in the northern industrial towns, because of the high proportion of the unemployed who are unskilled.

Since the passing of the 1969 Local Government Grants (Social Need) Act there has been an urban programme through which the Government gives money, in addition to the rate support grant and housing subsidies, to provide facilities in deprived areas which, without the extra money, would not normally be available; for example, day nurseries, centres for the elderly, community centres, language classes for immigrants, etc. The Government pays 75 per cent of the cost of an approved project, the local authority 25 per cent. There is usually a time limit on this kind of government funding. Voluntary organisations, including community care groups, are also involved. The 1978 Inner Urban Areas Act increased resources for urban aid and laid more emphasis on encouraging economic activities. The administration of urban aid at local level takes different forms. In severely deprived large city areas there are inner city partnerships where there is a co-ordinated approach between central and local government. In other deprived areas, local authorities make their own programmes and a project may be carried out by the local authority or a voluntary organisation. In some areas projects are initiated by voluntary organisations – community groups, for example, with the money allotted to them by the local authority. Since 1981 enterprise zones have been set up with an expected life of ten years. In these zones firms can carry on business free of rates and development tax plus income tax and corporation tax concessions.

Arising from urban riots in 1981, money for the urban programme was again increased and a much more radical attempt at urban renewal was attempted by the creation of two urban development corporations for the London and Merseyside docklands respectively. At the Conservative Party Conference 1986 it was announced that the urban development corporation concept was to be extended to other areas. Another response to the riots was the concept of task forces for the inner cities and on 6 February 1986 the Government announced the launching of eight new inner city task forces. Each would be allotted £1 million, which might seem a modest sum, but the aid would be concentrated in a comparatively small area of the inner cities. Like the earlier task forces they would support existing agencies and work closely with local communities. They would be involved with training, urban regeneration and industrial assistance. One very important aspect of urban development corporations, task forces and other development bodies is that, for certain schemes, private organisations have contributed. Thus the G-Mex centre in Manchester was financed by contributions not only from local government but from an insurance company and the European Regional Fund. A very successful operation involving a task force, the government funded Scottish Development Agency, private investment and the local community took place in the eastern part of Glasgow where industry had virtually disappeared and where housing had been knocked down and not replaced. In this area, over a period of ten years, 250 new factories and workshops have been opened and 150,000 houses rebuilt or modernised and an area where nobody wished to live is now a desirable residential area. Critics of the urban aid programme accept that it has slowed down urban decline but feel much larger amounts of public money are needed in the inner cities. They point out that although expenditure on urban aid has been maintained in real terms overall, money provided by the central government for local authorities has been reduced because of cuts in the rate support grant. In the meantime the Government might argue that public expenditure has to be kept under strict control and the urban aid programme is a means of concentrating expenditure where it is most needed. The Government might also argue that it has been successful in finding new sources of financial help from the private sector and stimulated local authorities to plan, if possible, developments with the private sector. But urban corporations, task forces, the MSC's involvement with vocational education, the new plan for technical colleges in inner city areas run by independent trusts do seem to imply, to say the least, a lack of confidence by the Government in local government.

The Countryside

Access to and preservation of the countryside have been of great interest to many people in the last 150 years, especially with the rapid advance of enclosures, including the enclosure of common land from around 1740. The 1949 National Parks and Access to the Countryside Act was the first major Act to deal with the problem. Large areas of land were designated National Parks, looked after by a National Parks Commission. It also empowered county councils to prepare maps showing public rights of way which must be preserved. Local authorities can also create paths. The 1968 Countryside Act set up a Countryside Commission for England and Wales (a 1967 Act set up one for Scotland) which took over the functions of the National Parks Commission. Its main job is to encourage facilities in the countryside so people will get the maximum pleasure from it – for example, the establishment of camping sites, picnic areas and long-distance footpaths. The actual provision of the sites is mainly the work of local authorities working together to form country parks. By 1985 there were in England and Wales, in addition to the National Parks, 200 country parks and 236 picnic sites. In addition the Forestry Commission (established by the Forestry Acts of 1919 and 1945), which is concerned with the conservation of trees and woodland, has opened seven of its forest parks to the public, four of which are in Scotland. Voluntary bodies also play a large part in preserving the amenities of the countryside. For example, the National Trust owns and protects much land and many historic houses for the benefit of the public. In addition, there are approximately 202 national nature reserves in Great Britain supervised by the Nature Conservancy Council, set up in 1973.

The 1971 Dangerous Litter and 1972 Poisonous Waste Act strengthen the provisions for the control of dangerous litter, much of which is dumped in the countryside. A permanent Royal Commission on Environmental Pollution has issued a number of reports, and further legislation will undoubtedly follow.

The 1974 Control of Pollution Act gives wide powers to local authorities and water authorities to control industrial waste and protect water supplies as well as to ensure clean air and control of noise.

The central government gives substantial grants to local authorities to get rid of objects disfiguring the countryside.

In spite of the planning legislation there has been increasing concern in recent years over the destruction of certain types of wild life and areas of special scientific interest. Such destruction has sometimes been carried out by certain farmers in what they consider to be in the interest of farming. For the same reasons hedgerows have been destroyed changing the rural landscape. The 1981 Wildlife and Countryside Act aims to preserve sites of special scientific interest from destruction but for it to be effective farmers and conservationists must work harmoniously together.

Regional Planning

Under the principles first laid down by the 1934 Special Areas Act, financial inducements are offered to businessmen to set up business in depressed areas (called 'development areas' under the 1945 Distribution of Industry Act) in order to help reduce unemployment and obtain balanced economic development nationwide. Increasing aid to development areas led to political pressure for aid to other areas, and following the Report of the Hunt Committee of 1969 (*The Intermediate Areas*) the government designated seven 'intermediate areas' to qualify for financial aid.

Since joining the European Economic Community help for these areas also comes from the European Regional Development Fund and the European Regional Social Fund. The term 'assisted areas' is now used for three different types of areas, which, because of their long-term structural problems, are able, with government help, to offer financial incentives to attract firms. They are – in order of priority – special development areas, development areas and intermediate areas.

In spite of all the acts of Parliament to encourage the more depressed areas of the country to become more prosperous relative to other areas, the disparities between regions are greater than ever. The only consolation is that without these acts (the 1960 Local Employment Act which replaced the 1945 Distribution of Industry Act which, in turn, superseded the 1934 Special Areas Act), the problem might have been much worse. The 1972 Industry Act and urban renewal policies are later attempts to lessen economic imbalance between regions, particularly between the north and south of the country.

Problems Today

Administration

Over the years there has been continuing criticism of the long time it takes for decisions to be made on planning applications. It is hoped that by giving publicity to the number of applications received by the Department of the Environment and local authorities and the time it takes to deal with them it will speed up planning procedures. However, it must be remembered that it is very important for the *right* decision to be made.

But it is not only for the length of time some inquiries take but also their cost. For example, the public inquiry to decide whether to build a nuclear power station at Sizewell lasted 2½ years and the estimated cost to the Central Electricity Generating Board (CEGB) was £50 million and the cost to the Friends of the Earth who opposed the building of the power station was £140,000. The Commons Select Committee on the Environment in a report published September 1986 proposed a two-tier system of inquiry in appropriate cases for the purpose of speeding up inquiries. There would be a first hearing at which national policy issues would be discussed and this would cover the need for the project. At the second hearing only local issues could be discussed. The Committee felt that this system of two hearings would avoid much repetition of the same argument. And an important recommendation to give objectors a fairer crack at the whip was that objectors, who had been asked to give evidence, should have their costs paid by the State.

In the past it has been felt that the professional planners have imposed their ideas on the public. The reason for this, it has been suggested, is that often planners see themselves as servants of the developers. It is now much more appreciated that planners must make decisions the community at large supports. And this implies taking into consideration all the social implications of the plan. To this end, consultation with the public is very necessary. The trouble is that, while everyone supports democratic consultation in theory, comparatively few members of the public participate in it in practice, and the vocal minority does not necessarily reflect the views of the 'silent majority'.

The procedure of public inquiries has been changed to give objectors a fairer chance. One example is that at motorway inquiries objectors can challenge the *need* for the motorway and not just the proposed route as was previously the case.

However, in recent years, there has developed in central government circles the viewpoint that, for certain large projects, the public inquiry procedure is not suitable because these projects are what the Government considers to be in the national interest which must take precedence over regional and local interests. Hence the guardians of the national interest – the democratically elected Government and Parliament – must decide these projects. According to this view, the decision as to what type of power station to build at Sizewell – whether nuclear or non-nuclear – should be decided by the CEGB, subject to the approval of the Government and Parliament. All the public inquiry would have been concerned with would have been where to put the power station.

Green belts

In recent years controversy has arisen over the future of green belt land, particularly in south-east England. House prices are exceptionally high in London and what aggravates the situation is that land for housebuilding is scarce. Many a young couple wanting to set up a home cannot afford to buy a house in London but can afford one in areas beyond the green belt where land is considerably cheaper and where many housing estates have developed. But they then have the problem of travelling a long distance to their work in London. High house prices in London also contribute to inner-city decay because, like the young couple, many people move out to areas where houses are cheaper. Private housebuilders want to build new villages in the Essex green belt arguing that there will be a housing shortage in the south-east unless new homes are built (see John Herington, 'The Outer City Problem', *New Society*, 9 August 1985). In other areas of the country there is pressure from builders to build on green belt land and this is also causing concern. In an address to leaders of the construction industry the Prince of Wales is reported to have said (*Guardian*, 29 October 1986) that farmland was being lost at a rate which would see its disappearance in 200 years.

Summary

Planning is the responsibility of local government supervised by the central government.

Planning arose form the need to mitigate the problems of bad sanitation and unhealthy housing created by the rapid growth of towns (especially industrial towns) in the nineteenth century. It later became concerned with the layout of towns from an aesthetic point of view.

In spite of legislation for land development going back to the first Planning Act of 1909, only 3 per cent of Britain had planning schemes before 1939, but a start had been made with regional development under the 1934 Special Areas Act.

The big advance in planning came after the Second World War with the 1945 Distribution of Industry Act, the 1946 New Towns Act and the 1947 Town and Country Planning Act.

Today planning is not just concerned with land use but with the total environment, including the problem of pollution. The problem of pollution has become much more worrying with the development of nuclear power.

The new towns have been in general, a success, though to begin with there were problems in connection with the development of community life. Some people, especially older people, missed the homeliness of their old environment even though its physical side was perhaps not very attractive.

Urban renewal, particularly in the inner cities, offers perhaps the biggest planning problem. There are, especially in the industrial towns, still vast areas of drab, shabby housing and industrial and commercial premises that need replacing. Paradoxically land is often expensive in these inner-city areas, even though it is derelict, making it often more economical for an industrialist to build a factory or plant on the more virgin and cheaper land outside the town. The enterprise zones and now the urban development corporations might partially remedy this. The motor-car has also made the problem of urban renewal even more difficult. Regional policies have failed to lessen disparities between the regions as far as the pleasantness of the environment and business activity are concerned. Some people argue that as far as business activity is concerned regional inequalities are inevitable because under an economic system based mainly on private capitalist enterprise businesses will locate where costs are lowest. In a market orientated economy, it will always be a problem to reconcile the drive for business profit with the wider needs of a civilised community life.

A beginning has been made to integrate the countryside and the urban areas for planning purposes, and the local government structure introduced in 1974 should speed up this integration and ensure the countryside is developed, bearing in mind the needs of both the country people and the people in the towns.

Assignments

1. Think about the town in which you live (or your nearest town). Discuss whether it is well planned and, in doing so, make suggestions for improving it. If possible, consult the development plan of the local planning authority.
2. What provisions exist for protecting the beauty of the countryside? Include in your answer not only the work of statutory bodies but also the work of voluntary bodies. Obtain literature on the work of one of these voluntary bodies. For example, you could obtain information on the work of the National Trust by writing to its Director-General at the Trust's headquarters in London.
3. Discuss the purpose of new towns. Write to the offices of one of the new town development corporations to try to find out what they have to offer for residents and commercial and industrial interests.
4. Why in some towns is there what is called an 'inner-city problem'? What is being done to resolve the problem? If you write to the Department of Environment, you might get assistance with this question.

Reading

Britain 1987: An Official Handbook (HMSO).

Gordon C. Cameron (ed.), *The Future of the British Conurbations* (Longman, 1980).

Gordon E. Cherry, *The Evolution of British Town Planning* (Leonard Hill Books, 1974).

Gordon E. Cherry, 'New Towns and Inner-City Blight', *New Society* (8 February 1979).

Control of Pollution Act 1974 (HMSO).

Countryside Commission, *Annual Report*.

W. Harvey Cox, *Cities: The Public Dimension* (Penguin, 1976).

J. B. Cullingworth, *Town and Country Planning in Britain* (Allen & Unwin, 1976).

David Donnison and Paul Solo, *The Good City – A Study of Urban Development and Policy in Britain* (Heinemann, 1980).

Martin J. Elson, *Green Belts: Conflict Mediation in the Urban Fringe* (Heinemann 1986).

John Herington, 'The Outer City Problem', *New Society* (9 August 1985).

HMSO, *Pollution: Nuisance or Nemesis?* (HMSO, 1972).

House of Commons, Inner Cities debate (*Hansard*, vol. 88, no. 26, 11 December 1985).
Lionel March, 'Why Have New Towns?', *New Society* (8 June 1972).
New Science, *Environment: New Society Social Studies Reader* (New Science Publications, n.d.).
Reports of the Royal Commission on Environmental Pollution (HMSO).
Frank Schaffer, *The New Town Story* (Paladin, 1972).

17 Probation and After-Care Service

History

Probation – that is, the release of an offender providing he or she promises to be good – is a legal procedure which has been used for centuries. In more formal language the offender enters into recognisance to be of good behaviour. This means the probation order requires the offender's consent. The recognisance procedure was increasingly used in the nineteenth century, especially for young offenders, reflecting a growing humanity in the treatment of law-breakers. Unfortunately very few offenders had someone to keep a parental eye on them during recognisance, though by the end of the nineteenth century there were a fair number of voluntary workers for this work – part of what was called the Police Court Mission.

The first Act to provide for statutory provision and guidance of offenders outside the penal institutions was the 1907 Probation of Offenders Act. It covered offenders of all ages and a wide range of offences. It provided for the appointment of probation officers by the courts to be paid for out of public funds. It laid down a maximum period of probation of three years, which still stands, but no minimum. The present minimum is six months (Scotland 12 months).

Although put on probation, an offender might be made to pay compensation for damages or injury. Since the passing of the 1907 Act there have been periodic reports followed by legislation which have extended the role of the service, but the 1907 Act still forms the basis of the service today. But since 1971 probation orders have been abolished for persons under 17 (Scotland 16) and replaced by supervision orders (see p. 117).

If the probationer (offender) fails to comply with the terms of the order, the probation officer may bring him or her before the court to be dealt with for the original offence. The terms of the order may require attendance at a day training centre or a stay at a probation hostel or other place of residence, or willingness to accept psychiatric treatment. For offenders who have committed more serious offences which would normally mean a prison sentence, a community service order may be made, though community service is also a sentence in its own right (see p. 120). The terms may also require the offender to report to the probation officer and notify any change of address. Failure to comply with the probation order may result in a fine or the requirement to attend an attendance centre, in which case the probation order may still continue but, if some other sentence is given, probation terminates. The probationer may also be dealt with for the original offence if he or she commits a further offence while on probation. But if the probationer responds well, he or she may be discharged early.

The growing humanity towards law-breakers was also reflected in prison reform. The Report of the Departmental Committee (the Gladstone Committee), published in 1895, recommended that reformation as well as deterrence should be the purpose of prisons. The 1895 Prison Act implemented its main recommendations – unproductive labour was abolished, prisoners were able to earn money, and so on. In more recent times the 1948 Criminal Justice Act abolished penal servitude, hard labour, corporal punishment and extended the possibilities of non-institutional treatment. It underlined again that penal policy should be reformation and restoration of prisoners to a normal life. The 1967 Criminal Justice Act abolished corrective training. Since 1965 capital punishment has been abolished for murder. However, the overcrowding and degrading conditions in many prisons do not encourage reformation.

Offenders whose punishment is a fine, whether paid by instalments or not, can be sent to prison if they default on payment. The 1914 Criminal Justice Act gave the court power to put such a person, if between the age of 16 and 21, under supervision until the fine was paid in an attempt to reduce the number of young persons sent to prison for non-payment. Legislation was eventually passed (the latest being the 1952 Magistrates Act) which laid down that courts should consider supervision before sending defaulters under

21 to prison, and also gave the courts authority to use supervision for adult defaulters if they wished. At the same time, probation officers were designated by the Home Office as suitable supervisors.

The after-care service was mainly confined to young people before the Second World War, particularly to those leaving borstals, but arrangements for supervision were made locally with various (including voluntary) agencies. Since 1945 after-care has been extended to older offenders and compulsory after-care now covers, among others, those leaving youth custody centres and detention centres, and those released from prison on licence (parole), young prisoners and those released from life imprisonment. Since the mid-1960s any prisoners on leaving prison can, on a voluntary basis, seek the help of the probation officer in the first year of their release. The probation officer must 'advise, assist and befriend' these ex-prisoners in the same way as he or she must, by statute, 'advise, assist and befriend' any other person needing help. The parole system for prisoners – even those who had committed serious offences – was introduced by the 1967 Criminal Justice Act. The probation service is represented on the Parole Board and local review committees and therefore has some say on the choice of prisoners for parole. But the probation service is responsible for their supervision.

Before sentence is passed on an offender, a probation officer may be asked by the court to make a report on the offender's home surroundings, education, and so on. This only became a statutory duty with the 1948 Criminal Justice Act; previously the reports had been made on a voluntary basis. These probation reports often influence the sentence passed by the magistrates. Under the 1982 Criminal Justice Act a social inquiry report must normally be considered by the court before a custodial sentence is given on an offender under 21.

Since 1966 probation officers can act as prison welfare officers.

Marriage counselling goes back to pre-1914 days and arose from trying to get husbands and wives to settle amicably those matrimonial disputes they were bringing to the courts. It was not until 1937 that statutory authority was given to probation officers to do this work.

Apart from marriage counselling, which the service is now rarely called upon to provide, probation officers may be asked by the magistrates courts or divorce courts to report on the circumstances of the parties and their children in cases of divorce where access to or custody of the children is in question. In adoption proceedings the court can nominate a probation officer (more usually it nominates a local authority social worker) to act as *guardian ad litem* and, under the 1975 Children Act, which is concerned with adoption, the duties of the *guardian ad litem* are extended.

Probation officers are concerned with young people aged 14–17 rather than children, whether offenders or simply those in need of care. The 1908 Children Act set up juvenile courts to keep children away from criminals and set up remand homes for children awaiting trial. It abolished imprisonment for children under 16, raised to 17 by the 1933 Children and Young Persons Act. Delinquents, or simply children needing care, could be brought before these courts under the 1933 Children and Young Persons Act and the 1948 Children Act and put into the care of a fit person which might be a local authority or probation officer (see Chapter 9).

Under the 1969 Children and Young Persons Act the aim is to keep children and young people out of the juvenile court but if, in spite of everything, they have to be brought before one, the court may make out a supervision order under which the child will remain at home under the supervison of the local authority or probation officer. But for a child under 14 the probation officer is not normally involved. Eventually it is the intention of the Act that probation officers will not look after children under 17 – they will be dealt with by local authority social workers. A supervison order may involve 'intermediate treatment' where, under supervision, the delinquent is given constructive activities. Private organisations, particularly youth groups, are encouraged to provide 'intermediate' treatment facilities and are helped financially to do so (see Chapter 13). But the probation and after-care service has 'intermediate' treatment facilities of its own.

Under the 1969 Act it was intended to raise the age of criminal responsibility from 10 to 12 but it still remains 10.

A child over 10 and under 17 can have a criminal prosecution made against him or her but cannot be sent to prison. This has applied ever since the 1933 Act. But a custodial sentence may be given for serious offences, including murder. Normally no young person under 21 is sent to prison unless the Court is satisfied no other option is suitable.

Administration

Although the probation and after-care service is a local one, it is not run by local authorities. The country is divided into probation and after-care areas, and each area has a probation and after-care committee of magistrates appointed by the courts in the area. It is these probation and after-care committees that are directly involved in the running of the service, with chief probation officers acting as advisers and administrators. The committees are required to co-opt non-magistrates with knowldege of prisoners and after-care. The committees are autonomous and not accountable to the courts. There is a Central Council of Probation and After-Care Committees.

The central authority is the Home Office, which has a Probation and After-Care Department. It is advised by an advisory council for probation and after-care. There is also a National Association of Probation Officers formed in 1912. The Home Office also has an inspectorate for the service.

Problems Today

Has the probation and after-care service too many duties?

In the last decade new duties have been imposed on the probation and after-care service – voluntary after-care, parole and prison welfare. The 1972 Criminal Justice Act introduced community service orders and suspended sentence supervision orders, which placed even more work on the probation service. If the Home Office and the criminologists who advise it see the development of non-institutional care as a means of keeping down crime in the long run, then the probation and after-care service is best fitted to do the work and the extra duties should be willingly accepted providing more staff are provided in sufficient quantities to cope. Probation officers in their jobs of helping the people they supervise must have close contacts with other people who might be able to assist their clients; e.g. local authority social workers and housing officers, public employees in central goverment departments, voluntary organisations and employers. In the last decade the service has more than doubled. There are now about 5,600 probation officers in England and Wales who supervise around 147,000 offenders. But the increase in numbers is not simply due to extra duties; there has been a very big increase in the number of demands for court reports (over a quarter of a million are now provided each year) and other reports. However, probation and after-care officers are aided by ancillary workers who do such things as court and escort duties, maintaining registers of employers and lodgings and helping in community service schemes. Help with community service schemes is also given by voluntary organisations and individual volunteers. These volunteers are given training and also do such duties as taking wives by coach to visit their husbands in prison or helping families with visits to long-term prisoners.

Should the probation and after-care service be part of the local government Social Services Department?

The idea behind the introduction of social services departments of local government was to integrate all the personal social services concerned with individual welfare into one department to ensure, by better co-ordination between the different social workers, a more effective family service. Naturally when it was formed there was concern among probation officers, who preferred the existing set-up, that they would become part of the social services department, especially as local government shared 20 per cent of the cost of the probation service with the central government and yet has no say in how it is run. Official thinking seems to favour its retention by the courts, though in Scotland it is a local government service – but Scotland has a different legal system. But the type of work the probation service does is very much concerned with the courts. Would it not perhaps lose its judicial independence, so necessary as part of the administration of justice, if it became part of local party politics? All criminal law reformers of all political shades are in agreement on the need for more non-institutional (non-custodial) penalties. Hence it is a service which, in the future, will be responsible for a wide range of treatment in the community for offenders. The specialist nature of its work and its extent would seem to justify its separate administrative structure. A local authority with a wide range of other services for other groups of people might not be willing to give the same priority to offenders. On the other hand, the work of the service depends for much of its success on the co-operation of the local community. For example, in order to do his or her best for the client, a probation officer must contact social workers in the local authority and government departments. In this connexion, probation officers sit on official committees of the local authority social services department.

Is probation effective?

The total number of indictable offences increases each year and about half of those found guilty are under 21 (but less than half of the offences are cleared up). But the growing increase in crime is due to factors outside the control of the probation service. A more effective test would be to check the numbers who are put on probation and find out what proportion are not reconvicted within a given period.

In 1980 in England and Wales 33,016 persons were put on probation and only about a quarter of them were known to have had no previous conviction (*Probation and After-Care Statistics, England and Wales, 1980*).

To try to make it more effective the 1972 Criminal Justice Act introduced a scheme of community service and an expansion of day training centres for those on probation. Quite apart from the Act, the government launched a programme of new probation hostels for adults. Furthermore, probation committees are able to provide after-care hostels; previously they had only been provided by voluntary bodies. Research and experiments are continually going on to make non-custodial treatment more effective. The most exciting development is the imposition of community service orders where offenders have to do useful work helping families in need, the elderly, and so on, or simply do work to improve the community's environment. For the first time they have helped other people instead of being on the receiving end of help. Some offenders have discovered a new purpose to their lives and gone straight.

Summary

Once a system of supervising offenders as an alternative to prison was introduced, then it was only a matter of time before there developed a variety of ways of supervising to suit the different categories of law-breaker.

The main duties of the problem and after-care service are as follows:

(1) *Probation*

(a) maintain contact with the offender placed on probation at home (and the offender must contact the probation office when asked to do so)

(b) 'advise, assist and befriend' the offender, which can include advice with any domestic difficulties, including the finding of lodgings, help in finding a job, and encouragement generally – some offenders placed on probation must attend a day training centre or stay at a probation hostel or do community service.

(2) *Reports*. Probation officers may be asked, before sentence is passed on an offender brought before the court and found guilty, to provide the court with a report on the offender's home surroundings, education, health and general social conditions.

(3) *Supervision of juvenile offenders aged 14–17.*

(4) *Supervision of offenders given a suspended sentence.* Unlike a probation order, a suspended sentence does not need the offender's consent.

(5) *After-care*. Probation officers provide after-care for a wide range of offenders and must 'advise, assist and befriend' any discharged prisoners who voluntarily come for help during their first year of release.

(6) *Prison welfare*. Probation officers act as prison welfare officers.

(7) *Marriage guidance*. Probation officers were usually asked to meet those who came before the courts or who applied to the magistrates courts for separation orders. They often acted as marriage guidance counsellors to these people and in fact gave advice on marriage to all who voluntarily approached them. But work in connection with marriage guidance is no longer significant. What has become an important part of probation officers' work in cases of matrimonial breakdown is the preparation of welfare reports on the custody and access of children.

(8) *Children*. Children who come before the courts needing care and protection are normally put in the care of the local authority, but they can be put in the care of a probation officer if aged over 13.

(9) *Divorce and family court work* where access to or custody of children is in dispute.

As non-custodial treatment is extended in line with modern criminology, the service will continue the expansion which has been going on ever since it was first created in 1907. (Non-custodial treatment is very much cheaper than custodial treatment – see John Harding). It will continue to need the co-operation of other social workers and the community at large. Volunteers will continue to play an important role in the service.

Assignments

1. Write to the administrator of your local probation and after-care service and ask if you can have a copy of the service's *Annual Report* for the area. From your reading of the report discuss what you consider to be its most interesting contents.
2. Why must the probation and after-care officer be involved with the personal social services run by the local authority? Give examples where co-operation with these services may be necessary.
3. How far is the probation and after-care service an agency in the war against crime?

Reading

Britain 1987: An Official Handbook (HMSO).
Paul Cavadino, 'Criminal Justice Act 1982, A Pragmatic Compromise', *Community Care* (11 November 1982).
First Report of the Select Committee on Expenditure in Session 1971–2, *The Probation and After-Care Service* (HMSO).
John Harding, 'Probation in the Community: "Twelve Pounds a Week"', *The Listener* (19 September 1985).
HMSO, *Report on the work of the Probation and After-Care Department, 1972–1975*, Cmnd 6590 (HMSO, August 1976).
Joan King (ed.), *The Probation and After-Care Service* (Butterworth, 1969).
Mark Monger, *Casework in Probation*, 2nd edn (Butterworth, 1972) ch. 1.
Report of Her Majesty's Chief Inspector of Constabulary (HMSO).
Report of the Advisory Council on the Penal System, *Sentences of Imprisonment: A Review of Maximum Penalties* (HMSO, 1978).

Lord Scarman's Report, *The Brixton Disorders*, Cmnd 8427 (HMSO, 1981).
Wendy Taylor (compiler), *Probation and After-Care in a Multi-racial Society* (Commission for Racial Equality, 1981).

18 The Future of the Social Services

Until the beginning of this century the only help for those in need outside that of family and friends was that provided by the Poor Law and voluntary organisations. In this century income maintenance and other services have developed outside the Poor Law. Income maintenance includes a comprehensive system of National Insurance, child benefit and other miscellaneous benefits, augmented, where necessary, by supplementary benefit paid for out of taxation – the Poor Law having been abolished in 1948. From a system where most ordinary people, when sick, only reluctantly, because of its cost, sought medical help from an impoverished doctor, there has developed a comprehensive and virtually free National Health Service paid for mainly out of taxation. There has also developed a wide range of community social services covering health and welfare, many of which were previously the concern of the Poor Law authorities. Parallel with these developments, educational advance has resulted in secondary education for all and higher education for all who want it and who can benefit from it, made possible, for children of poorer parents, by a system of grants. At least this was so until cuts in education finance in 1981. Housing standards have risen, and there has been a big increase in the nation's housing stock, though still nearly a sixth of it is substandard.

Since 1945 we have been trying for the first time, under a comprehensive planning system, to make the best use of the land and, more recently, planning has come to include not just land use but concern for the environment as a whole, including its pollution. Finally, the humanising of the penal system has led to a much greater use of probation and after-care for offenders and a corresponding increase in the duties of the probation and after-care service. The black spot is the severe overcrowding in our Victorian-built prisons.

Community care, which involves treatment in the home or neighbourhood instead of an institution – first considered in relation to mentally handicapped people – has been applied on an ever-increasing scale to other categories of people needing help. The concept has been given administrative expression by the creation of a local authority social services department to provide a community-based service in support of the family. Many social problems arise from a bad home environment and the social services department is an attempt to prevent problems arising in the first place by trying to keep the home situation of 'families at risk' as sound as possible. It involves the co-operation of many types of workers from the range of helping services. Community care will continue to develop and the social services department could become the focus of community service. It necessitates the co-operation of the ordinary citizen, as one of the assumptions of community care is that problems cannot be solved by professional social workers alone. Is there enough community spirit to ensure its success? Community spirit will certainly be put to the test when community care is developed on a much greater scale than now for law-breakers. Already the normal treatment for young offenders is rehabilitation, supervision and accommodation, all in the local community, and if present trends continue this will become the standard treatment for grown-up offenders as well, with prison being reserved for a much smaller number of hard-core law-breakers. In other words, in the future the community will be asked to accept greater responsibility for all types of people who need help, including criminals.

We tend to assume that all doctors, dentists, opticians, teachers, social workers, planners, etc., in their own particular sphere, know what is best for us or our children. Greater community participation in the social services, which will inevitably follow from a greater acceptance of responsibility by the community for those in need, will probably make us much more critical of professionals' advice. They will be asked more and more to explain the assumptions and theories which guide their methods of work and influence their conclusions.

The biggest problem affecting the future of the social services will continue to be the problem of resources. There never will be enough money to do all that is needed, and hence it is a question of making the best use of the money available. The reasons for the increasing cost of the services, apart from the paying out of more unemployment benefit, are: improved services due to the use of more equipment and the employment of more workers in the social services; the continuing increase in the proportion of old people in the population; the increasing proportion of people claiming means-tested benefits, as the official policy of giving more publicity for the services continues; the increasing wage bill, which will be difficult to reduce as the social services rely on people to operate them, and hence, as the wage bill increases, greater use cannot be made of machinery as happens in industry; and finally, an awareness of new needs that had previously been overlooked.

The increasing cost of social services has given rise to the criticism that they necessitate high taxation to pay for them, and this is one of the reasons why industrial profits fell in the 1960s and 1970s leading to a fall in investment and hence lower productivity, accelerating the lack of competitiveness of British industry. Put more colloquially, the welfare state has stimulated private demand and public consumption beyond the means of the economy and hence expenditure on the welfare state must be reduced to what the country can afford.

This has led to the main controversy surrounding the welfare state – the degree of selectivity there should be or how far benefits should be given to everyone irrespective of their circumstances. At the present time we have both universal benefits and selective benefits – perhaps far more selective benefits than is generally realised. Nobody has suggested that all benefits should be universal, though there are those who say all benefits should be selective. Selectivity is an easier policy to put across than the defence of the universal principle mainly because it seems so obvious – why give benefits to those who do not need them? Not to give benefits to those who do not need them would reduce government expenditure and allow more to be given to the needy. This seems a difficult argument to counter. One practical point against any extension of selectivity is, of course, that the take-up will be nothing like 100 per cent – it will perhaps be as low as 60 per cent in some cases – and many are still left in need. But the real arguments for and against selectivity are political. They centre upon the kind of society we want and what we think the aims of the social services should be.

The supporters of more selectivity tend to see the social services simply as means for helping the weaker members of the community. The richer we become, the more the riches will go to those in work and hence the state must step in to help the old, the sick, the unemployed and the large family, in order to redress the balance. On the other hand, the defenders of the universal principle see the social services as a means to a more homogeneous and egalitarian society. They see selectivity as a divisive force in our society. In any case selectivity imposes burdens of form-filling and feelings of humiliation on people who have already had a poor deal, while the more fortunate ones are free from all this. The change in government economic thinking from Keynesian demand management to monetarism due to the economic recession combined with a high rate of inflation strengthened the hand of those who wanted more selectivity.

A system of negative income tax is seen by some as a means of making the unversalist–selectivist argument obsolete, but is a comprehensive system administratively and financially feasible?

Within the present system of universal and selective benefits there is room for manoeuvre without going to one extreme or the other. It is possible to introduce bigger selective benefits for special categories of poorer people, bigger child benefit, greater reliance on private insurance and perhaps a more modest scheme of negative income tax.

But the future of the social services will, to a large extent, be affected by whichever of the two main political parties happens to be in power because of their contrasting political philosophies. For example, the Conservative Party supports leaving the running of a business or a service to private enterprise if it can do it satisfactorily on the grounds that the less state control there is, the greater the amount of individual freedom and the less burden on the finances of the state. The state should simply act as umpire to ensure fair play. On the other hand, the Labour Party sees the economic order run mainly by private enterprise as creating so many economic and social evils that the state must play a very powerful role to ensure a sound economy and a just society. Within each political party there are of course differences in the degree to which the particular viewpoint is held:

1. In the sphere of *social security* we can see this difference in political philosophy is reflected in the universalist–selectivist

argument, but with the Alliance Party putting much greater faith in the eventual merging of the tax and benefit systems, thus permitting the abolition of universal benefits whilst avoiding all, or most of, the pitfalls of the present means-tested system.

2. In *health* we can see why the Conservative Party encourages the development of private health insurance and private hospitals, while the Labour Party fears the effect of this development on the National Health Service.

3. In *welfare* we can see why the Conservative Party places great stress on the importance of voluntary action, while the Labour Party, although encouraging voluntary action, does not want it to be at the expense of the statutory services.

4. In *education* we can see why the Conservative Party strongly supports the independent sector and greater choice and participation by parents in the maintained sector, while the Labour Party attacks the divisive nature of the independent sector.

5. In *employment* we can see the reason for the greater caution displayed by the Conservative Party to any proposals for increasing public expenditure to combat unemployment – proposals favoured by both opposition parties and some members of the Conservative Party.

6. In *housing* we can see why the Conservative Party puts much greater stress on the expansion of owner-occupation than the Labour Party – the Labour Party fears that local authority housing will become a kind of ghetto for the poor.

7. In *planning* we can see why the Conservative Party is much more reluctant than the Labour Party to extend the powers of local authorities to acquire land for the control of future development.

But in more general terms the future will depend on two main factors. Firstly, the outcome of the economic argument between the monetarists and the Keynesians and, secondly, perhaps the most important factor of all – the future of East–West relations.

In a just society command of the country's welfare resources should be based on need, and the more they are controlled by private organisations the greater the danger that money will play too great a role in their use, with the rich getting an unfair proportion of them compared with the poor.

Assignments

1. Give the main advantages and disadvantages of the following
   agencies for the administration of social services:
   (a) local authorities
   (b) central government departments
   (c) voluntary bodies.
2. 'The future of the social services depends more on the economists than the professional people in the social services.'
   Discuss.
3. Write to the headquarters of each of the main political parties
   asking for the party's policies for the future of the welfare state.
   From the replies, which may include party literature on the
   welfare state, make your own summary of the views of the
   respective parties.

Reading

Robert Bacon and Walter Eltis, *Britain's Economic Problem: Too Few
   Producers* (Macmillan, 1978).
David Blake and Paul Ormerod (eds), *The Economics of Prosperity* (Grant
   McIntyre, 1980).
Muriel Brown and Nicola Madge, *Despite the Welfare State* (Heinemann,
   1982).
Peter Donaldson, *A Question of Economics* (Penguin, reprint 1986).
Frank Field, *Poverty and Politics* (Heinemann, 1982) chs 11 and 12.
George Gilder, *Health and Poverty* (Buchan & Enright, 1982) ch. 11.
Ian Gough, *The Political Economy of the Welfare. State*, reprint
   (Macmillan, 1981).
David Graham and Peter Clarke, *The New Enlightenment the rebirth of
   liberalism* (Macmillan, 1986).
M. Penelope Hall, *The Social Services of Modern England*, 9th rev. edn
   (Routledge & Kegan Paul, 1975).
Martin Loney, *The Politics of Greed: the New Right and the Welfare State*
   (Pluto Press, 1986).
Robert Pinker, *Social Theory and Social Policy* (Heinemann, 1971) ch. 5.
Arthur Seldon, 'Thaw in the Welfare State', *Lloyds Bank Review* (July
   1972).
J. F. Sleeman, *The Welfare State* (Allen & Unwin, 1973).
Peter Taylor-Gooby and Jennifer Dale, *Social Theory and Social Welfare*
   (Edward Arnold, 1981) ch. 9.
R. M. Titmuss, *Essays on the Welfare State*, 3rd edn (Allen & Unwin,
   1976).
Jim Tomlinson, *Monetarism: Is There an Alternative?* (Basil Blackwell,
   1986).

Appendices

1 Some of the Main Social Security Weekly Benefit Rates (beginning 6 April 1987)

Unemployment Benefit	(£)
Over pension age	
single rate	39.50
adult dependency addition	23.75
Under pension age	
full rate	31.45
adult dependency addition	19.40
Sickness Benefit	
Over pension age	
single rate	37.85
adult dependency addition	22.70
Under pension age	
full rate	30.05
adult dependency addition	18.60
Retirement Pension	
On own insurance	39.50
On spouse's insurance	23.75
Widow's Benefit	
Widows' allowance	55.35
Widowed mothers' allowance	39.50
Widows' pension – standard rate	39.50
Invalid Care Allowance	23.75
Adult dependency addition	14.20
Invalidity Benefit	
Invalidity pension	39.50
Invalidity allowance	
higher rate	8.30
middle rate	5.30
lower rate	2.65
Maternity Benefit	
Maternity allowance	
full rate	30.05
adult dependency addition	18.60
Child dependency additions	
For each child with:	
retirement pension, widows benefit, invalidity benefit, invalid care and severe disablement allowance, higher rate industrial death benefit, unemployability supplement and sickness or unemployment benefit if beneficiary over pension age	8.05

Child Benefit
    Each child   7.25

One-parent Benefit   4.70

Supplementary Benefit (leaflet SBI)
Scale rates
  ordinary rates

single householder	30.40
couple	49.35
non-householder 18 or over	24.35
non-householder 16–17	18.75

  long-term rates

single person living alone	38.65
couple	61.85
non-householder 18 or over	30.95
non-householder 16–17	23.70

  dependent children

over 18	24.35
16–17	18.75
11–15	15.60
under 11	10.40

(The scale for blind people is slightly more than the above rates. Persons on supplementary benefit receive in addition to the above basic scales an amount from the local authority for rent or rates, and interest on mortgage repayments from the DHSS plus extra to meet special and additional requirements.)

Family Income Supplements (leaflet FIS 1)

Prescribed amount for one-child family,
  where child is aged

under 11	100.70
11–15	101.75
16 and over	102.80

Increase for each additional child

under 11	11.90
11–15	12.95
16 and over	14.00

Maximum amount for one-child family
  where child is aged

under 11	25.85
11–15	26.40
16 and over	26.90

Increase for each additional child

under 11	2.60
11–15	3.15
16 and over	3.65

Source: *House of Commons Hansard*, vol. 102, no. 160, 22 October 1986.

2 Expenditure on Social Security Benefits for Great Britain 1985–6, and Estimated Number of Recipients 1979–80 and 1985–6

	Expenditure (£s million cash)	*Recipients (000s)*	
	1985–6	*1979–80*	*1985–6*
National insurance benefits			
Pension benefits			
Retirement pensions	16 440	8 680	9 410
Invalidity benefit	2 262	620	840
Industrial disablement benefit	389	200	180
Widow's benefits and industrial death benefit	882	520	450
Lump-sum payment to contributory pensioners	105	9 600	10 500
Other benefits			
Unemployment benefit	1 611	550	980
Sickness benefits	276	490	170
Death grant	17	600	620
Maternity allowance	174	115	125
Non-contributory benefits			
Pension benefits			
Non-contributory retirement pensions	41	55	35
War pensions	564	370	290
Attendance allowance and invalid care allowance	651	290	530
Severe disablement allowance	295	165	290
Mobility allowance	429	140	405
Lump-sum payment to non-contributory pensioners	6	500	600
Other benefits			
Supplementary pensions	892	1 720	1 720
Supplementary allownaces	5 715	1 200	2 925
Child benefit	4 435	13 330	12 210
Family income supplement	140	80	220
One-parent benefit	133	370	590
Maternity grant	18	660	720
Housing benefit–rent rebates and allowances	2 889	1 425	4 780
Administration and miscellaneous services	1 735		

Source: *Social Trends, 1986* (HMSO).

3   Cost of the Health and Personal Social Services for Great Britain, 1985–6 (£ million at current prices)

	1985–6
National Health Service	
Current expenditure	
Hospitals and community health services	11 664
Family practitioner services	4 102
Central health and miscellaneous services	701
Capital expenditure	
Hospitals and community health services	913
Family practitioner services	4
Central health and miscellaneous services	45
Total	17 429
Personal social services	
Current expenditure	
Central government	29
Local authorities	3 254
Capital expenditure	
Central government	3
Local authorities	99
Total	3 385
Total gross expenditure	20 814
Less income from charges	1 002
Total net public expenditure on health and personal social services	19 812

Source: *Social Trends 1986* (HMSO).

4 Manpower in the National Health Service in the United Kingdom in 1979 and 1983

	Thousands	
	1979	*1983*
Regional and District Health Authorities		
Medical and dental	45.3	48.9
Nursing and midwifery (excluding agency staff)	449.2	502.0
Professional and technical (excluding works)	74.1	84.6
Administrative and clerical	121.8	131.0
Other staff (including ancilliary, works, maintenance, and ambulance)	272.4	269.1
Total Regional and District Health Authorities	962.8	1 035.5
Family practitioner services		
General medical practitioners	28.5	31.3
General dental practitioners	14.4	16.2
Ophthalmic medical practitioners, ophthalmic opticians, and dispensing opticians	8.8	9.3
Total family practitioner professionals	51.7	56.8
Dental Estimates Board and Prescription Pricing Authority/Prescription Pricing Division	4.6	4.6

Source: *Social Trends, 1986.*

5   Education: Numbers of Students in 1984 in the United Kingdom (in thousands)

		Projection for 1996
Nursery schools		
Public sector	95	99
Primary schools		
Public sector	4 655	5 117
Secondary schools		
Public sector	4 385	3 586
Assisted and independent schools (nursery, primary and secondary)	603	557
Special schools (full time)	138	130
Higher education (full time)		
Universities	268 ⎱ In addition 46.6	
Other higher education	265.9 ⎰ overseas students	
Higher education (part time)		
Universities	36.3	
Open University	76.2	
Further education advanced courses		
Part time day	151.1	
Evening only	49	

In addition to the above there are students at further education colleges taking courses up to 'A' level and intermediate professional level.

Source: *Social Trends, 1986* (HMSO).

6 Pupils in Secondary Education in 1984 in England, Wales, Scotland and Northern Ireland

Percentages and thousands

	1984
England (percentages)	
Maintained secondary schools	
Middle deemed secondary	6.9
Modern	4.7
Grammar	3.2
Technical	0.1
Comprehensive	84.4
Other	0.7
Total pupils (= 100%) (thousands)	3 646
Wales (percentages)	
Maintained secondary schools	
Middle deemed secondary	0.1
Modern	0.9
Grammar	0.7
Comprehensive	98.0
Other	0.3
Total pupils (= 100%) (thousands)	232
Scotland (percentages)	
Public sector secondary schools	
Selective	
Comprehensive	96.7
Part comprehensive/part selective	3.3
Total pupils (= 100%) (thousands)	390
Northern Ireland (percentages)	
Public sector secondary schools	
Secondary intermediate	88.4
Grammar	11.6
Technical intermediate	
Total pupils (= 100%) (thousands)	117
United Kingdom	
Assisted and independent schools	
Pupils aged 11 or over (thousands)	380

Source: *Social Trends, 1986* (HMSO).

7   Students in Further Education in 1983–4 in the United Kingdom taking Courses up to 'A' Level and Intermediate Professional Level

	Males	Females
	1983–84 (000s)	*1983–84 (000s)*
Student enrolments in major establishments		
By type of course		
Full-time and sandwich		
From the United Kingdom	180	221
From abroad	6	2
Total	185	223
Day release	311	117
Part-time day	92	174
Evening only	287	433
Total student enrolments	874	947
Student enrolments on courses in local authority adult education centres	597	1 297
Student enrolments on other courses of adult education	195	284

Source: *Social Trends 1986* (HMSO).

8 Public Expenditure on Education for the United Kingdom, 1983–4

£s million cash and percentages

	1983–4
Current expenditure (£s million)	
Schools	
Nursery	67
Primary	3 377
Secondary	4 675
Special	583
Further and adult education[1]	2 157
Training of teachers: tuition	86
Universities[1]	1 497
Other education expenditure	656
Related current expenditure	
Meals and milk	519
Youth service and physical training	209
Maintenance grants and allowances to pupils and students	825
Miscellaneous expenditure	459
Total current expenditure	15 110
Capital expenditure (£s million)	
Schools	
Nursery	6
Primary	141
Secondary	232
Special	20
Further and adult education	141
Training of teachers	2
Universities	139
Other education expenditure	14
Related capital expenditure	22
Total capital expenditure	717
Total government expenditure (£s million)	15 827
Of which, expenditure by local authorities	13 605
Gross domestic product at market prices (£s million)	304 814
Expenditure as a percentage of GDP	5.2

[1] Includes tuition fees.
Source: *Social Trends, 1986* (HMSO).

9   Stock of Dwellings in the United Kingdom: by Tenure

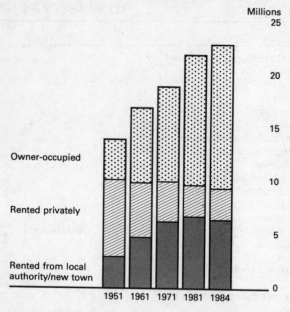

Source: *Social Trends, 1986.*

10 Persons Supervised by the Probation Service: By Type of Supervision in England and Wales, 1971, 1981, 1984

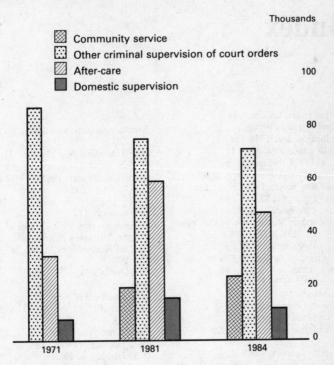

Source: *Social Trends, 1986.*

Index

adjudication officers 34
administrative tribunals 35
Adoption Act, 1958 111
adult education 138,142
Advisory, Conciliation and
  Arbitration Service (ACAS) 192
Advisory Council on Child Care 116
after-care 81, 232
after-care hostels 231
Albermarle Report, 1960 (The Youth
  Service) 177, 178
ambulance service 81
approved societies 18, 26
area health authorities 86, 87
Assistance Board 22
assisted areas 219
Assisted Place Scheme 148
attendance allowance 36, 39
attendance centres 120, 226

Barclay Report, 1982 129, 132
Barlow Committee Report, 1940 (on
  population distribution) 211, 212
Barlow Committee Report, 1946 (on
  scientific manpower) 156
basic income schemes 48, 49, 59
Bevan, Aneurin 71
Beveridge, Sir William 22, 24, 25,
  43, 44
Beveridge Report, 1942 (on social
  insurance and allied
  services) 22-3, 26, 44, 70
binary system 154, 159
births registration 69
Black Report, 1980 (*Inequalities in
  Health*) 94
Blanesburgh Committee, 1927 (on
  unemployment insurance) 20
Board of Education Act, 1899 136-7
Boer War 14, 16, 68, 109
Booth, Charles 14
borstals 118, 119, 227

Bourneville 200
British Association of Social Workers
  120
British Medical Association 71, 100
British Youth Council 178
Buchanan Report, 1963 (*Traffic in
  Towns*) 215

care orders 117
Careers Service 192-3, 196
Central Midwives Board 69
Central Redundancy Fund 38, 39,
  197
Chamberlain, Joseph 200
chemists 76
child abuse 131
child benefit 35, 39, 43, 47-8, 54,
  235
Child Care Act, 1980 120-1, 122
child guidance clinics 115
child labour 6, 10
child-minders 110
Children Act, 1908 17, 116, 228
Children Act, 1948 116, 120, 121
Children Act, 1975 111, 121, 228
Children and Young Persons Act,
  1933 116, 228
Children and Young Persons Act,
  1963 122
Children and Young Persons Act,
  1969 117-20, 121, 228
children in need of care and
  protection 115-22
children's services 2
child's special allowance 36
Chronically Sick and Disabled Persons
  Act, 1970 123, 187, 195
church schools 135, 136, 138, 143,
  148, 152
Churchill, Sir Winston S. 18
city technology colleges 162
Civic Amenities Act, 1967 215

Civil Service 8
clinics 80, 109, 110
College of the Air 147, 161
colleges of education 147, 154
Commission for New Towns 214
community care 56, 77, 94, 97, 98,
    125, 127, 128–31, 216, 236
community health councils 79, 98
community health physician 78
community health services 76, 79–
    84, 86, 97–8
community homes 119
Community Industry Scheme 189
Community Nursing Review, 1986 97
Community Programme 189
community service orders 120, 226,
    229, 230, 231, 232
community services for the mentally
    handicapped 127–8
complaints in the NHS 98–100
comprehensive education 144, 146,
    159, 162–6, 171, 173
consensus management 87–8, 89, 92
conservation areas 215
Control of Pollution Act, 1974 215,
    218
co-operative societies 7
Council for Education and Training in
    Youth and Community
    Work 181
Council for National Academic
    Awards 154, 159
council houses 206, 208
Council on Tribunals 35
country parks 218
Countryside Act, 1968 218
court reports 230, 232
Criminal Justice Act, 1914 226
Criminal Justice Act, 1948 226, 227
Criminal Justice Act, 1967 226, 227
Criminal Justice Act, 1972 229, 231
Criminal Justice Act, 1982 117, 118,
    119, 120, 227
criminal responsibility age 228
Crowther Report, 1959 (15–18-year-
    olds) 160
Curtis Report, 1946 (on care of
    children) 116
custodial treatment 120

dame schools 135
Dangerous Litter Act, 1971 218
day nurseries 110

day release 138, 142, 144, 162, 195
day training centres 231, 232
death grant 36, 56, 58
denationalisation 9, 44
dentists 76
Derelict Land Act, 1982 214
detention centres 118, 119, 227
Development Land Tax Act, 1976 213
Dickens, Charles 14
direct grant schools 141, 147, 168
disablement benefit 39
Disabled Persons (Employment) Act,
    1944 187, 188
Disabled Persons (Employment) Act,
    1958 123, 187
disablement resettlement officers 187
discretionary payments 34, 57, 58
Disraeli, Benjamin 14
Distribution of Industry Act, 1945
    211, 219, 222
district health authorities 74, 75, 76–
    8, 109, 114, 189
district management team 78, 86, 87
Dr Barnado's 115
doctors 66–7, 68, 70, 71, 74–6, 82,
    88, 95–7, 100, 109, 110, 126, 127,
    128, 187, 235, 236
domestic system 6
Donnison Report, 1970 (on
    independent schools) 168
Duke of Edinburgh's Award Scheme
    179

Early Leaving (Report of Ministry of
    Education's Central Advisory
    Council, 1954) 163
earnings-related benefits 25, 27, 30–
    1, 43, 45
education 2, 8, 14, 16, 68, 109, 135–
    174
Education Act, 1870 135–6, 143
Education Act, 1902 137–8, 144
Education Act, 1918 136, 138–9
Education Act, 1944 112, 113, 114,
    140, 142–4, 150, 151, 160, 176
Education Act, 1980 148
education administration 150
Education (Administrative Provisions)
    Act, 1907 16, 112
education advisory bodies 151
education and local authorities 151
Education (Choice of Employment)
    Act, 1910 192

Education (Defective and Epileptic) Act, 1899   114
education finance   149–50, 157–9, 169, 170
Education (Provision of Meals) Act, 1906   16, 112
education voucher system   172–3
educational opportunity   169–73
educational pressure groups   151, 152
educational priority areas   171
elderly   78, 81, 83, 94, 105–8
Elementary Education (Blind and Deaf Children) Act, 1893   114
Emergency Hospital Service   70
Employment and Training Act, 1948   193
Employment and Training Act, 1973   184, 193
Employment and Training Act, 1981   162, 186
Employment Medical Advisory Service   191
Employment Protection Act, 1975   192
Employment Protection (Consolidation) Act, 1978   192
employment rehabilitation centres   187
Enterprise Allowance Scheme   190
employment services   2, 194–8
enclosures   6, 7
enterprise zones   216, 222
environmental health   6, 64, 65, 78, 81, 84
Equal Pay Act, 1975   191, 192
European Regional Development Fund   219
European Regional Social Fund   219

factories   6, 8, 10, 17
Factories Act, 1961   191
Factory Act, 1833   135
family   8, 10
family allowances   35, 47
Family Allowances Act, 1945   23, 27
family credit   3, 50–1, 55, 60, 113
family income supplement   1, 2, 35–6, 39, 48, 50–1, 54, 60, 113
Family Income Supplement Act, 1970   35–6
family planning   81
family practitioner committees   68, 74–6, 82, 98–9

Fleming Report, 1944 (on public schools)   167
Forestry Commission   218
Forster, W. E.   136
foster homes   121
French Revolution   7
Freud, Sigmund   125
Friedman, Milton   9, 43
friendly societies   7
further education   147

General Certificate of Secondary Education (GCSE)   165–6
general improvement areas   205
General Medical Council   75
Gingerbread   112
Gladstone Committee Report, 1895 (on prisons)   226
grammar schools   135, 137, 140, 144, 163–5
Green, T. H.   15
green belts   213, 221
Griffiths Report, 1983 (on NHS management)   88
group practice   96
guardian's allowance   36
guardians of the poor   12, 13, 15, 20, 66, 135

Hadow Report, 1926 (on education of the adolescent)   139–40, 144
half-time system   136
handicapped children   114–15, 149
Harris, Dr Drew   69
health and safety at work   191–2
Health and Safety at Work Act, 1974   191
Health and Safety Commission   191
Health and Social Services and Social Security Adjudication Act, 1982   116, 119, 125, 126
health care planning teams   78
health centres   82, 96
health insurance   19, 67, 71
Health Service Commissioner   99
health service finance   89–95, 101–2
Health Service Management Board   88
Health Service Supervisory Board   73, 88
Health Services and Public Health Act, 1968   73, 106
health visiting   80, 109
higher education   154–160

Historic Buildings and Monuments Commission for England (English Heritage) 215
home helps 82, 127
homeless 33, 208
home nursing 80
Hospital Patients' Association 100
hospitals 65–6, 70, 76–9, 91, 92, 94
household means test 20, 26
houses built 203
housing 2, 78, 200–8, 235
Housing Act, 1930 201
Housing Act, 1949 202, 203
Housing Act, 1957 205
Housing Act, 1969 205
Housing Act, 1974 205
Housing Act, 1980 200, 202, 203
housing action areas 205
Housing and Planning Act, 1986 206
Housing and Town Planning Act, 1919 201
housing associations 203
housing benefit 37–8, 50, 55
Housing Corporation 203
Housing Finance Act, 1972 37, 206, 207
Housing (Homeless Persons) Act, 1977 203
housing officers 229
housing stock 204, 208
Housing Town Planning Act, 1909 211
Hunt Committee Report, 1969 (on intermediate areas) 219

improvement grants 202
income support 2, 37, 38, 55–8, 59
independent schools 147, 148, 167–8
index linking 27, 31
Industrial Injuries Advisory Council 31
Industrial Revolution 8
Industrial Training Act, 1964 162, 192
industrial training boards 162, 186, 195
industrial tribunals 192
Industry Act, 1972 211, 219
Infant and Nursery School Report, 1933 167
infant mortality rate 68
informal carers 129
Ingleby Report, 1960 (on children and young persons) 122

inner cities 215, 221, 222
inner city partnerships 216
Inner Urban Areas Act, 1978 216
Insurance Fund 31
Inter-Departmental Committee on Physical Deterioration, 1903 16
intermediate treatment 118, 179, 228
invalid care allowance 37
invalidity benefit 29, 31, 39, 48

James Report, 1972 (on teacher education and training) 160
jobcentres 184, 190, 194
jobclubs 190
Job Restart Programme 190
Job Start Allowance 190
Job Training Scheme 186, 188, 190
joint committees 86, 98
joint financing 78
juvenile courts 116–122
Juvenile Employment Report, 1917 138

Kerr, James 69
Keynesian economics 9, 23, 44, 157, 238, 239
Kingsley, Charles 14

Labour Exchange Act, 1909 17, 184, 192
laissez-faire 15
Letchworth Garden City 200
liberty 15
Lister, Joseph 65
Lloyd George 18, 26, 71
local authority health services 68, 69
Local Authority Social Services Act, 1970 129
Local Employment Act, 1960 211, 219
Local Government Act, 1871 12
Local Government Board 65, 67
Local Government Grants (Social Need) Act, 1969 216
Luddites 6
Lunacy Act, 1890 125
Lunatics Act, 1845 125

Magistrates Act, 1952 226
maladjusted children 115
Manpower Services Commission (MSC) 146, 147, 161, 173, 184–90, 194–8, 217

marriage counselling 227–8, 232
Maternity and Child Welfare Act,
    1918 69, 109
maternity benefits 30, 39, 56, 58
Mayhew, Henry 14
means testing 52–4, 61
Mearns, Rev. Andrew 14
Medical Appeals Tribunal 31
medical boards 32
Medical Practices Committee 75
Medical Relief (Disqualification
    Removal) Act, 1885 15
Mental Health Act, 1959 125
Mental Health Act, 1983 125, 126,
    127
Mental Health Commission 126
Mental Health Review Tribunal 126,
    127
Mental Treatment Act, 1930 125
mentally disordered 81, 82, 94, 124–
    8, 131
Metropolitan Poor Act, 1867 13, 66
midwifery service 81
Midwives Act, 1902 69, 109
Midwives Act, 1936 69
Milk Act, 1934 112
Mill, John Stuart 15
Mines Act, 1842 191
Mines and Quarries Act, 1954 191
minimum wage 51
Ministry of Health 12, 67, 68
Ministry of National Insurance 26
mobility allowance 36, 39
Monetarism 9, 43, 51, 101, 198, 238,
    239
money supply 9
Morant, Robert 138
mothers and young children 109–12

National Advisory Council on
    Employment for the Disabled
    187
national assistance 23, 24, 26, 33, 42
National Assistance Act, 1948 22,
    23, 33, 105, 106, 122, 123
National Assistance Board 22, 23
National Association of Youth Clubs
    178, 189
National Council for One-Parent
    Families 111
National Council for Vocational
    Qualifications (NCVQ) 162

National Council for Voluntary Youth
    Services 178
National Economy Act, 1931 20
National Health Service 2, 19, 22,
    26, 67, 70–1, 73–102, 235
National Health Service Act, 1946
    23, 66, 68, 69, 73, 109, 115, 122
National Housebuilding Council 204
national insurance 1, 2, 23, 24, 26,
    29–32, 43, 235
National Insurance Act, 1911 17–18,
    19, 25, 67, 70
National Insurance Act, 1946 23
National Insurance Act, 1959 30
National Insurance (Old Persons' and
    Widows' Pensions and
    Attendance Allowance) Act, 1970
    37
national parks 217, 218
National Parks and Access to the
    Countryside Act, 1949 217
National Parks Commission 218
National Trust 218
National Youth Bureau 178
National Conservancy Council 218
negative income tax 48–50, 59, 61,
    238
new towns 213–4, 222
New Towns Act, 1946 213
New Towns Act, 1959 213
New Towns (Amendment) Act 1976
    214
Newsom Report, 1963 (*Half Our
    Future*) 160
Nightingale, Florence 65
Norwood Report, 1943 (on curriculum
    and examinations in secondary
    schools) 144
Notification of Births Act, 1907 69
Nurseries and Child Minders'
    Regulation Act, 1948 110
nurses 88, 89, 109
nursing homes 80

occupational guidance 194
occupational pensions 45–7
Offices, Shops and Railway Premises
    Act, 1963 191
Old Age Pensions Act, 1908 17, 105
one-parent benefit 35, 54
one-parent families 24, 41
open-field system 6
Open Tech 195

Open University 154, 155
opthalmic services 76
Outdoor Relief (Friendly Societies)
    Act, 1894 15
owner-occupation problems 208

parole 227, 229
Pasteur, Louis 65
pensions 2, 21, 22, 30, 31, 41, 45, 55
Pensions Act, 1940 21
Percy Report, 1945 (on higher
    technological education) 156
personal pensions 45–7
personal practitioner services 68, 74–
    6, 82, 97, 98
personal social services 2, 97, 98,
    131–2
physically handicapped 85, 122–4,
    186–8
picnic sites 218
Piercy Committee Report, 1956 (on
    disabled people) 187, 196
planning 2, 211–222
Planning Act, 1968 212, 213
planning administration 212–3
planning and the countryside 217–8
Plowden Report, 1967 (*Children and
    Their Primary Schools*) 167
Poisonous Waste Act, 1972 218
Police Court Mission 225
polytechnics 147, 154
polyversities 159
Poor Law 8, 12–3, 15, 16, 17, 18,
    19, 22, 23, 25, 26, 33, 65, 66, 68,
    235
Poor Law Amendment Act, 1834 12
Poor Law Amendment Act, 1869 66
population 5, 6, 64
Port Sunlight 200
poverty 8, 14, 16, 41, 58, 65
poverty line 24, 27, 41
poverty trap 54–5
primary education 146, 167
primary health care 97–8
Primary School Report, 1931 (Board
    of Education Consultative
    Committee) 167
Prison Act, 1895 226
prison welfare 227, 229, 232
private education 147–9, 165, 167–
    8, 171, 172, 173
private health care 90–2, 102
privatisation 9, 44, 92, 93, 101

probation and after-care committees
    229
probation and after-care 16, 17, 225–
    33, 235
probation hostels 231
Probation of Offenders Act, 1907 16,
    225
probation orders 117, 118, 225, 226
professional and executive recruitment
    185, 194
Provision for Youth Report, 1975
    (DES discussion paper) 179
psychiatric social workers 127
public assistance committees 20, 21
public expenditure 9
Public Health Act, 1848 64
Public Health Act, 1875 64, 65, 200
public inquiries 219–21
public inquiry – Sizewell 220
public schools 135, 137
public works 16

Race Relations Act, 1976 191, 192
rate rebate 37, 54, 202, 203
Rathbone, William 69
Rating Act, 1966 37
redundancy payments 2, 38–9, 185,
    190
Redundancy Payments Act, 1965 38
Reform Act, 1867 136
regional health authorities 79, 86, 88
regional planning 218
Relief Regulation Order, 1930 19
Remploy Ltd 187
Rent Act, 1965 202
Rent Act, 1968 206
rent allowance 37, 54, 202
rent control 201, 202, 207
rented accommodation 202, 207
Representation of the People Act,
    1884 15
Representation of the People Act,
    1918 15, 26, 139
research councils 150, 151
resettlement units 33, 34
residential accommodation 105–6,
    108
Resource Allocation Working Party
    (RAWP) 93
Robbins Report, 1963 (on higher
    education) 155–7
Rowntree, B. Seebohm 14

Royal Commission on Environmental Pollution 218
Royal Commission on Health Insurance, 1924–6 67
Royal Commission on Lunacy and Mental Disorder 1924–6 125
Royal Commission on Medical Education 1965–8 96–7
Royal Commission on Public Health, 1869 64
Royal Commission on Secondary Education, 1895 137, 138
Royal Commission on the Laws relating to Mental Illness and Mental Deficiency, 1957 125, 128
Royal Commission on the National Health Service, 1976–9 73, 86, 87, 98, 100
Royal Commission on the Poor Law, 1905 18–19
Royal Commission on Unemployment Insurance, 1930 20

Sanitary Act, 1866 64
school boards 135, 137
school health service 16, 78, 81, 86, 114, 139
school meals 16, 112–14
school milk 112–13
schoolchildren 112–15
Scott Committee on Land Utilisation, 1941 211, 212
secondary education 142, 144, 146, 155, 160–6, 173
Seebohm Report, 1968 (on local authority and allied personal social services) 130, 131
selectivity 52–4, 237, 238
severe disablement allowance 36, 48
Sex Discrimination Act, 1975 191, 192
sheltered workshops 188
Shop Act, 1911 17
sickness benefit 29, 31, 39
single-parent mothers 111–12
single payments 33, 43, 57, 58
sixth form colleges 146
Skeffington Report, 1969 (*People and Planning*) 213
skillcentres 185–6, 188
slum clearance 206, 207
Social Fund 2, 56–7, 60

Social Security Act, 1966 33
Social Security Act, 1985 29
Social Security Act, 1986 2, 30, 37, 44, 45, 48, 50, 52, 113, 203
Social Security Advisory Committee 31, 33, 38, 52
Social Security Commissioner 34, 38
Social Security (Pensions) Act, 1975 31, 45
social security reviews 44, 48
social security tribunals 32, 33, 57
social workers 57, 60, 78, 84, 97, 111, 118, 119, 129, 130–2, 187, 228, 229, 231, 233, 236
Special Areas Act, 1934 211, 219, 222
speenhamland system 50
Spens Report, 1938 (on secondary education) 140, 144, 164
statutory sick pay 29
structure plans 212–3
sub-standard housing 205–6
supervision orders 118, 120, 225, 227, 228, 229
supplementary benefit 1, 2, 24, 31, 32–5, 36, 37, 38, 39, 41, 42, 43, 47, 48, 50, 52, 54, 55, 56, 60, 105, 113, 202, 203
Supplementary Benefits Commission 33, 34

task forces 216–17
tax allowances 44
tax-credit scheme 49–50, 59, 61
teachers' unions 152
Technical and Vocational Education Initiative (TVEI) 146, 147, 161, 195
technical colleges 138
Tomlinson Committee Report, 1943 (on disabled) 187
Town and Country Planning Act, 1932 211
Town and Country Planning Act, 1947 212, 222
Town and Country Planning Act, 1971 213
Town Development Act, 1952 214
Trade Board Act, 1909 17
trade unions 7
Training Opportunities Service 194
transitional benefit 20, 24, 26

unemployment 9, 13, 14, 20, 24, 42, 52, 188–90, 193–4, 198, 215
unemployed (helping the) 188–90
Unemployment Act, 1934 20
Unemployment Assistance Board 20, 22
unemployment insurance 18, 19, 20, 31, 39, 42, 52, 56
Unemployment Insurance Act, 1920 19
Unemployed Workers' Dependants Act, 1921 19
Unemployed Workmen Act, 1905 16
universities 141–2, 144, 148–9, 154, 160, 168
urban development corporations 216–7, 222
urban programme 216–17
urban renewal 214, 217, 222
Uthwatt Committee on Compensation and Betterment, 1941 211, 212

vocational training 185–6
voluntary schools 135, 136, 138, 148

wages councils 51, 196
war pension 37
Wheatley Act, 1924 (on local authority housing) 201
widows 21, 30, 31
Widows, Orphans and Old Age Contributory Pensions Act, 1925 21
Wildlife and Countryside Act, 1981 218
women workers 190–1
Workers' Educational Association (WEA) 168
workhouse schools 135

youth custody centres 118
youth leaders 178
Youth Service 176–82
Youth Service, Report of Committee of Inquiry, 1982 180
Youth Service Development Council 177
Youth Service Review Group 177
Youth Training Scheme 189